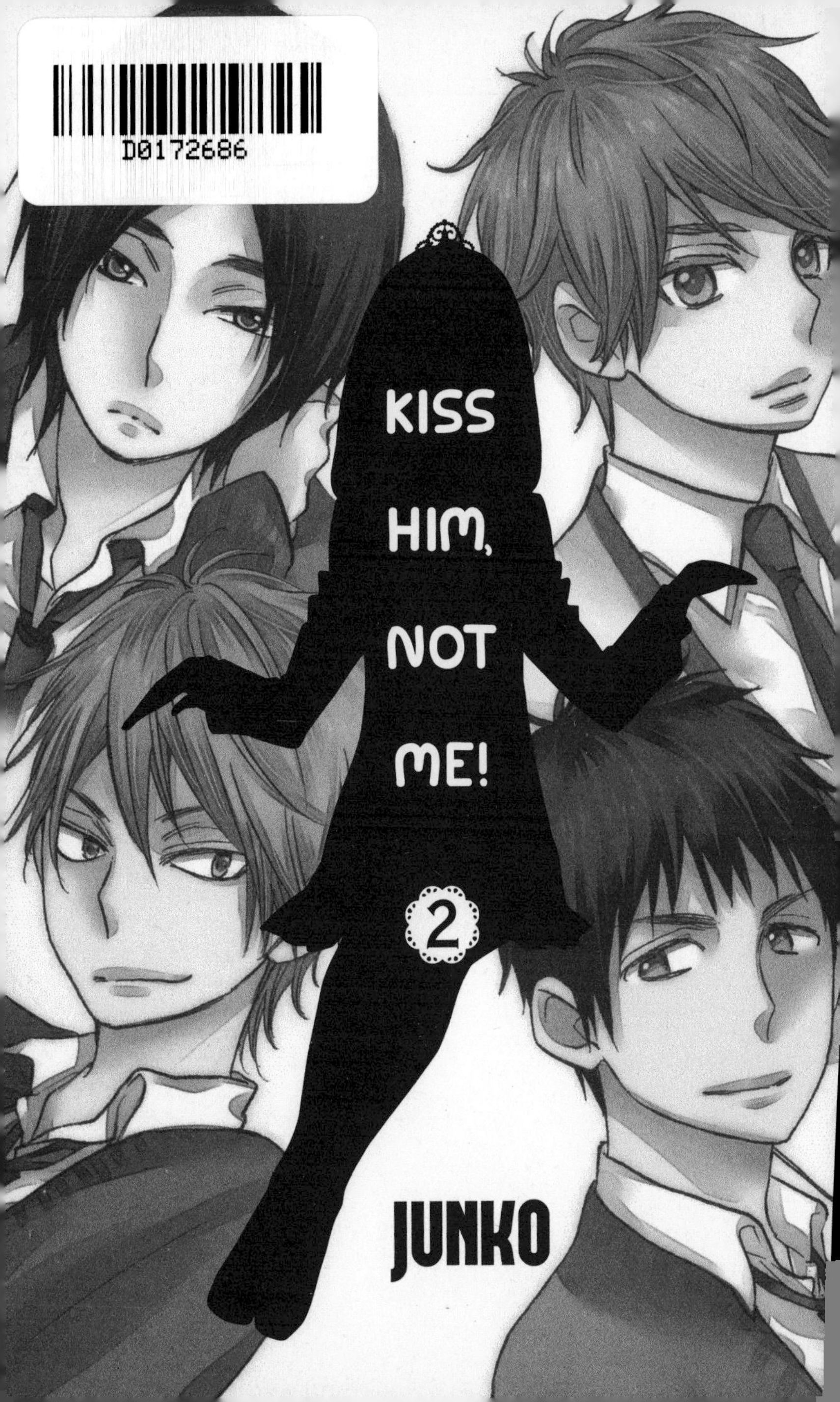
KISS HIM, NOT ME!
2
JUNKO

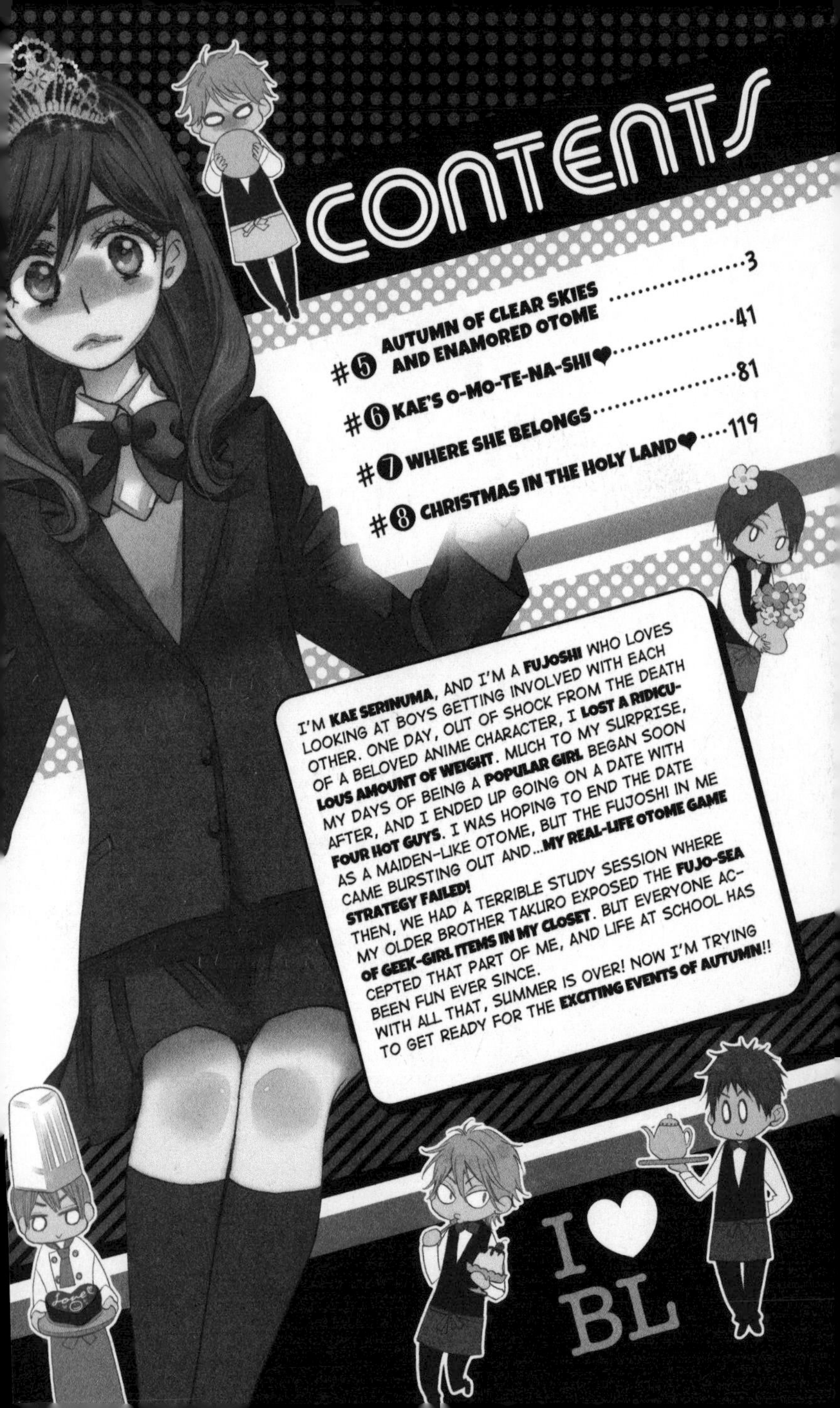
I ♥ BL

CONTENTS

I'M **KAE SERINUMA**, AND I'M A **FUJOSHI** WHO LOVES LOOKING AT BOYS GETTING INVOLVED WITH EACH OTHER. ONE DAY, OUT OF SHOCK FROM THE DEATH OF A BELOVED ANIME CHARACTER, I **LOST A RIDICULOUS AMOUNT OF WEIGHT**. MUCH TO MY SURPRISE, MY DAYS OF BEING A **POPULAR GIRL** BEGAN SOON AFTER, AND I ENDED UP GOING ON A DATE WITH **FOUR HOT GUYS**. I WAS HOPING TO END THE DATE AS A MAIDEN-LIKE OTOME, BUT THE FUJOSHI IN ME CAME BURSTING OUT AND...**MY REAL-LIFE OTOME GAME STRATEGY FAILED!**

THEN, WE HAD A TERRIBLE STUDY SESSION WHERE MY OLDER BROTHER TAKURO EXPOSED THE **FUJO-SEA OF GEEK-GIRL ITEMS IN MY CLOSET**. BUT EVERYONE ACCEPTED THAT PART OF ME, AND LIFE AT SCHOOL HAS BEEN FUN EVER SINCE.

WITH ALL THAT, SUMMER IS OVER! NOW I'M TRYING TO GET READY FOR THE **EXCITING EVENTS OF AUTUMN**!!

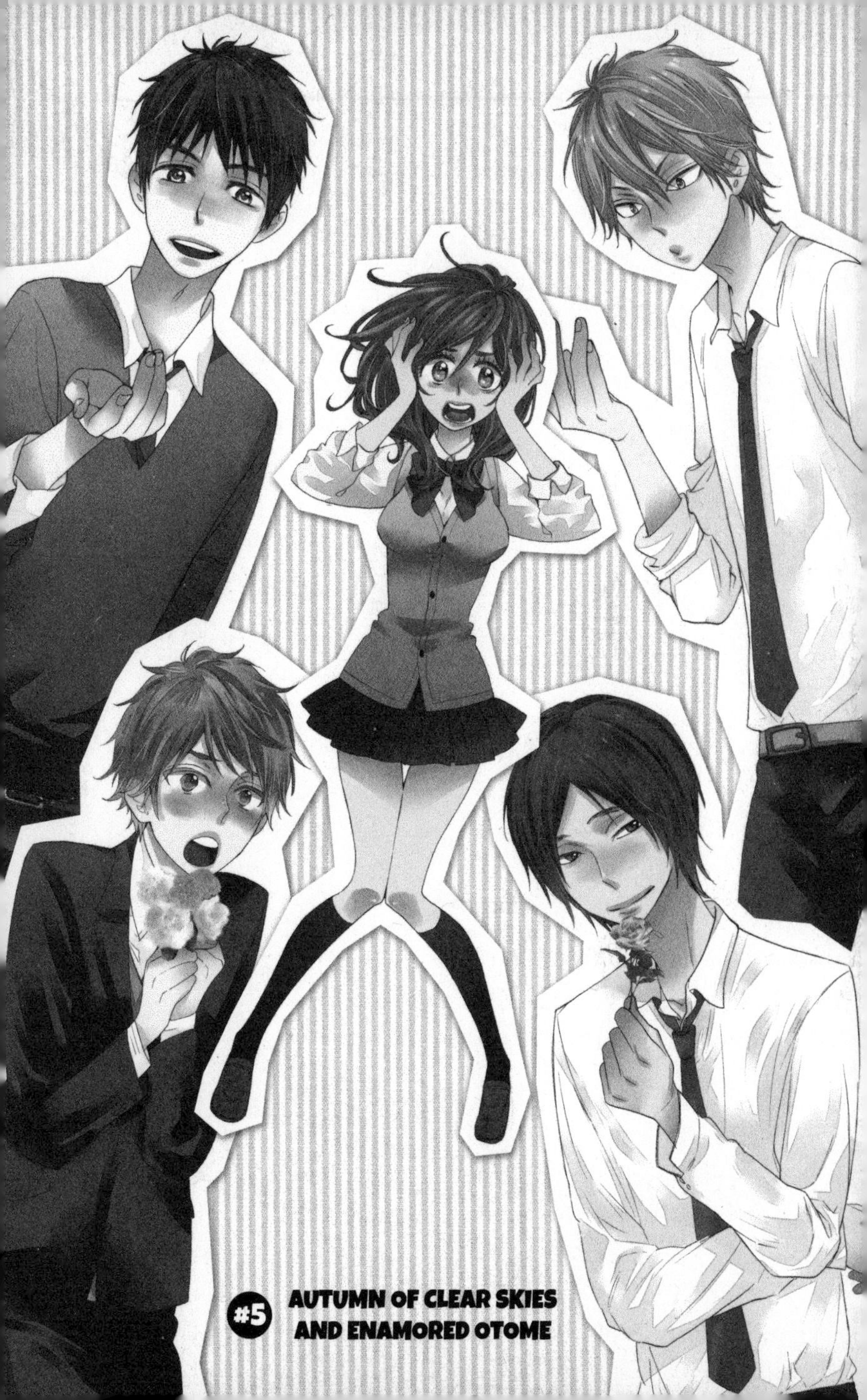
#5
AUTUMN OF CLEAR SKIES
AND ENAMORED OTOME

KISS HIM, NOT ME!

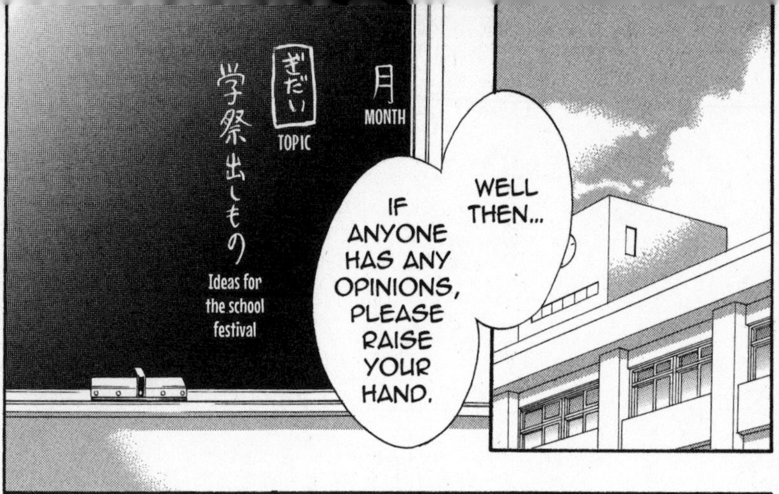
月
MONTH
ぎだい
TOPIC
学祭出しもの
Ideas for the school festival
WELL THEN... IF ANYONE HAS ANY OPINIONS, PLEASE RAISE YOUR HAND.

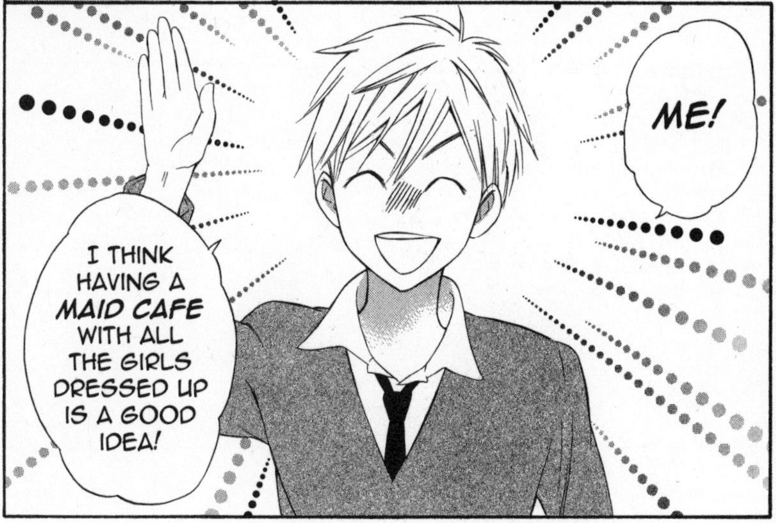
ME!
I THINK HAVING A MAID CAFE WITH ALL THE GIRLS DRESSED UP IS A GOOD IDEA!

KiSS HiM, NOT ME!

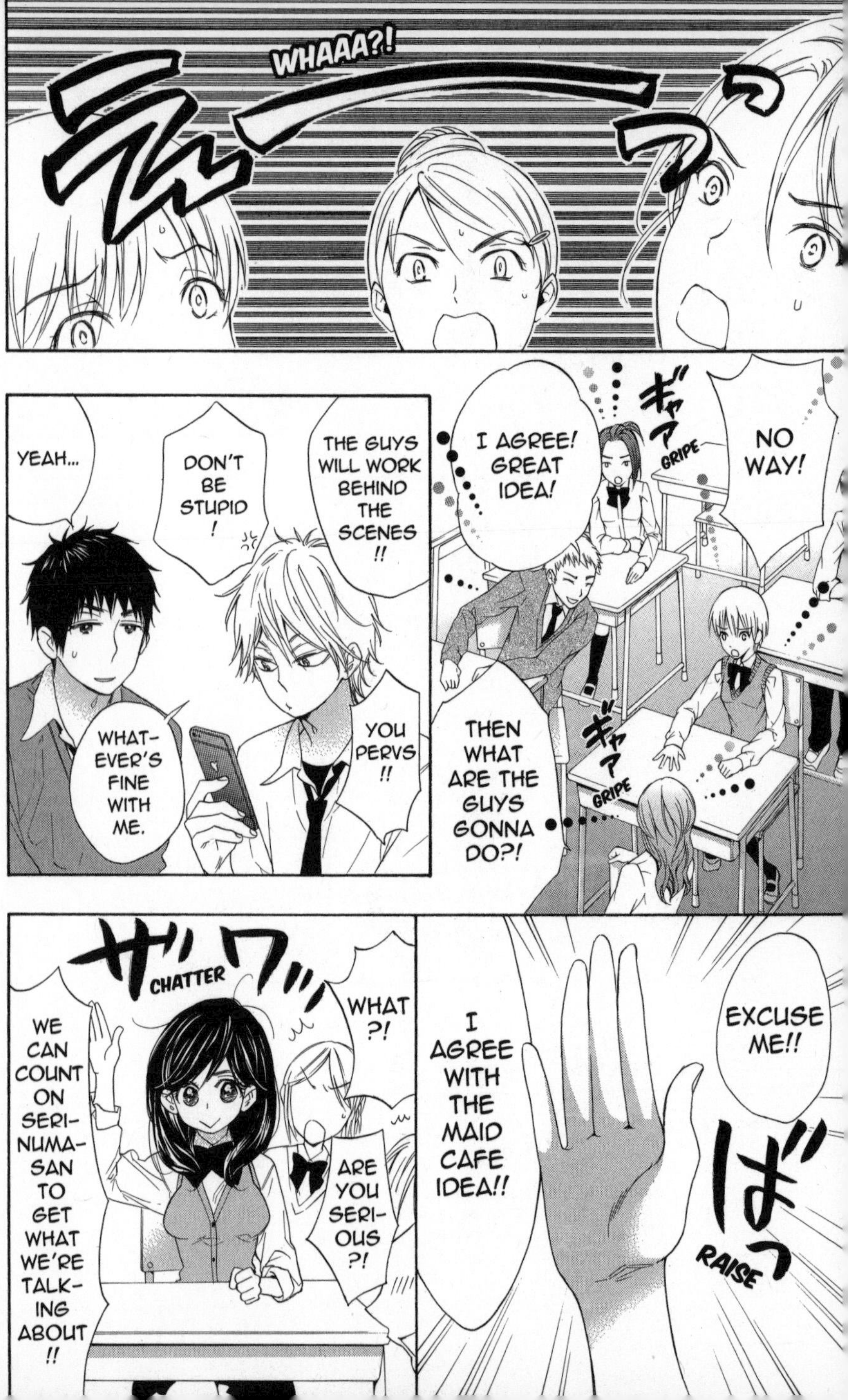
WHAAA?!
NO WAY!
GRIPE
I AGREE! GREAT IDEA!
THEN WHAT ARE THE GUYS GONNA DO?!
GRIPE
THE GUYS WILL WORK BEHIND THE SCENES!!
DON'T BE STUPID!
YEAH...
YOU PERVS!!
WHATEVER'S FINE WITH ME.
EXCUSE ME!!
RAISE
I AGREE WITH THE MAID CAFE IDEA!!
CHATTER
WHAT?!
WE CAN COUNT ON SERINUMA-SAN TO GET WHAT WE'RE TALKING ABOUT!!
ARE YOU SERIOUS?!

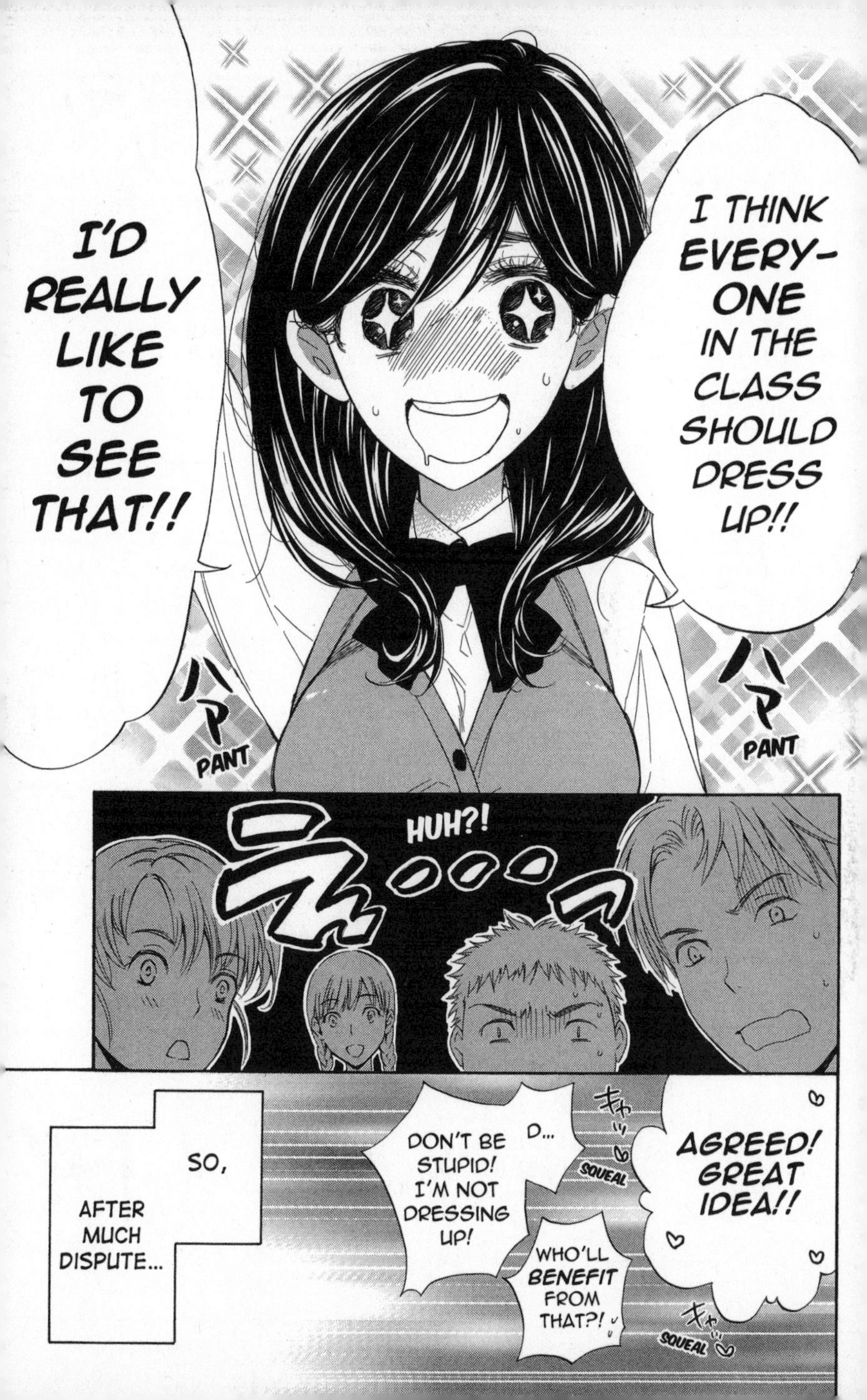
I THINK EVERY-ONE IN THE CLASS SHOULD DRESS UP!!
ハァ
PANT
I'D REALLY LIKE TO SEE THAT!!
ハァ
PANT
HUH?!
AGREED! GREAT IDEA!!
キャッ
SQUEAL
D...
DON'T BE STUPID! I'M NOT DRESSING UP!
WHO'LL BENEFIT FROM THAT?!
キャッ
SQUEAL
SO,
AFTER MUCH DISPUTE...

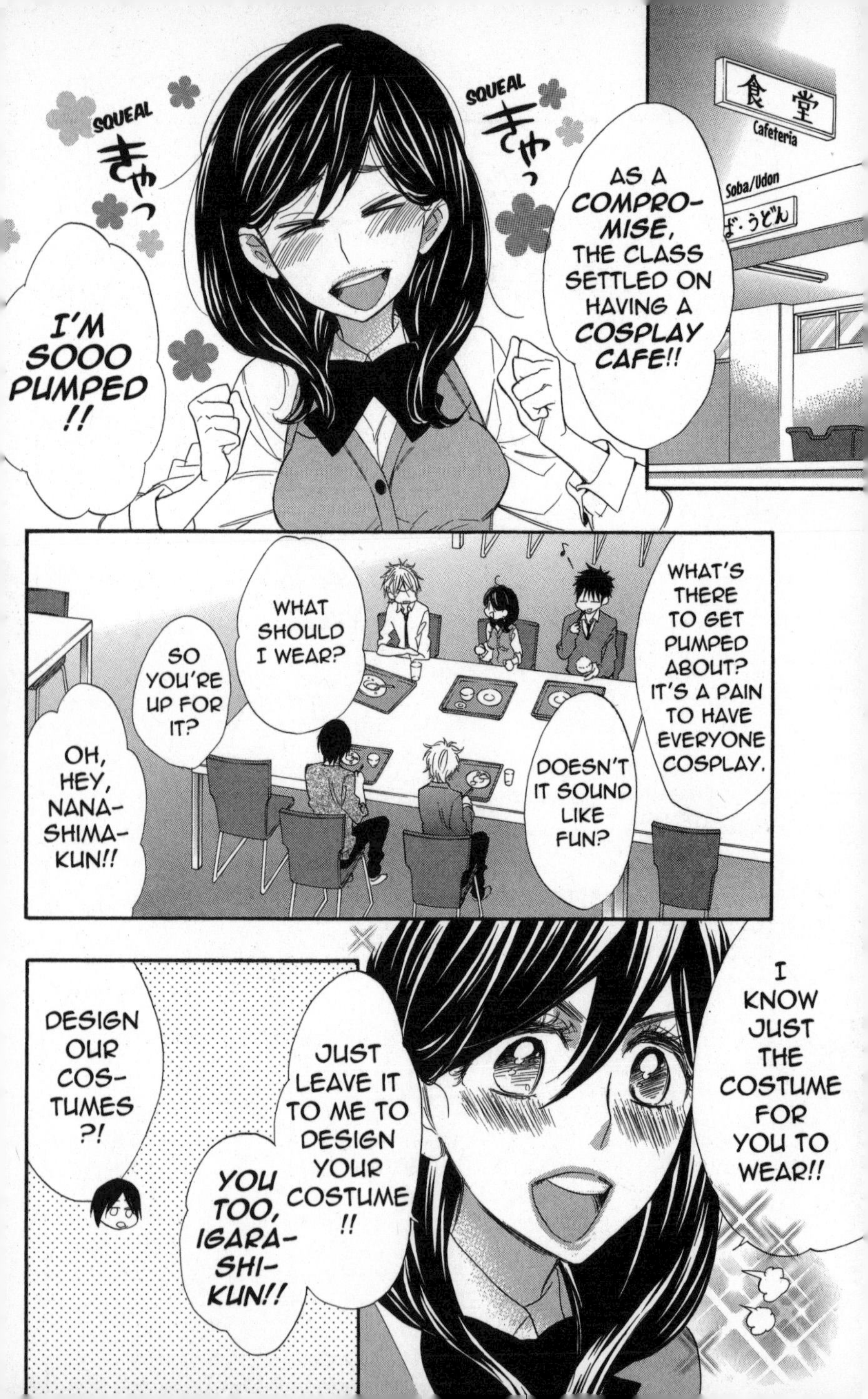
食堂
Cafeteria
Soba/Udon
ば・うどん
AS A COMPROMISE, THE CLASS SETTLED ON HAVING A COSPLAY CAFE!!
SQUEAL
きゃっ
SQUEAL
きゃっ
I'M SOOO PUMPED!!
WHAT'S THERE TO GET PUMPED ABOUT? IT'S A PAIN TO HAVE EVERYONE COSPLAY.
DOESN'T IT SOUND LIKE FUN?
WHAT SHOULD I WEAR?
SO YOU'RE UP FOR IT?
OH, HEY, NANASHIMA-KUN!!
I KNOW JUST THE COSTUME FOR YOU TO WEAR!!
JUST LEAVE IT TO ME TO DESIGN YOUR COSTUME!!
YOU TOO, IGARASHI-KUN!!
DESIGN OUR COSTUMES?!

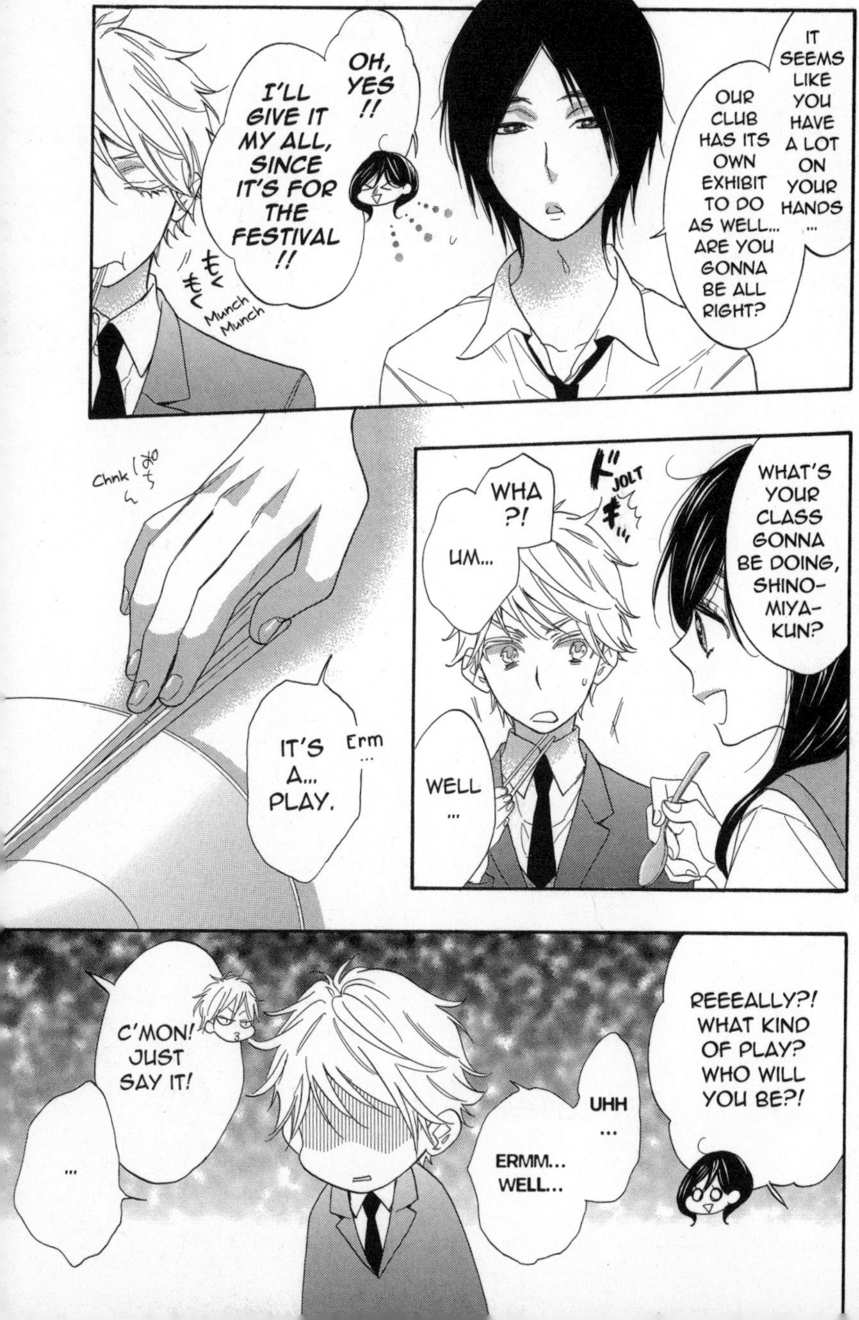
IT SEEMS LIKE YOU HAVE A LOT ON YOUR HANDS...
OUR CLUB HAS ITS OWN EXHIBIT TO DO AS WELL... ARE YOU GONNA BE ALL RIGHT?
OH, YES!!
I'LL GIVE IT MY ALL, SINCE IT'S FOR THE FESTIVAL!!
もぐもぐ Munch Munch
WHAT'S YOUR CLASS GONNA BE DOING, SHINOMIYA-KUN?
ドギ JOLT
WHA?!
UM...
WELL...
Erm...
IT'S A... PLAY.
ぽちん Chnk
REEEALLY?! WHAT KIND OF PLAY? WHO WILL YOU BE?!
UHH...
ERMM... WELL...
C'MON! JUST SAY IT!
...

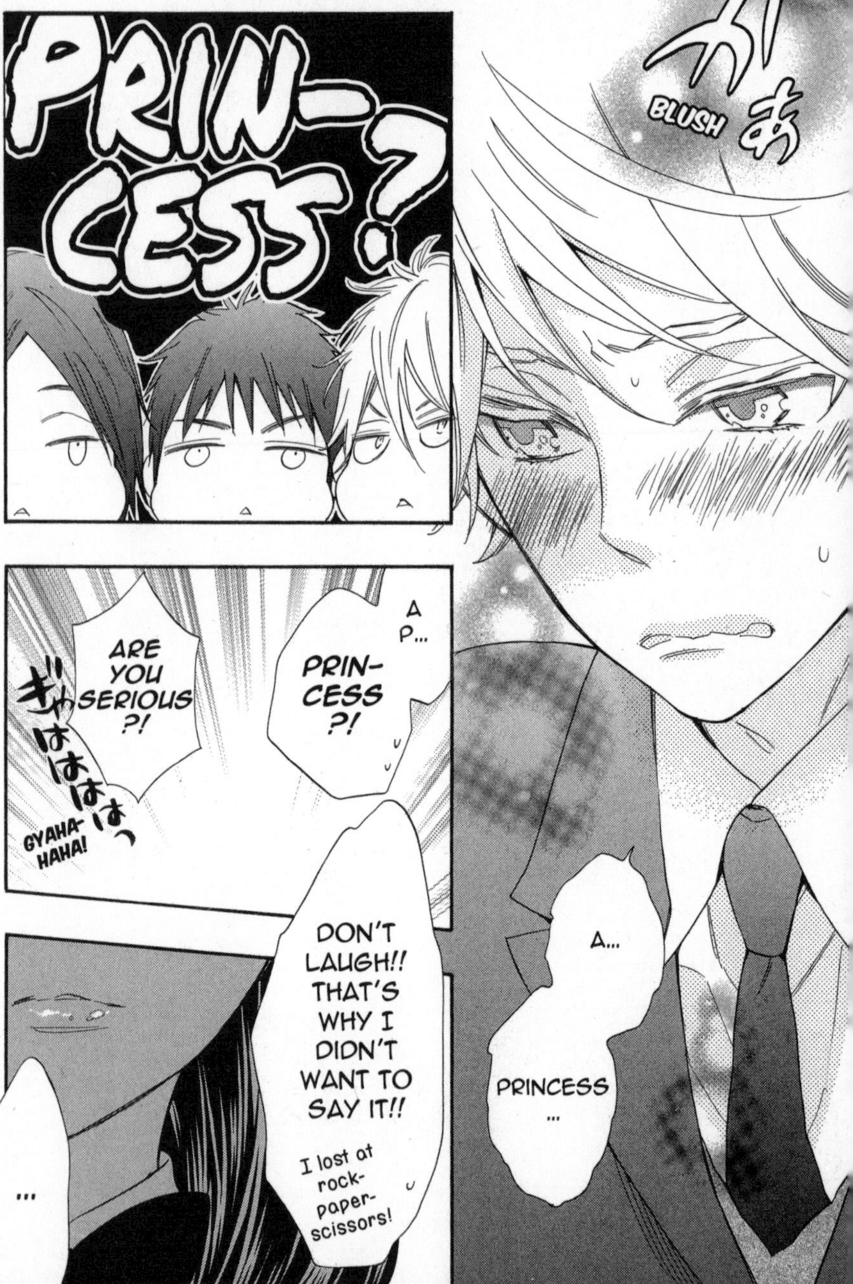
BLUSH
A... PRINCESS...
PRIN-CESS?
A P... PRIN-CESS?!
ARE YOU SERIOUS?!
GYAHA-HAHA!
DON'T LAUGH!! THAT'S WHY I DIDN'T WANT TO SAY IT!!
I lost at rock-paper-scissors!
...

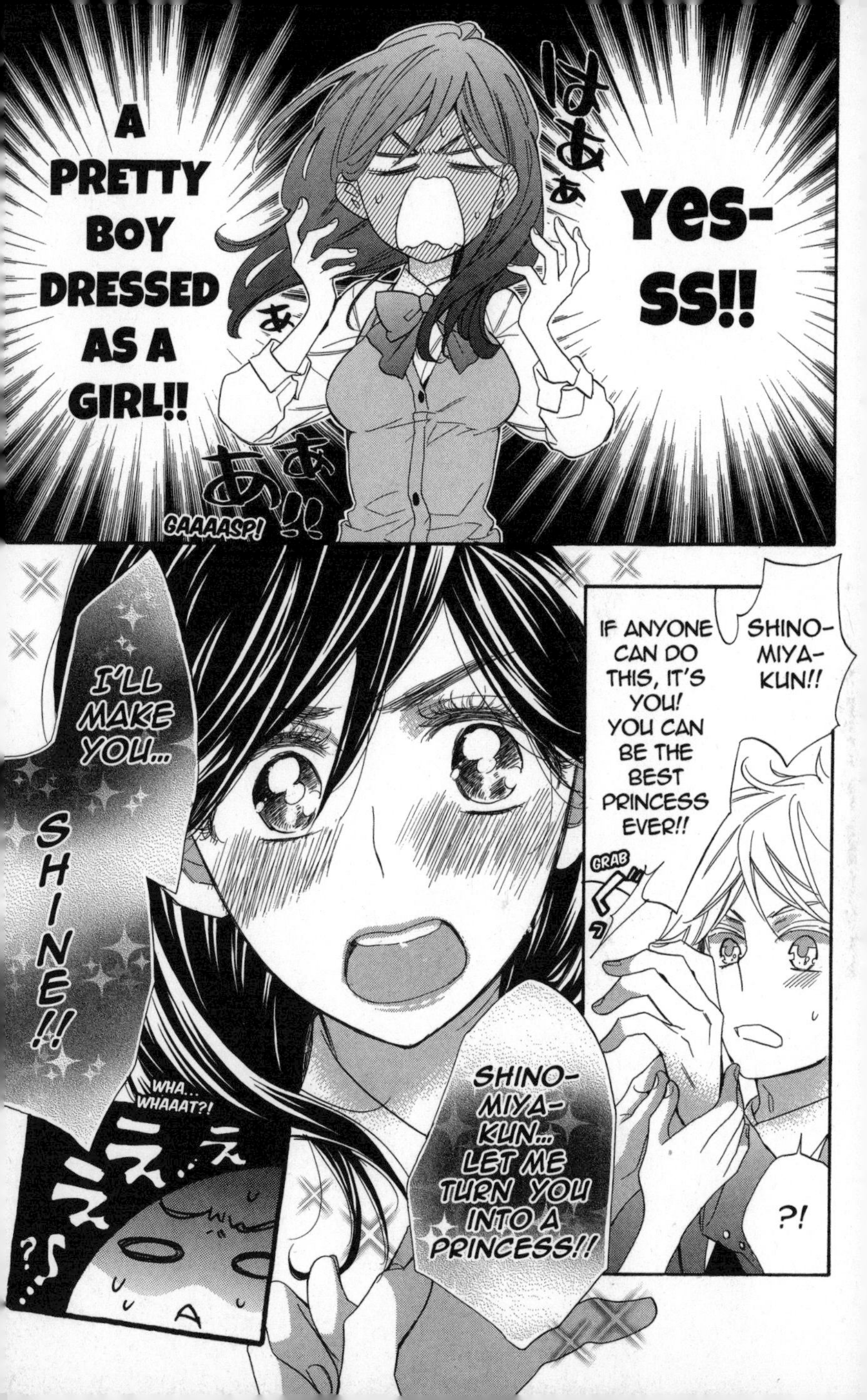はぁぁ
YES-SS!!
A PRETTY BOY DRESSED AS A GIRL!!
あ
ああ!!
GAAAASP!
SHINO-MIYA-KUN!!
IF ANYONE CAN DO THIS, IT'S YOU! YOU CAN BE THE BEST PRINCESS EVER!!
GRAB
?!
I'LL MAKE YOU... SHINE!!
SHINO-MIYA-KUN... LET ME TURN YOU INTO A PRINCESS!!
WHA... WHAAAT?!

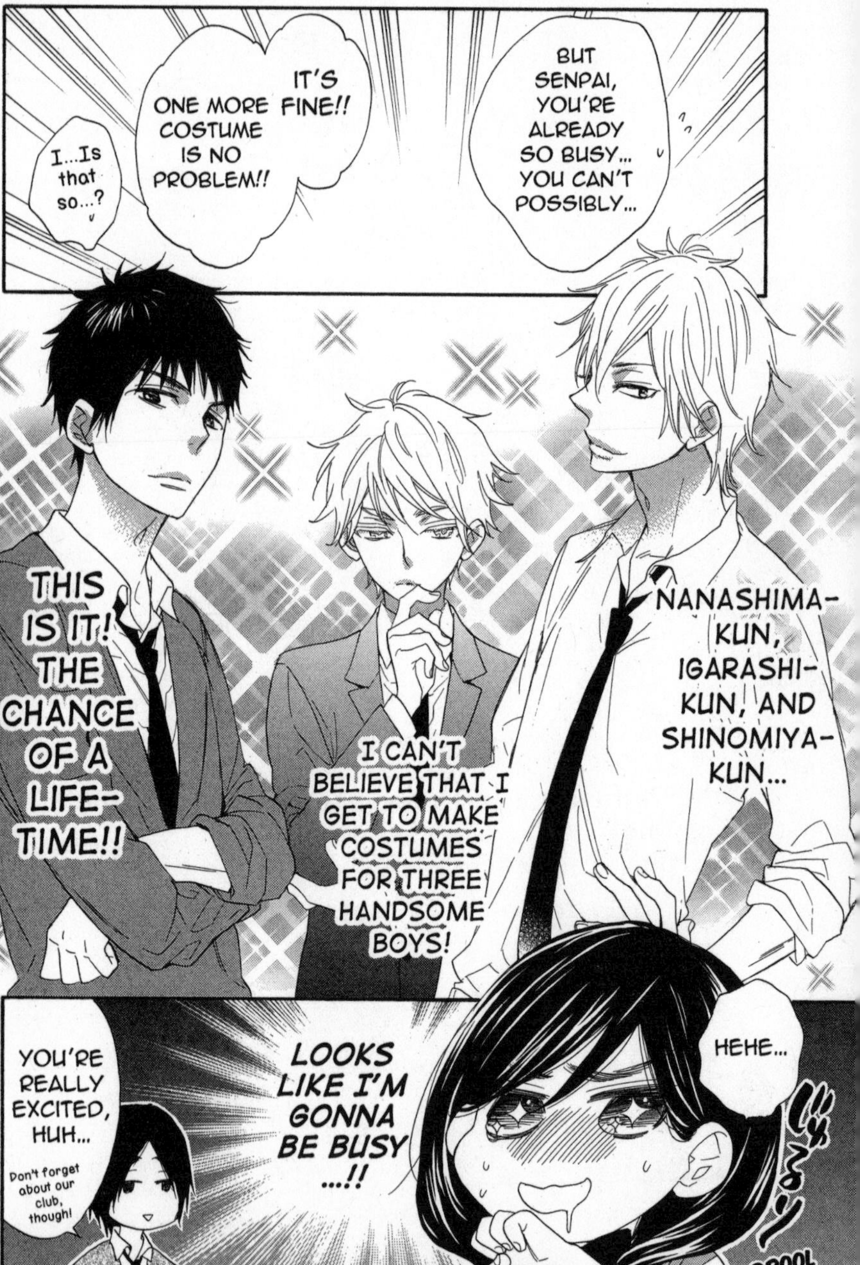
BUT SENPAI, YOU'RE ALREADY SO BUSY... YOU CAN'T POSSIBLY...
IT'S FINE!! ONE MORE COSTUME IS NO PROBLEM!!
I...Is that so...?
NANASHIMA-KUN, IGARASHI-KUN, AND SHINOMIYA-KUN...
I CAN'T BELIEVE THAT I GET TO MAKE COSTUMES FOR THREE HANDSOME BOYS!
THIS IS IT! THE CHANCE OF A LIFE-TIME!!
HEHE...
DROOL
LOOKS LIKE I'M GONNA BE BUSY ...!!
YOU'RE REALLY EXCITED, HUH...
Don't forget about our club, though!

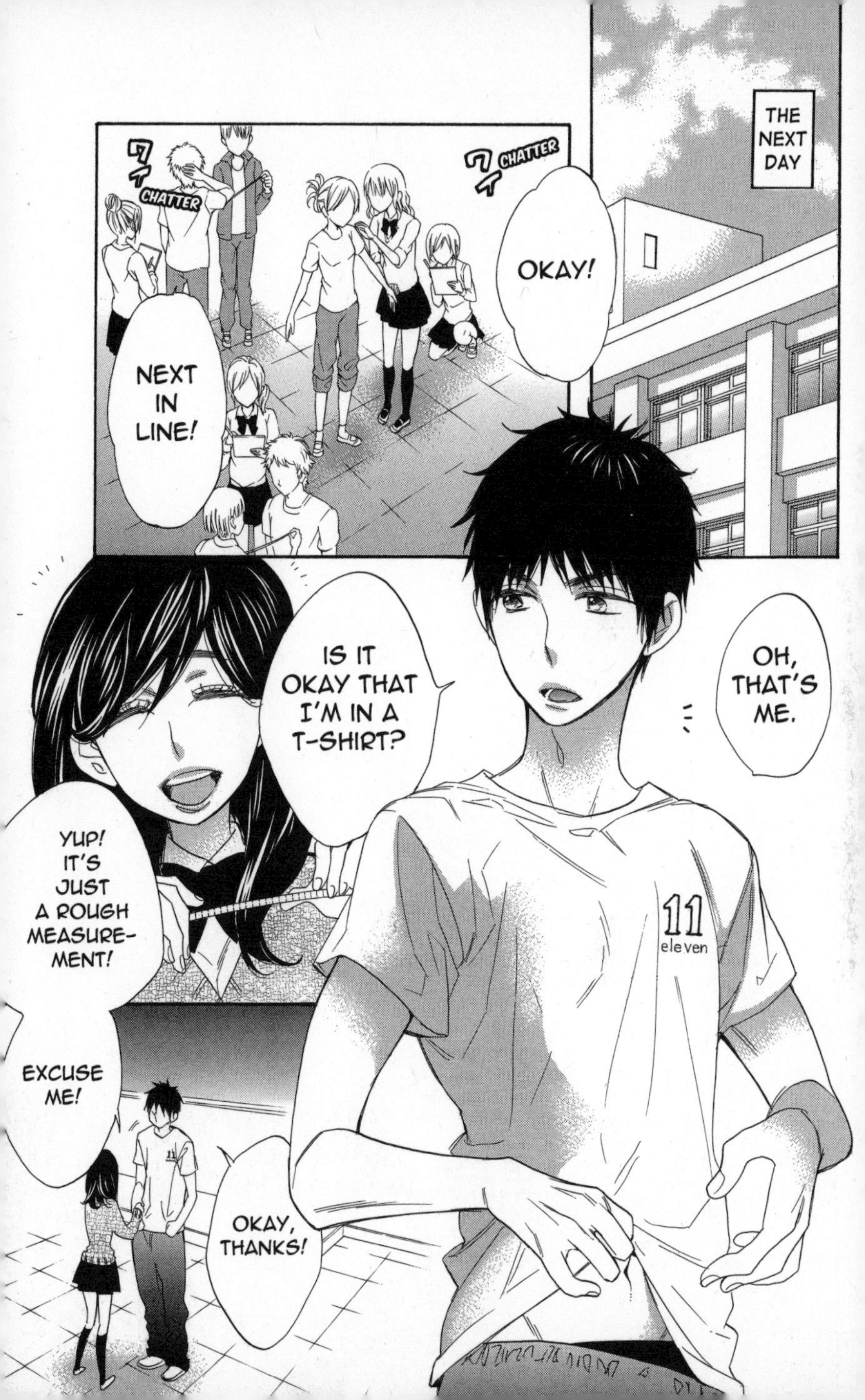
THE NEXT DAY
ワイ
CHATTER
ワイ
CHATTER
NEXT IN LINE!
OKAY!
OH, THAT'S ME.
IS IT OKAY THAT I'M IN A T-SHIRT?
YUP! IT'S JUST A ROUGH MEASUREMENT!
11 eleven
EXCUSE ME!
OKAY, THANKS!

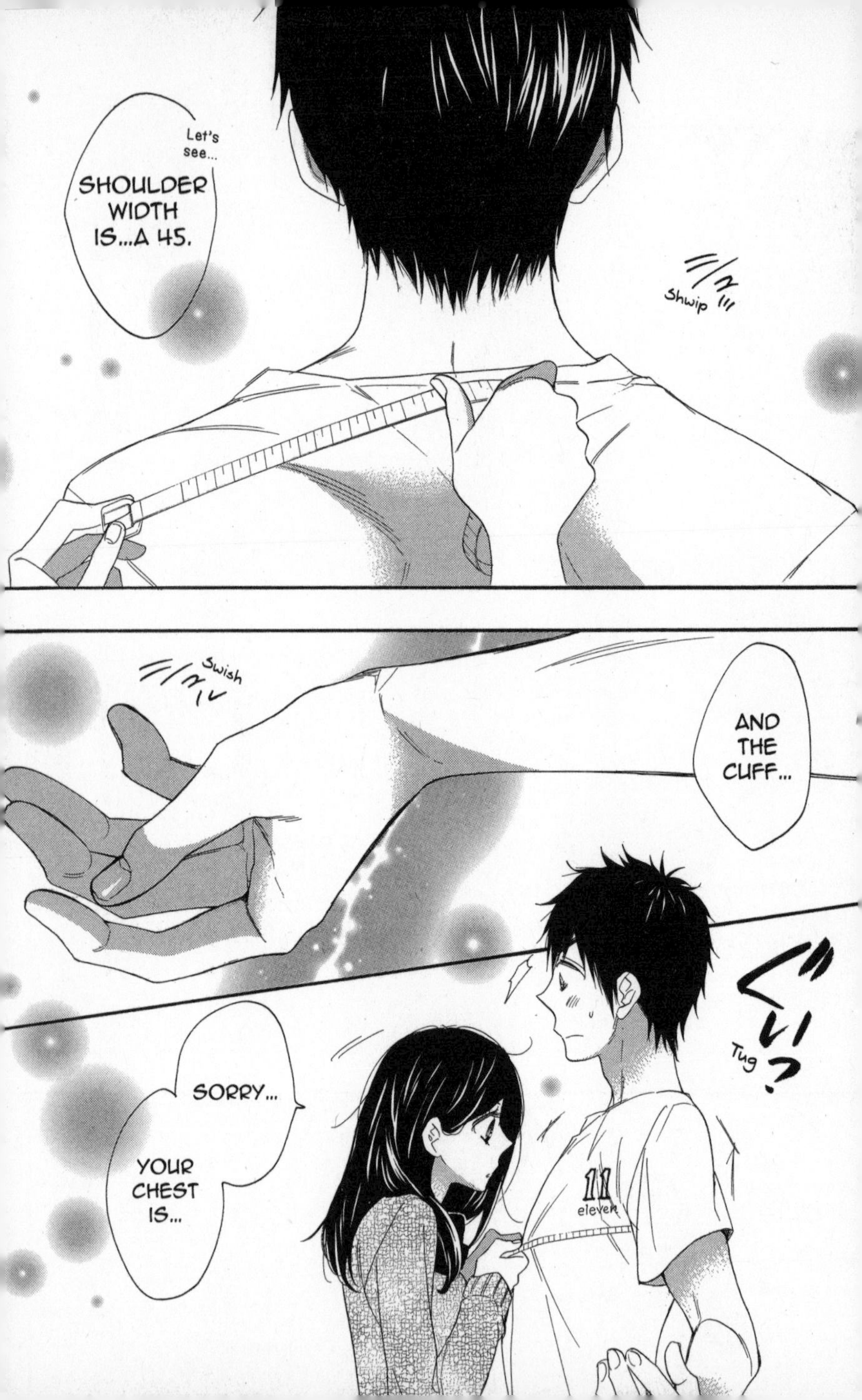
Let's see...
SHOULDER WIDTH IS...A 45.
Shwip
AND THE CUFF...
Swish
Tug ?
SORRY...
YOUR CHEST IS...
eleven

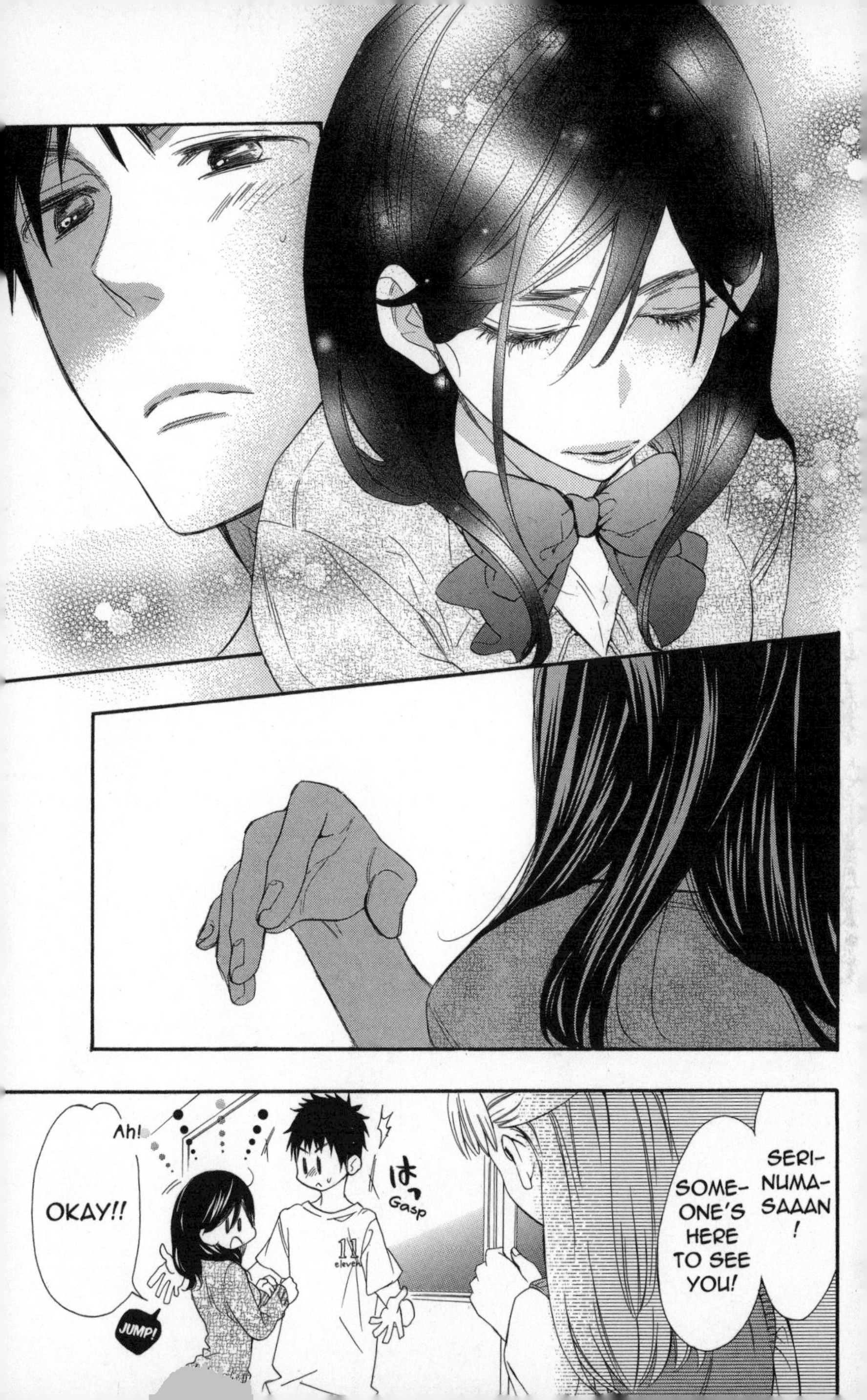
SERI-NUMA-SAAAN!
SOME-ONE'S HERE TO SEE YOU!
はっ
Gasp
Ah!
OKAY!!
JUMP!

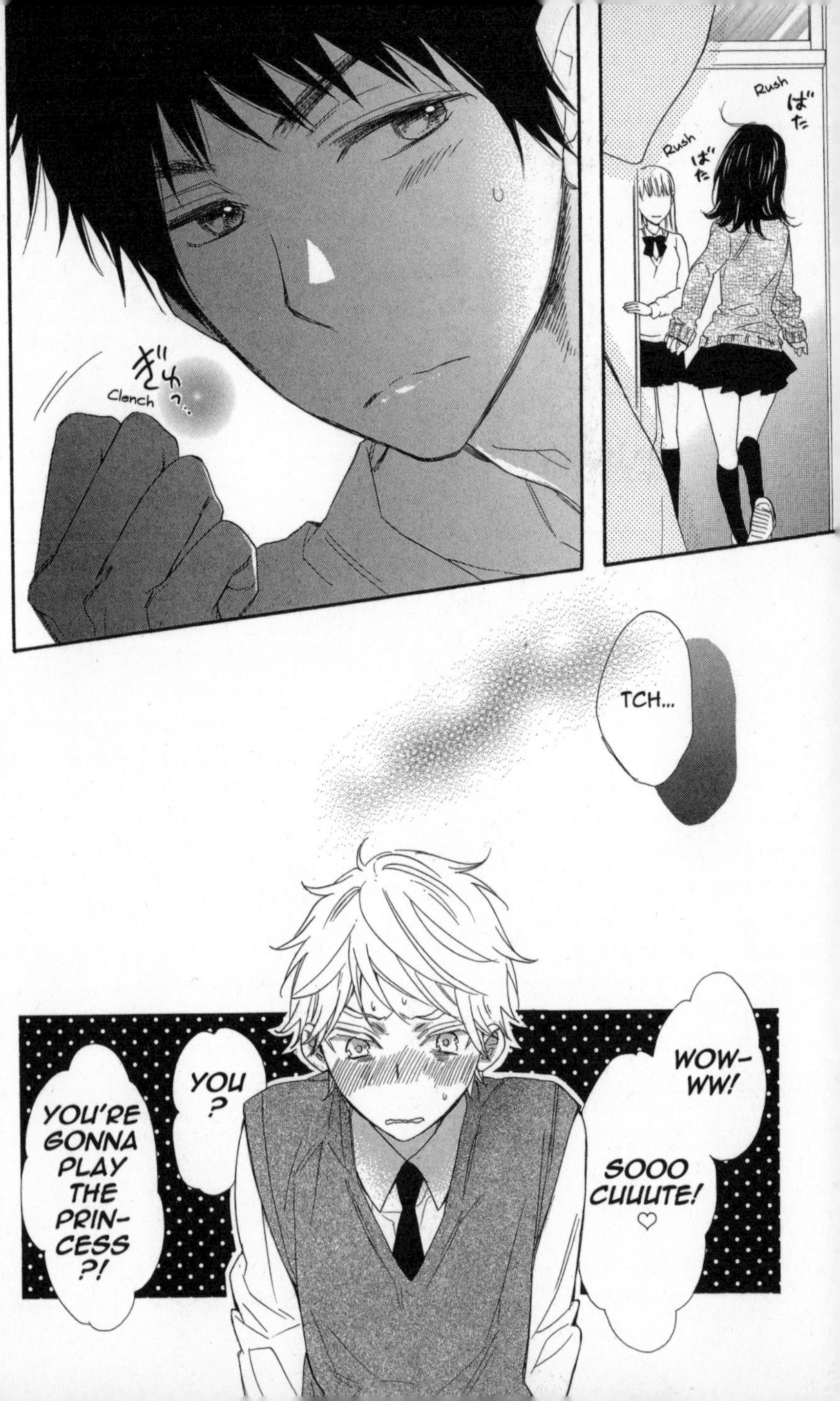
Rush
ばた
Rush
ばた
ぎゅっ…
Clench
TCH...
WOW-WW!
SOOO CUUUTE! ♡
YOU?
YOU'RE GONNA PLAY THE PRINCESS?!

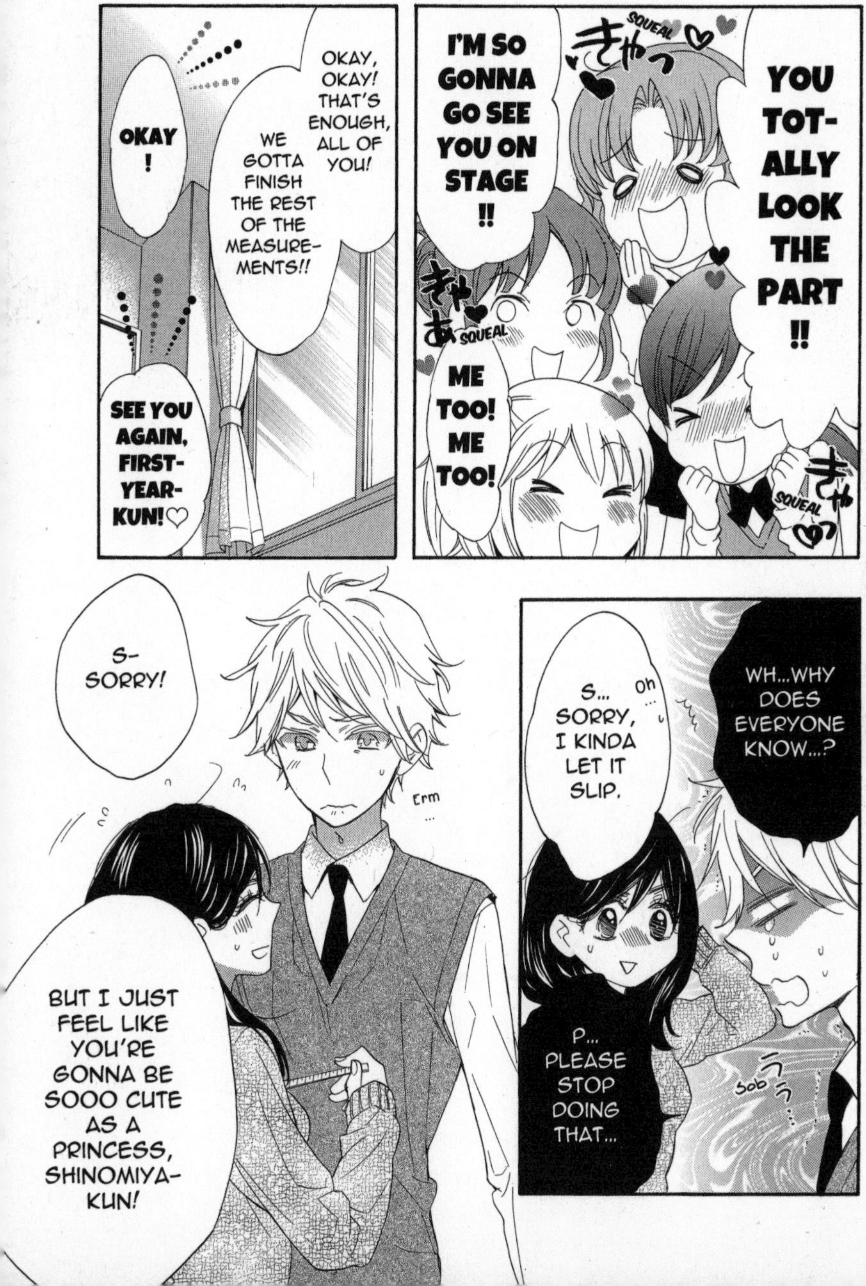
YOU TOTALLY LOOK THE PART!!
きゃっ SQUEAL
I'M SO GONNA GO SEE YOU ON STAGE!!
きゃ SQUEAL
きゃあ SQUEAL
ME TOO! ME TOO!
OKAY, OKAY! THAT'S ENOUGH, ALL OF YOU!
WE GOTTA FINISH THE REST OF THE MEASUREMENTS!!
OKAY!
SEE YOU AGAIN, FIRST-YEAR-KUN!♡
WH...WHY DOES EVERYONE KNOW...?
Oh...
S... SORRY, I KINDA LET IT SLIP.
Sob
P... PLEASE STOP DOING THAT...
S-SORRY!
Erm...
BUT I JUST FEEL LIKE YOU'RE GONNA BE SOOO CUTE AS A PRINCESS, SHINOMIYA-KUN!

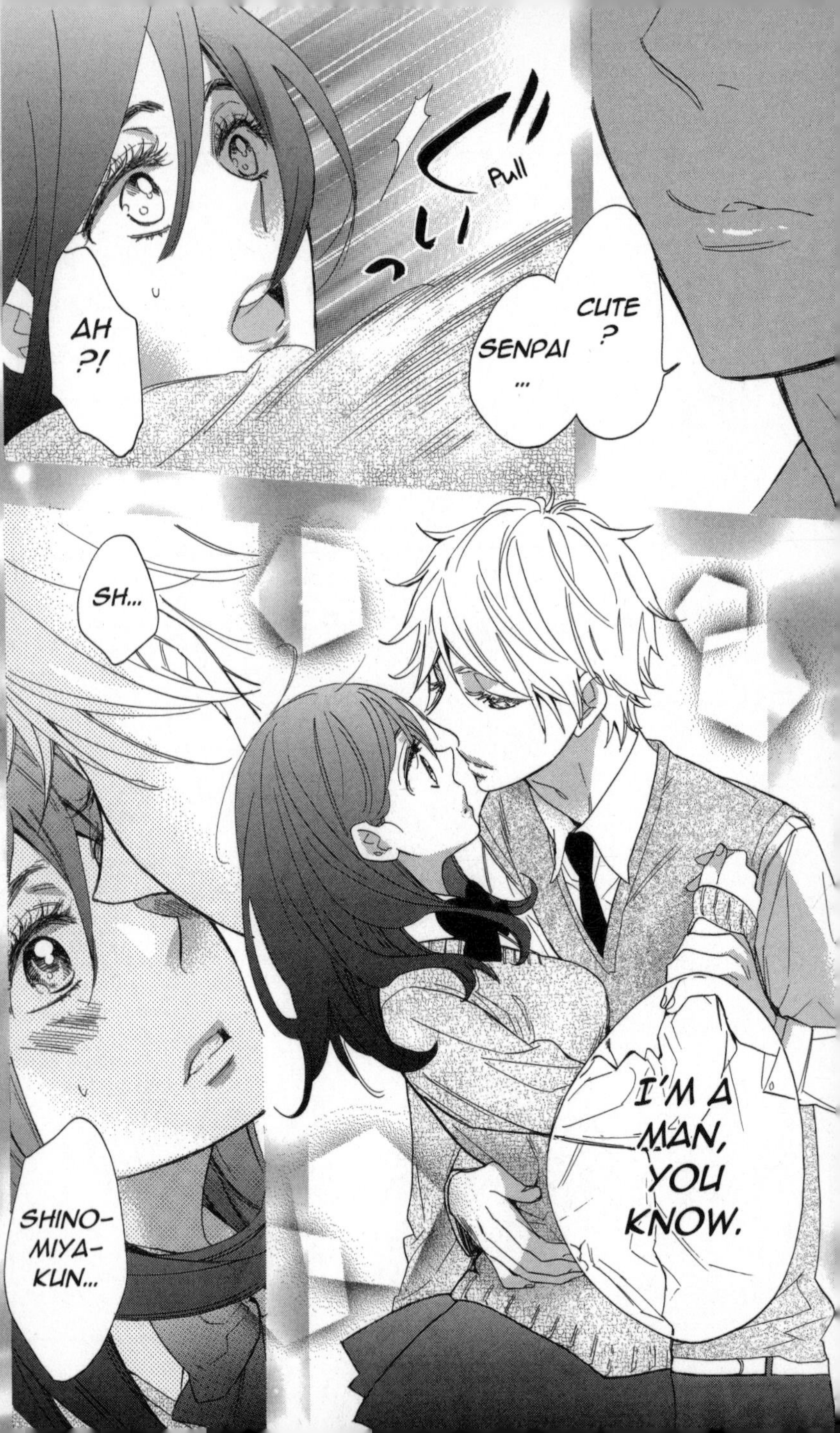
SENPAI ... CUTE ?
ぐいっ
Pull
AH ?!
I'M A MAN, YOU KNOW.
SH...
SHINO-MIYA-KUN...

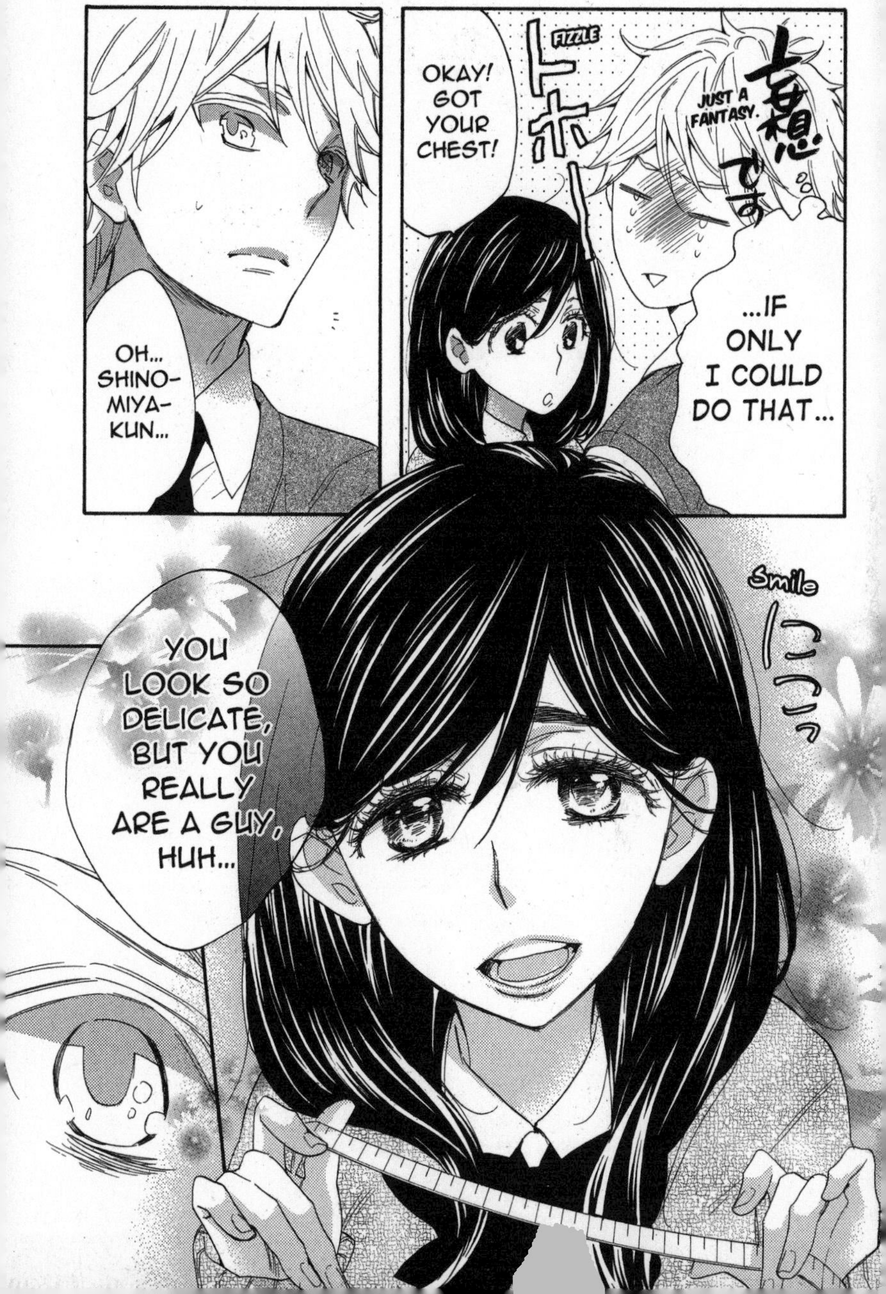
OKAY! GOT YOUR CHEST!
FIZZLE
JUST A FANTASY.
...IF ONLY I COULD DO THAT...
OH... SHINO-MIYA-KUN...
Smile
YOU LOOK SO DELICATE, BUT YOU REALLY ARE A GUY, HUH...

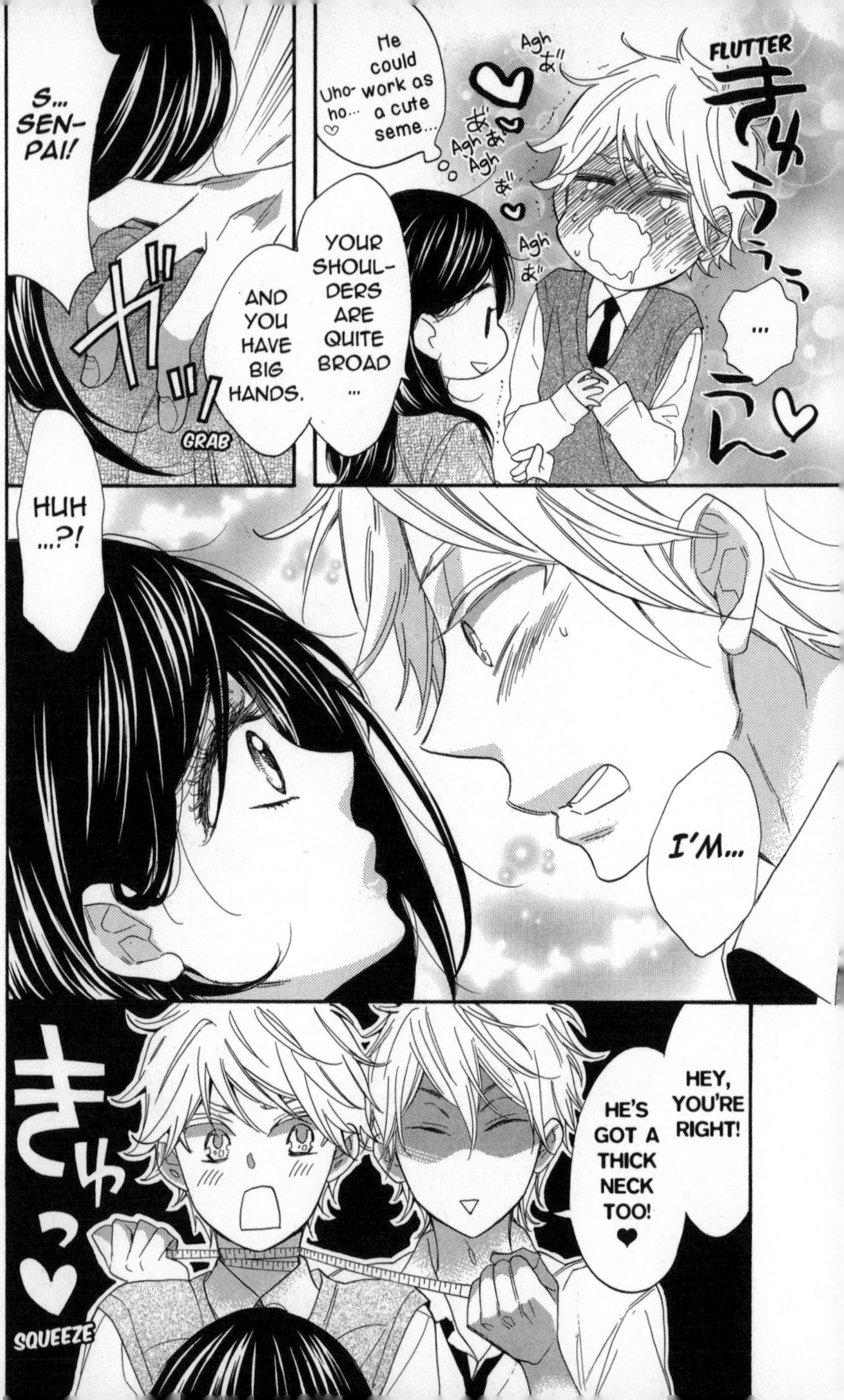
FLUTTER
...
Agh Agh Agh Agh Agh
He could work as a cute seme...
Uho-ho...♡
YOUR SHOULDERS ARE QUITE BROAD...
AND YOU HAVE BIG HANDS.
S... SEN-PAI!
GRAB
HUH...?!
I'M...
HEY, YOU'RE RIGHT!
HE'S GOT A THICK NECK TOO! ♥
SQUEEZE

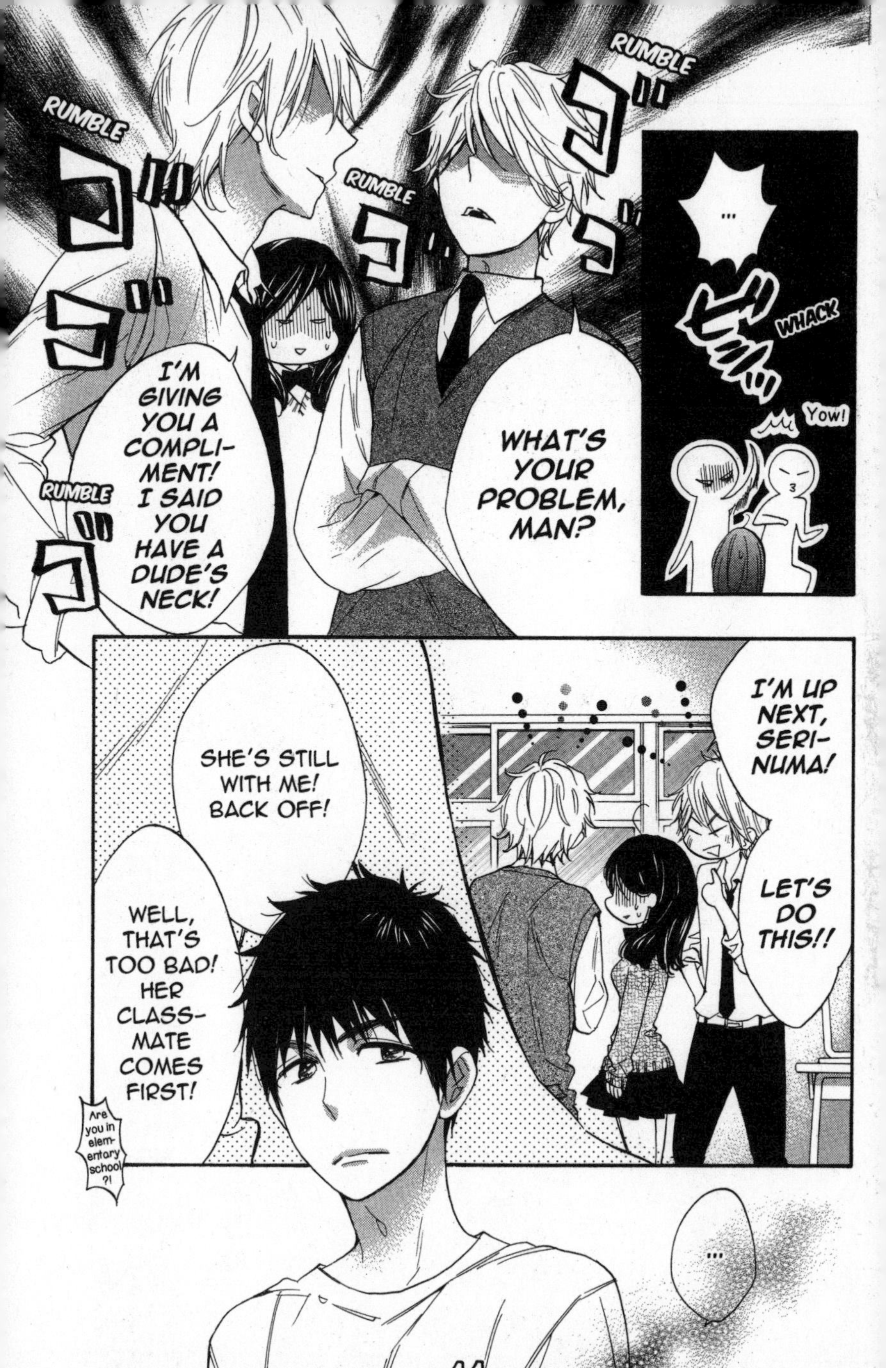
RUMBLE
RUMBLE
RUMBLE
WHAT'S YOUR PROBLEM, MAN?
I'M GIVING YOU A COMPLIMENT! I SAID YOU HAVE A DUDE'S NECK!
RUMBLE
...
WHACK
Yow!
I'M UP NEXT, SERINUMA!
LET'S DO THIS!!
SHE'S STILL WITH ME! BACK OFF!
WELL, THAT'S TOO BAD! HER CLASSMATE COMES FIRST!
Are you in elementary school?!
...

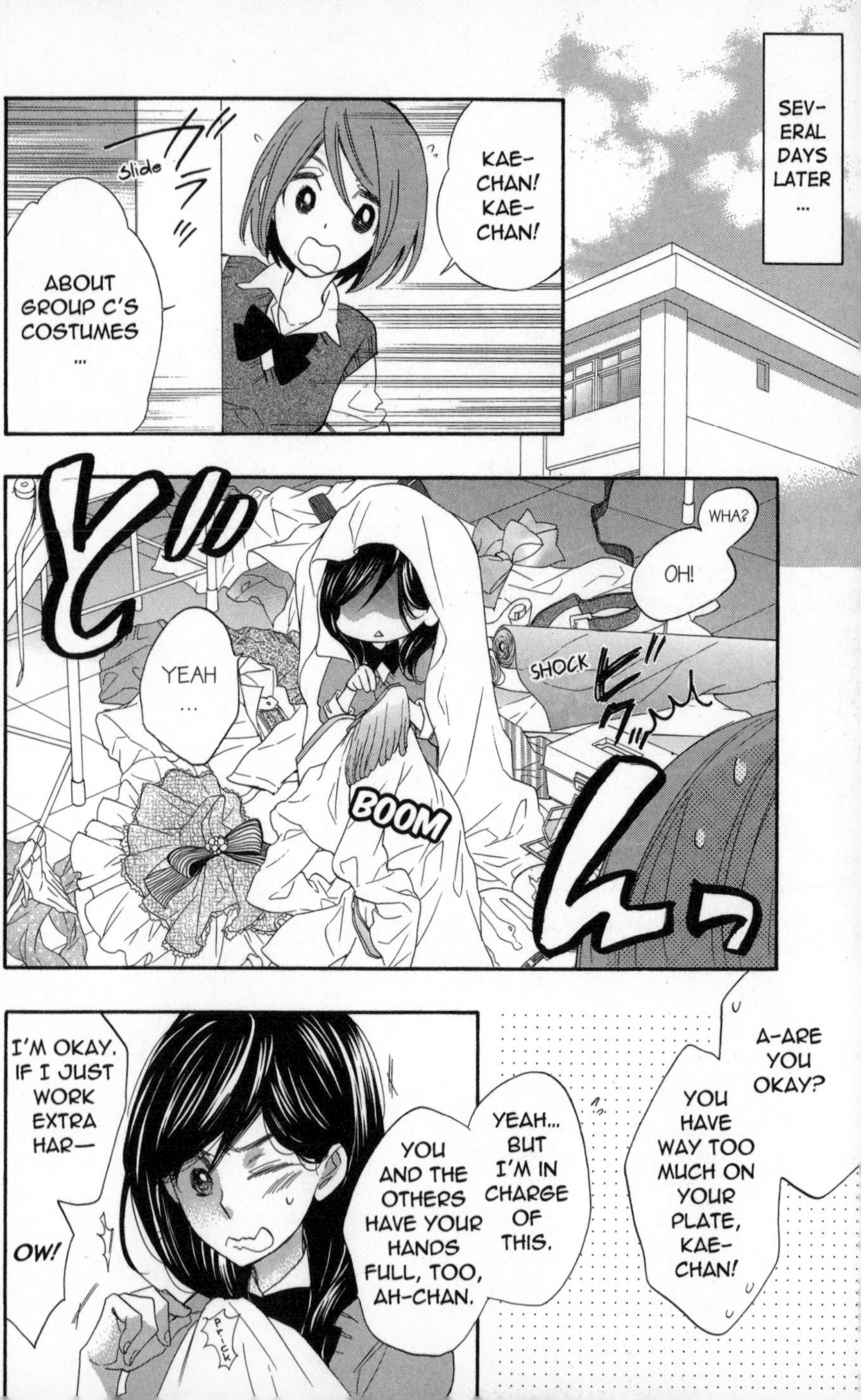
SEV-ERAL DAYS LATER ...
KAE-CHAN! KAE-CHAN!
Slide
ABOUT GROUP C'S COSTUMES ...
WHA?
OH!
SHOCK
BOOM
YEAH ...
A-ARE YOU OKAY?
YOU HAVE WAY TOO MUCH ON YOUR PLATE, KAE-CHAN!
YEAH... BUT I'M IN CHARGE OF THIS.
YOU AND THE OTHERS HAVE YOUR HANDS FULL, TOO, AH-CHAN.
I'M OKAY. IF I JUST WORK EXTRA HAR—
OW!
Prick

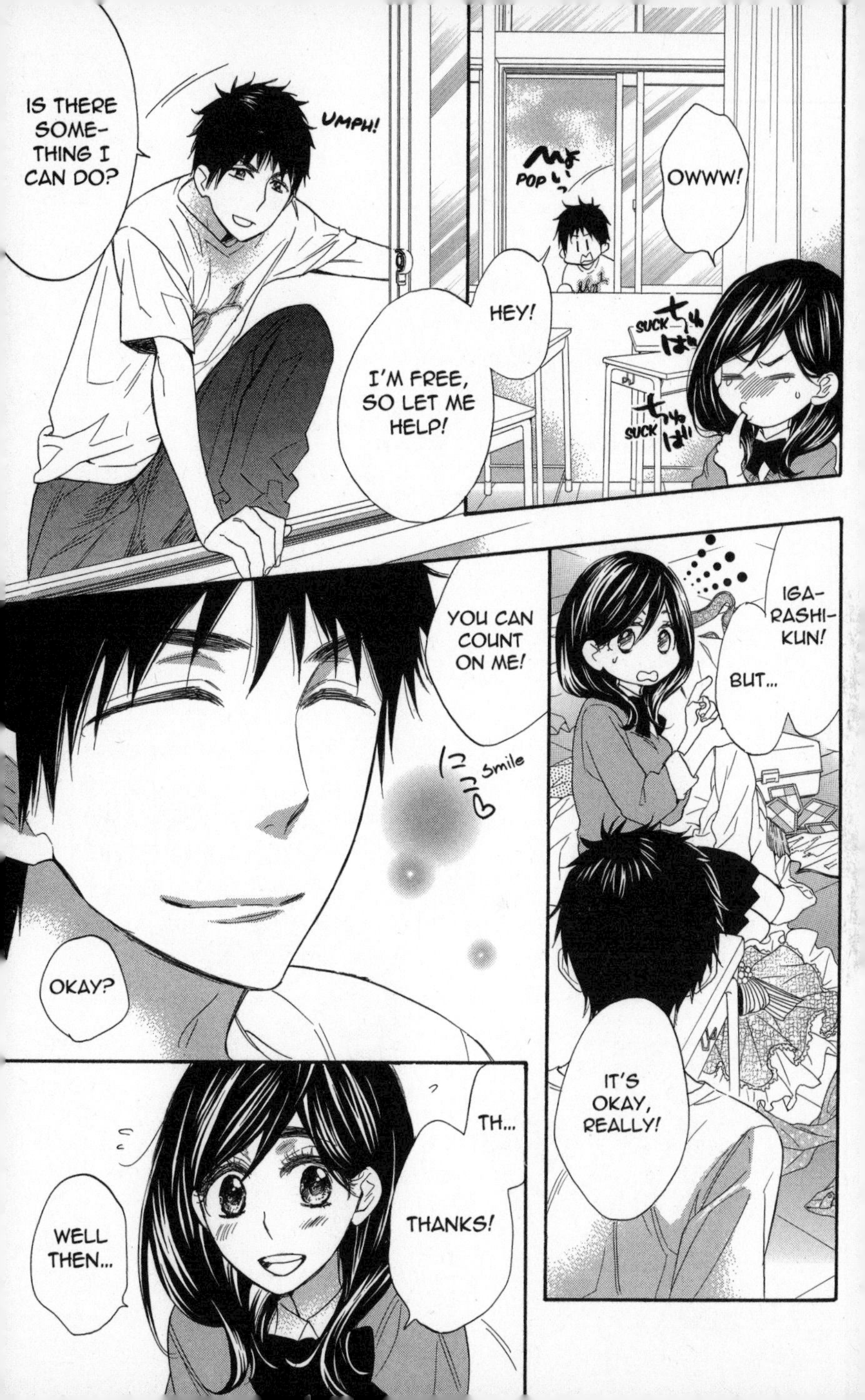
OWWW!
SUCK
SUCK
POP
HEY!
I'M FREE, SO LET ME HELP!
UMPH!
IS THERE SOMETHING I CAN DO?
IGA-RASHI-KUN!
BUT...
IT'S OKAY, REALLY!
YOU CAN COUNT ON ME!
Smile
OKAY?
TH...
THANKS!
WELL THEN...

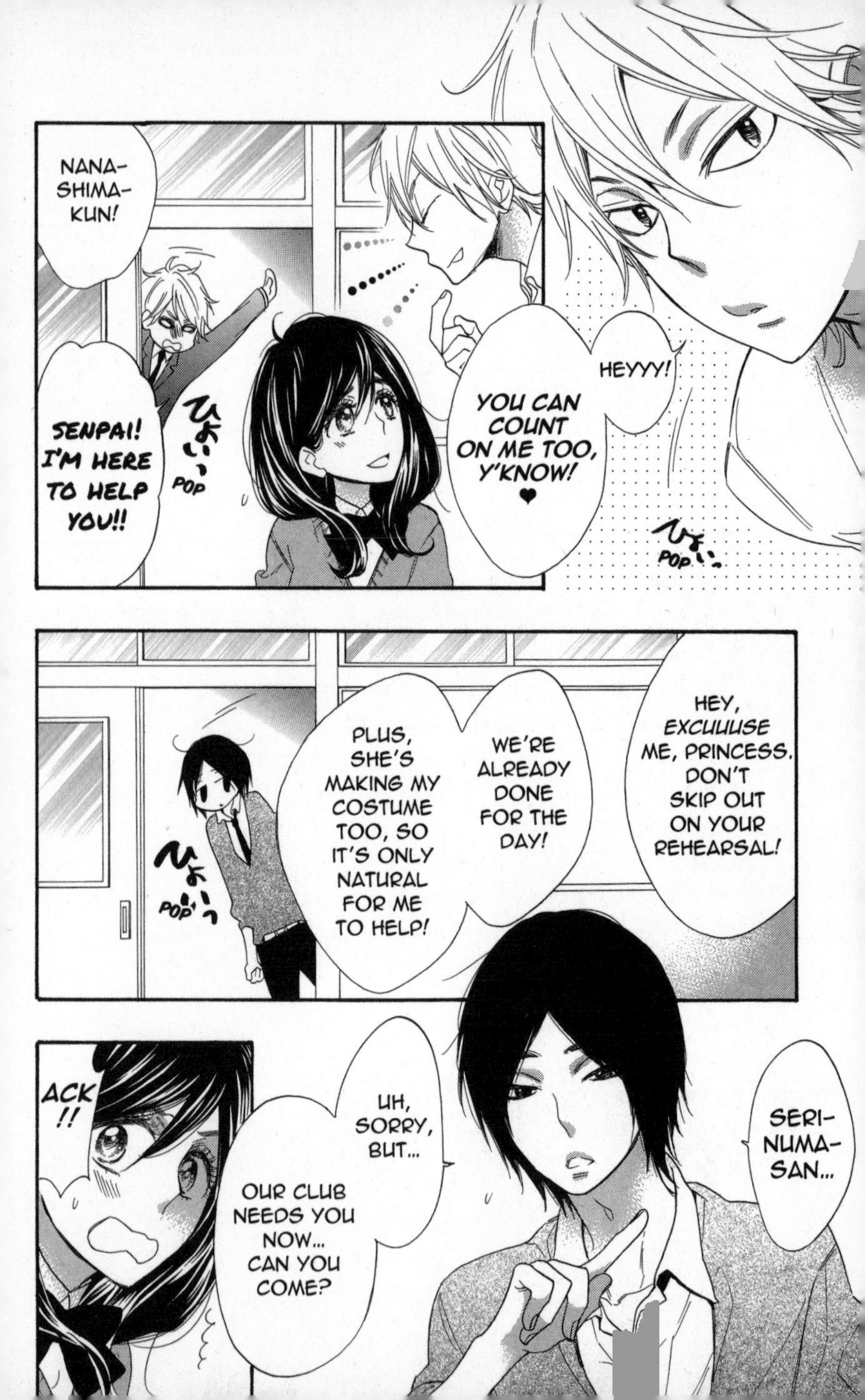
HEYYY!
YOU CAN COUNT ON ME TOO, Y'KNOW! ❤
ひょい POP
NANA-SHIMA-KUN!
SENPAI! I'M HERE TO HELP YOU!!
ひょい POP
HEY, EXCUUUSE ME, PRINCESS. DON'T SKIP OUT ON YOUR REHEARSAL!
WE'RE ALREADY DONE FOR THE DAY!
PLUS, SHE'S MAKING MY COSTUME TOO, SO IT'S ONLY NATURAL FOR ME TO HELP!
ひょい POP
SERI-NUMA-SAN...
UH, SORRY, BUT...
OUR CLUB NEEDS YOU NOW... CAN YOU COME?
ACK!!

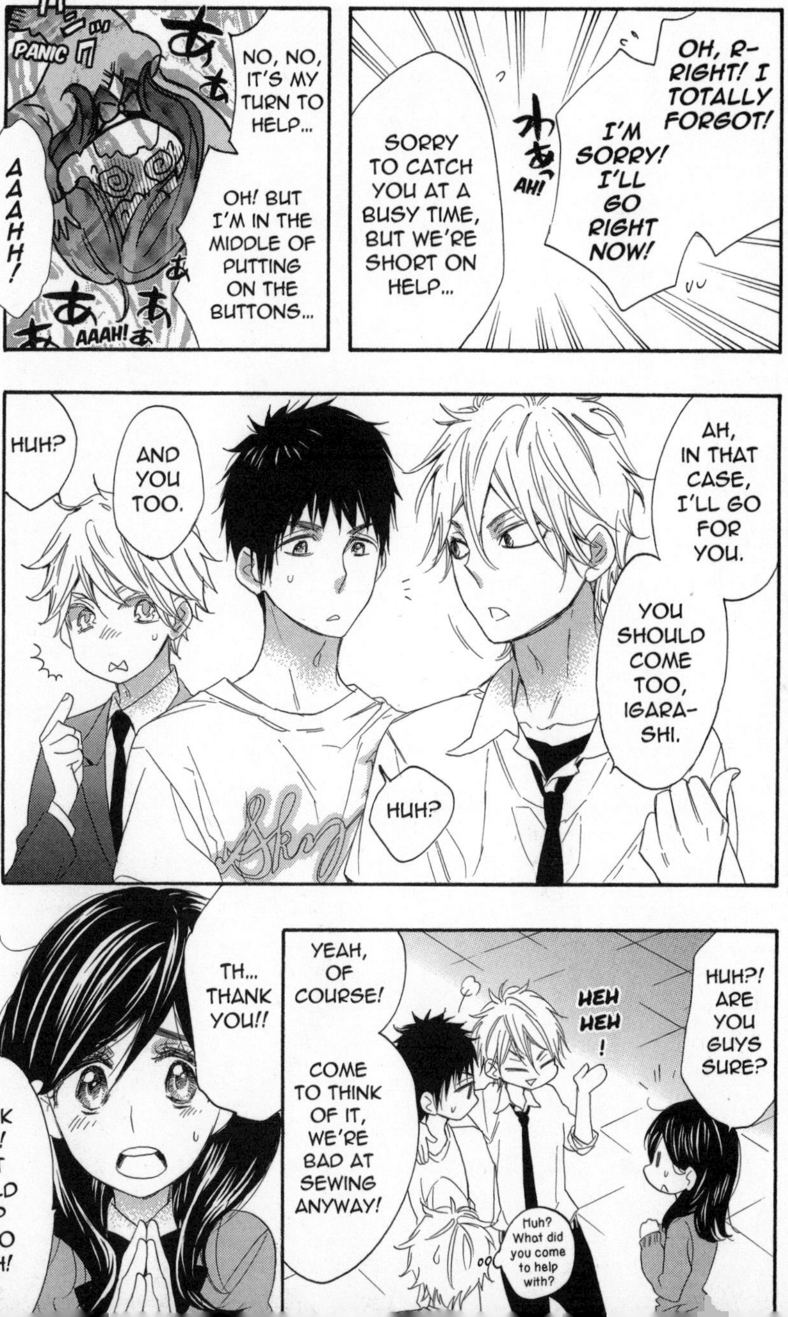

OH, R-RIGHT! I TOTALLY FORGOT!
I'M SORRY! I'LL GO RIGHT NOW!
わあ
AH!
SORRY TO CATCH YOU AT A BUSY TIME, BUT WE'RE SHORT ON HELP...
NO, NO, IT'S MY TURN TO HELP...
OH! BUT I'M IN THE MIDDLE OF PUTTING ON THE BUTTONS...
PANIC
AAAAHH!
AAAH!
AH, IN THAT CASE, I'LL GO FOR YOU.
YOU SHOULD COME TOO, IGARASHI.
HUH?
AND YOU TOO.
HUH?
HUH?! ARE YOU GUYS SURE?
HEH HEH!
YEAH, OF COURSE!
COME TO THINK OF IT, WE'RE BAD AT SEWING ANYWAY!
Huh? What did you come to help with?
TH... THANK YOU!!
THANK YOU! THAT WOULD HELP ME SO MUCH!

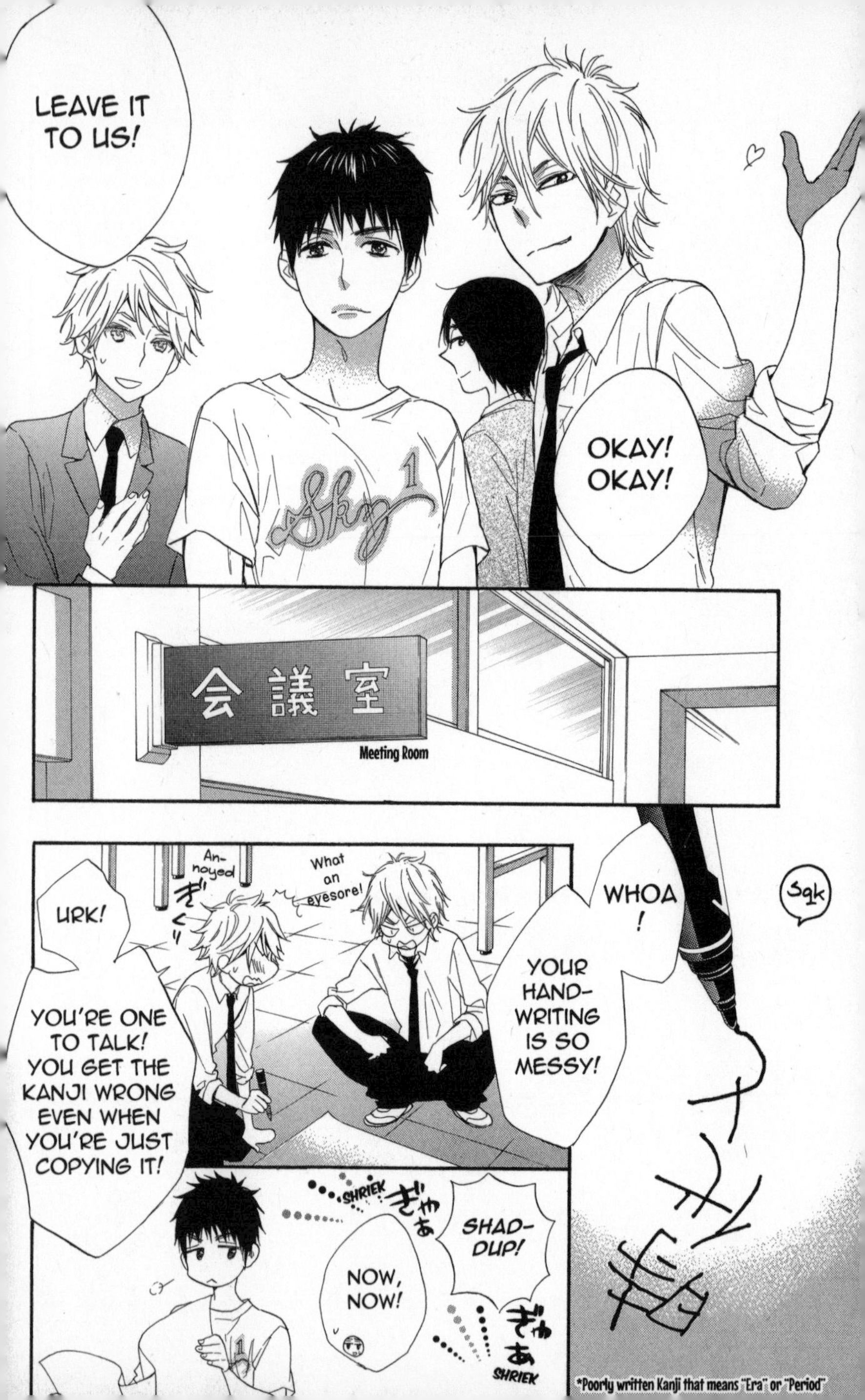
LEAVE IT TO US!
OKAY! OKAY!
会議室
Meeting Room
Sgk
WHOA! YOUR HAND-WRITING IS SO MESSY!
What an eyesore!
An-noyed
ぎくり
URK!
YOU'RE ONE TO TALK! YOU GET THE KANJI WRONG EVEN WHEN YOU'RE JUST COPYING IT!
SHRIEK
ぎゃあ
SHAD-UP!
NOW, NOW!
ぎゃあ
SHRIEK
*Poorly written Kanji that means "Era" or "Period"

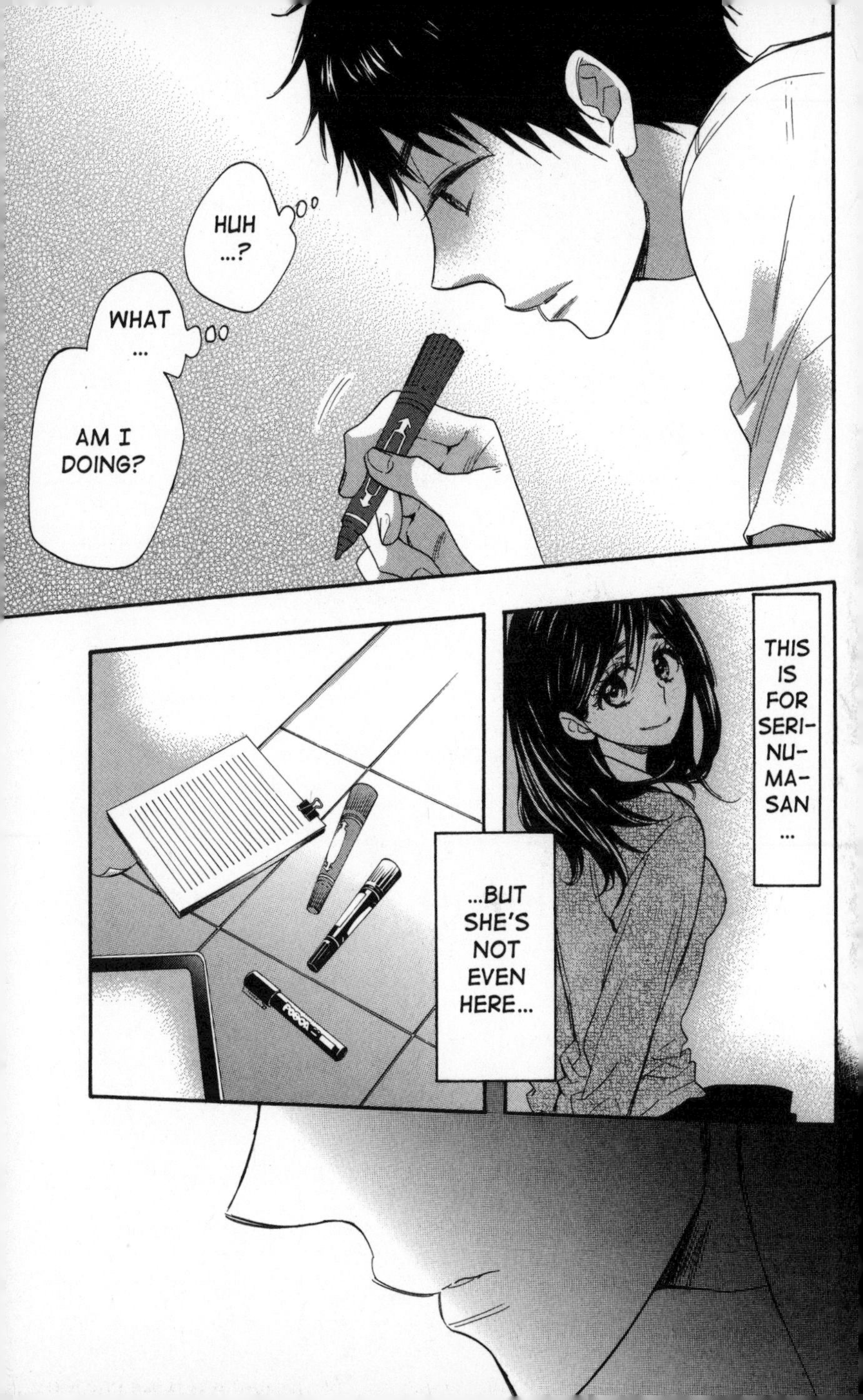
HUH ...?
WHAT ... AM I DOING?
THIS IS FOR SERI-NU-MA-SAN ...
...BUT SHE'S NOT EVEN HERE...

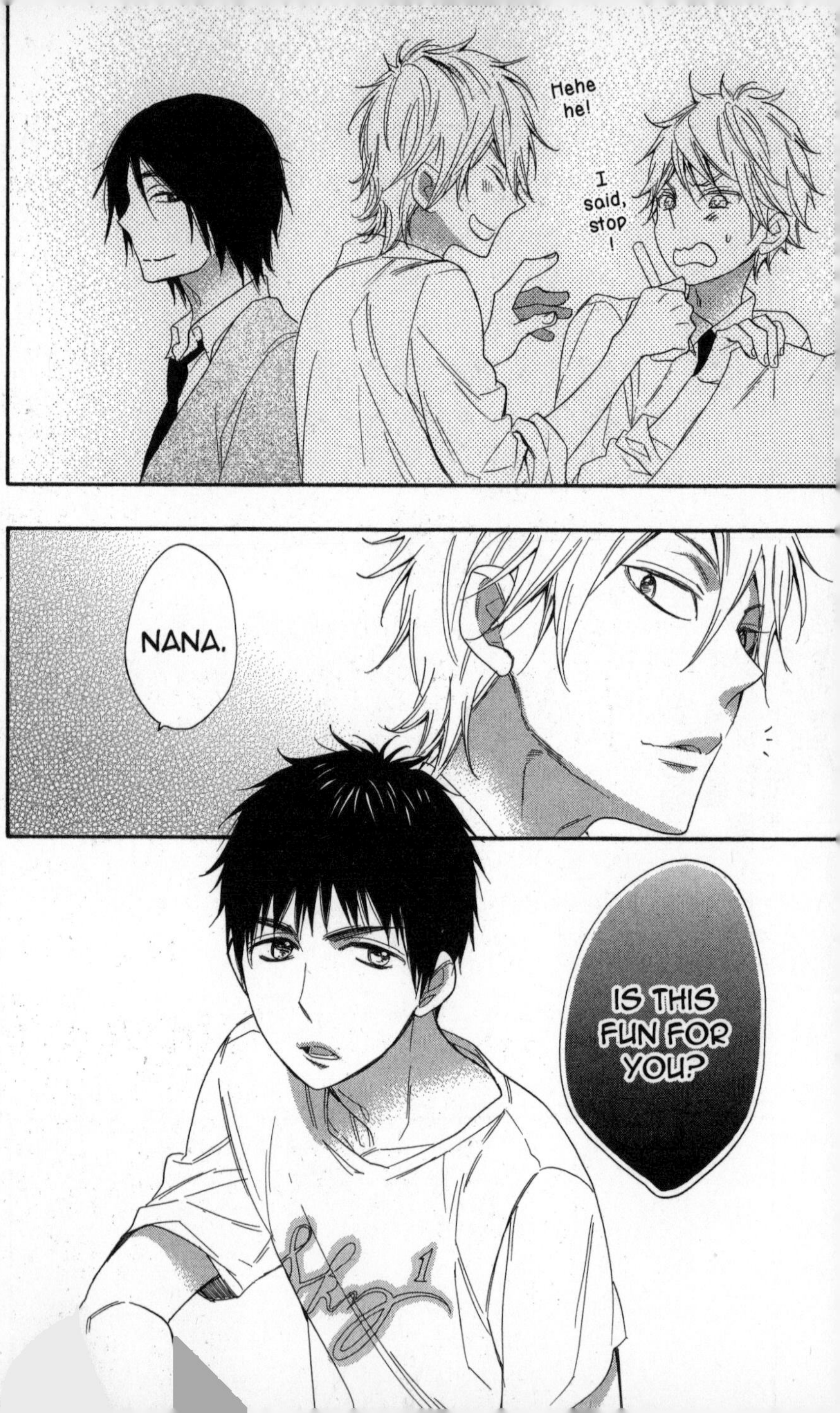
Hehe he!
I said, stop!
NANA.
IS THIS FUN FOR YOU?

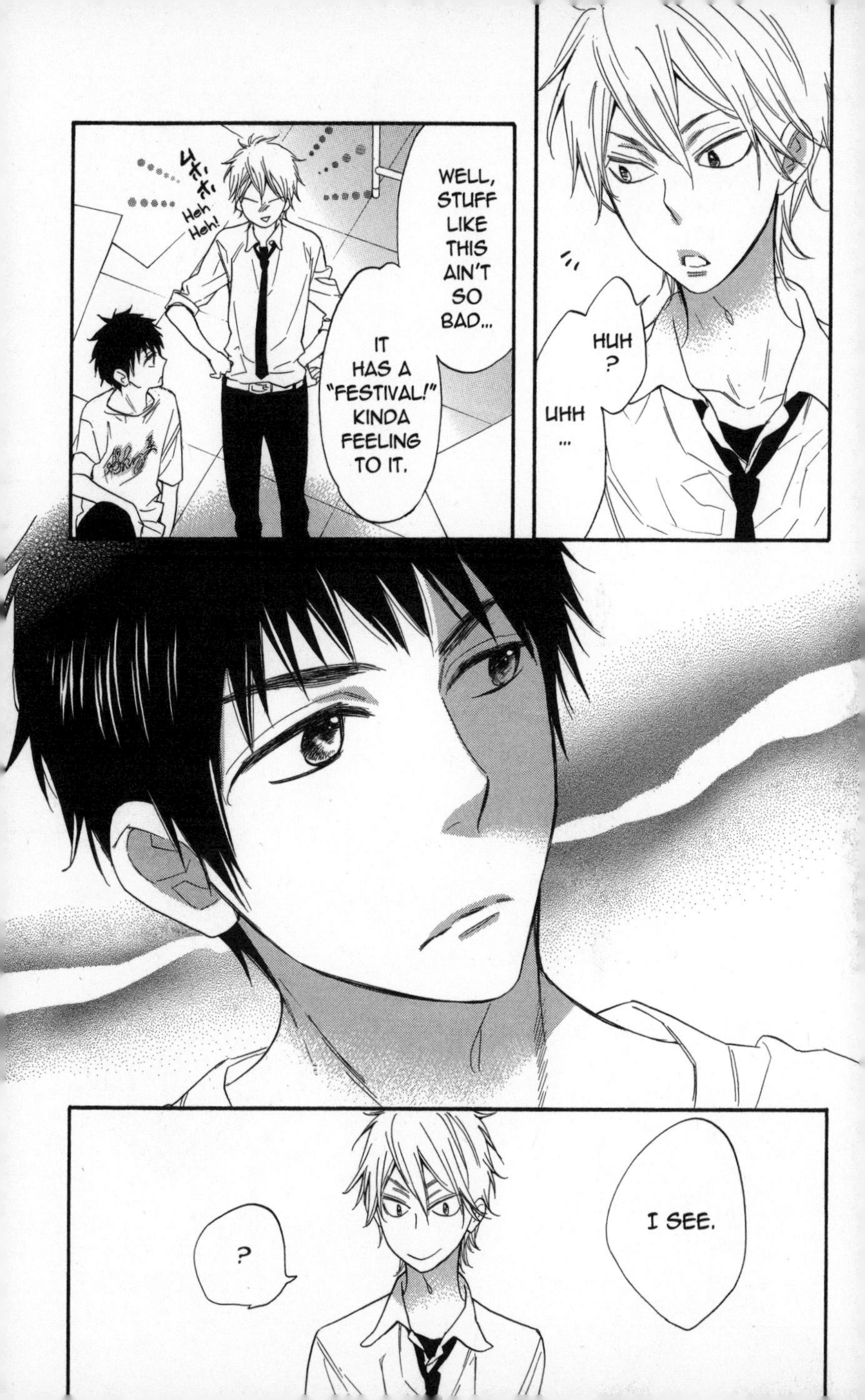
HUH?
UHH...
Heh Heh!
WELL, STUFF LIKE THIS AIN'T SO BAD...
IT HAS A "FESTIVAL!" KINDA FEELING TO IT.
I SEE.
?

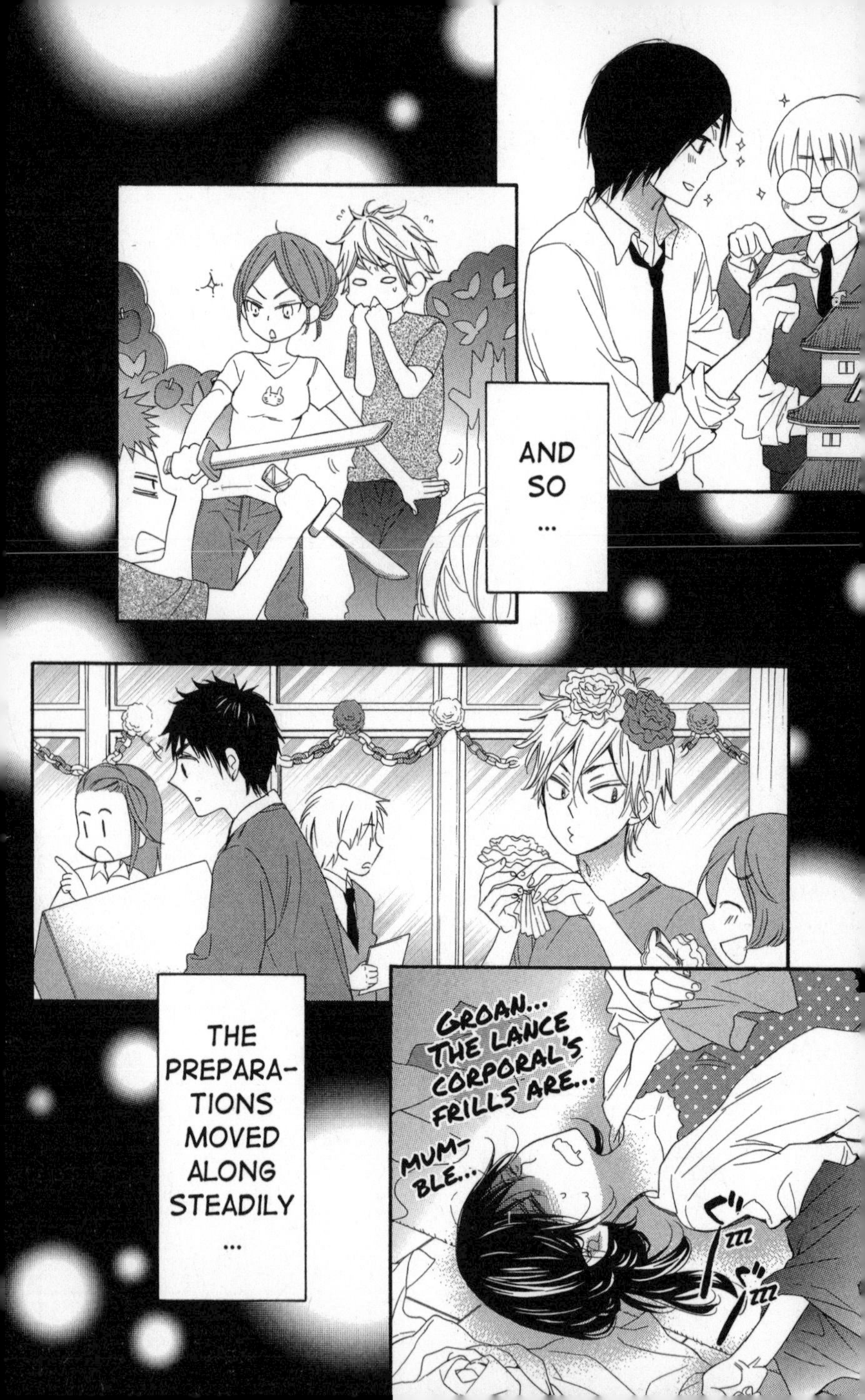
AND SO ...
THE PREPARATIONS MOVED ALONG STEADILY ...
GROAN... THE LANCE CORPORAL'S FRILLS ARE...
MUM-BLE...

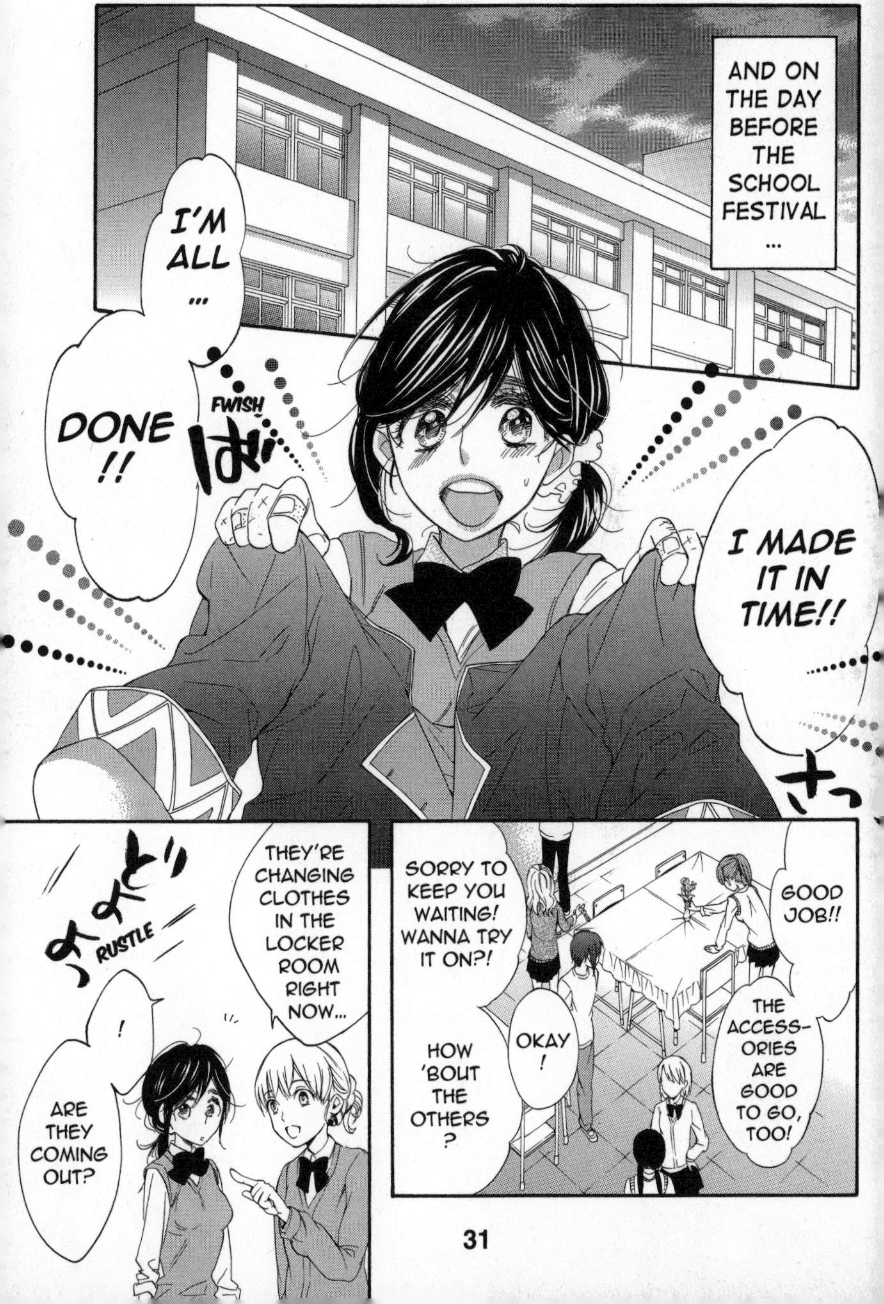
AND ON THE DAY BEFORE THE SCHOOL FESTIVAL ...
I'M ALL ... DONE !!
FWISH
I MADE IT IN TIME!!
GOOD JOB!!
SORRY TO KEEP YOU WAITING! WANNA TRY IT ON?!
THE ACCESS-ORIES ARE GOOD TO GO, TOO!
OKAY !
HOW 'BOUT THE OTHERS ?
THEY'RE CHANGING CLOTHES IN THE LOCKER ROOM RIGHT NOW...
RUSTLE
!
ARE THEY COMING OUT?

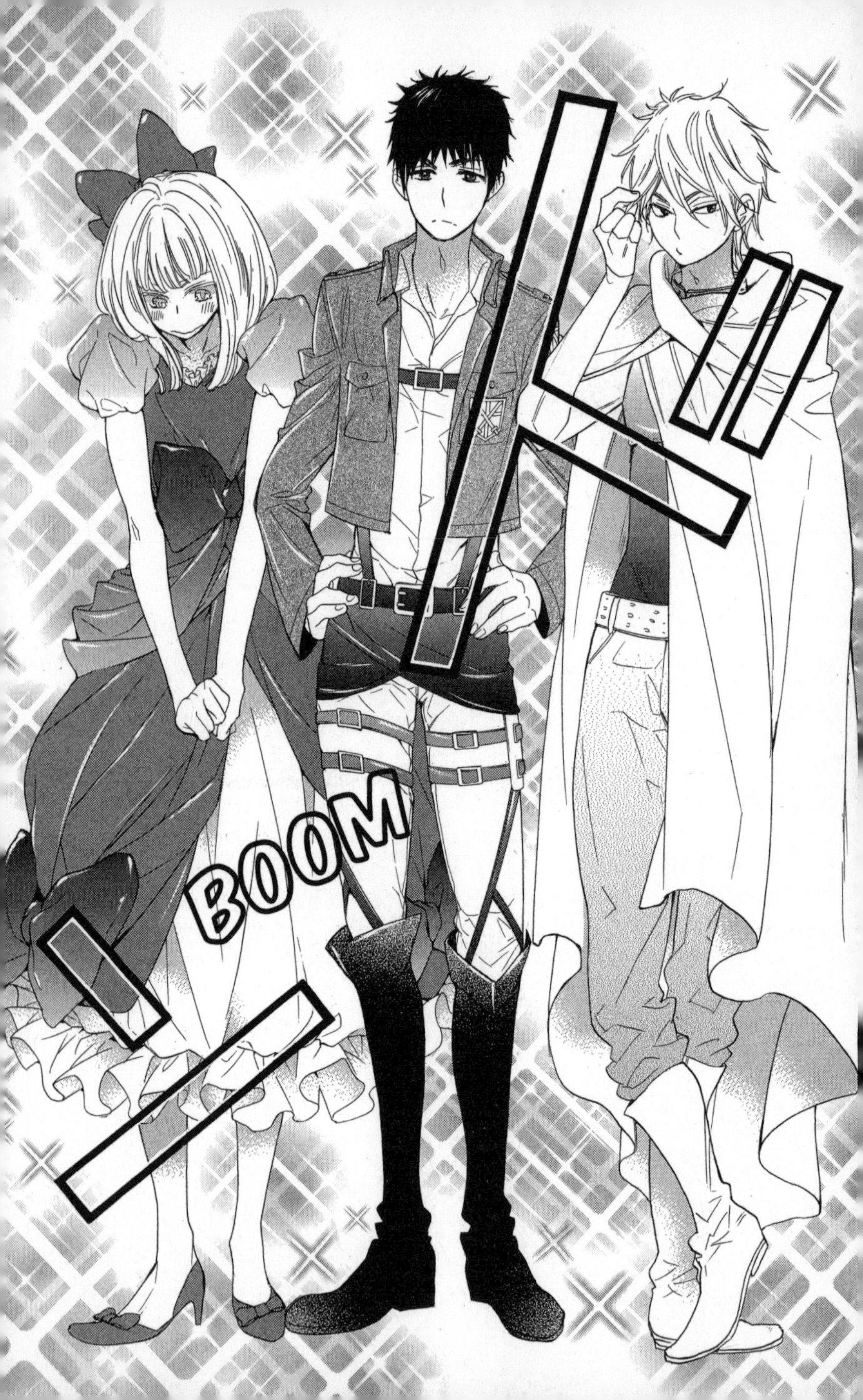
BOOM

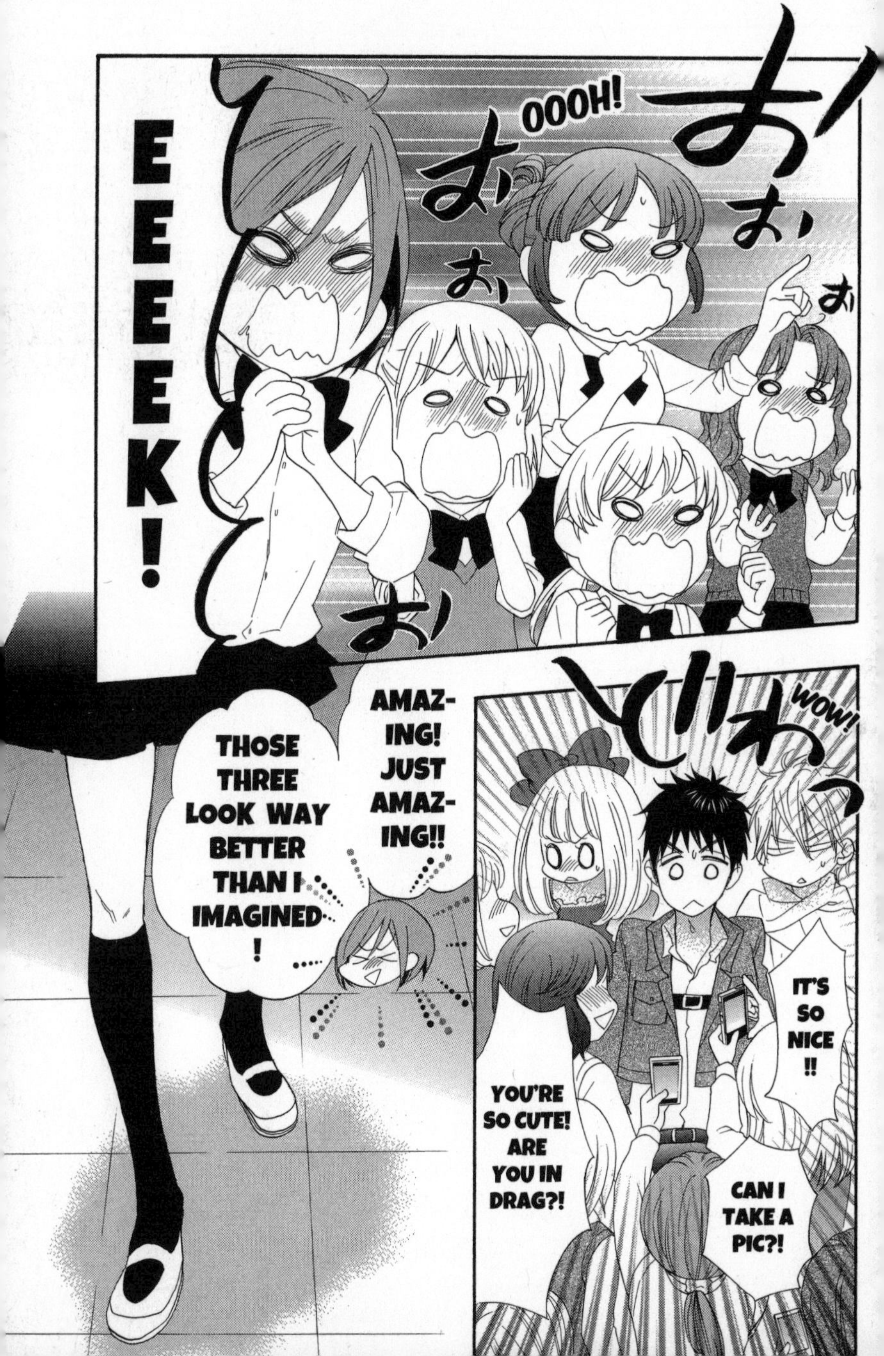
OOOH!
EEEEK!
WOW!
IT'S SO NICE!!
CAN I TAKE A PIC?!
YOU'RE SO CUTE! ARE YOU IN DRAG?!
AMAZ-ING! JUST AMAZ-ING!!
THOSE THREE LOOK WAY BETTER THAN I IMAGINED!

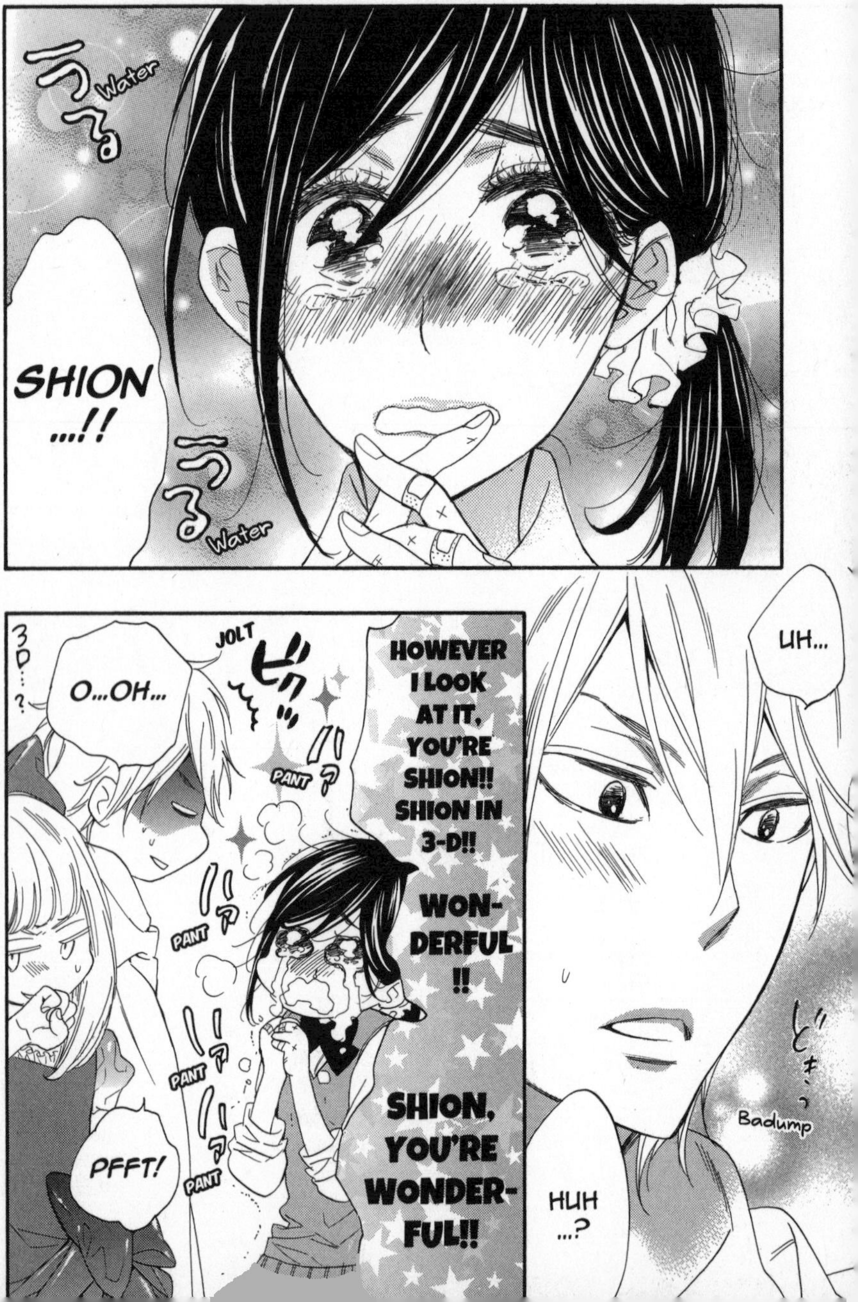

うる Water
SHION ...!!
うる Water
UH...
どきっ Badump
HUH ...?
HOWEVER I LOOK AT IT, YOU'RE SHION!! SHION IN 3-D!!
WON-DERFUL !!
SHION, YOU'RE WONDER-FUL!!
ハァ PANT
ハァ PANT
ハァ PANT
ハァ PANT
ビクッ JOLT
O...OH...
3D... ?
PFFT!

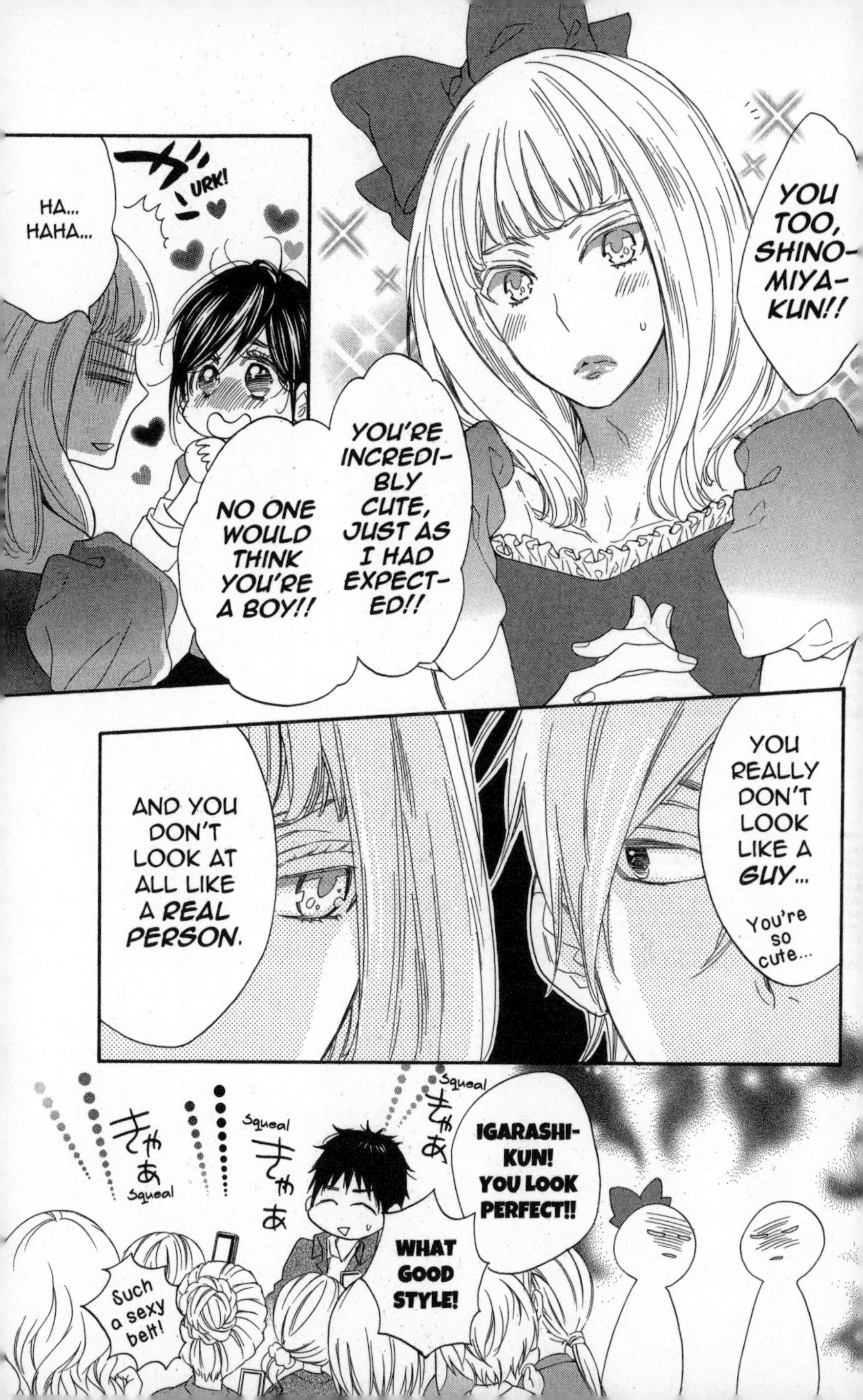
YOU TOO, SHINOMIYA-KUN!!
URK!
HA... HAHA...
YOU'RE INCREDIBLY CUTE, JUST AS I HAD EXPECTED!!
NO ONE WOULD THINK YOU'RE A BOY!!
YOU REALLY DON'T LOOK LIKE A GUY...
You're so cute...
AND YOU DON'T LOOK AT ALL LIKE A REAL PERSON.
IGARASHI-KUN! YOU LOOK PERFECT!!
Squeal
きゃあ
WHAT GOOD STYLE!
Squeal
きゃあ
きゃあ
Squeal
Such a sexy belt!

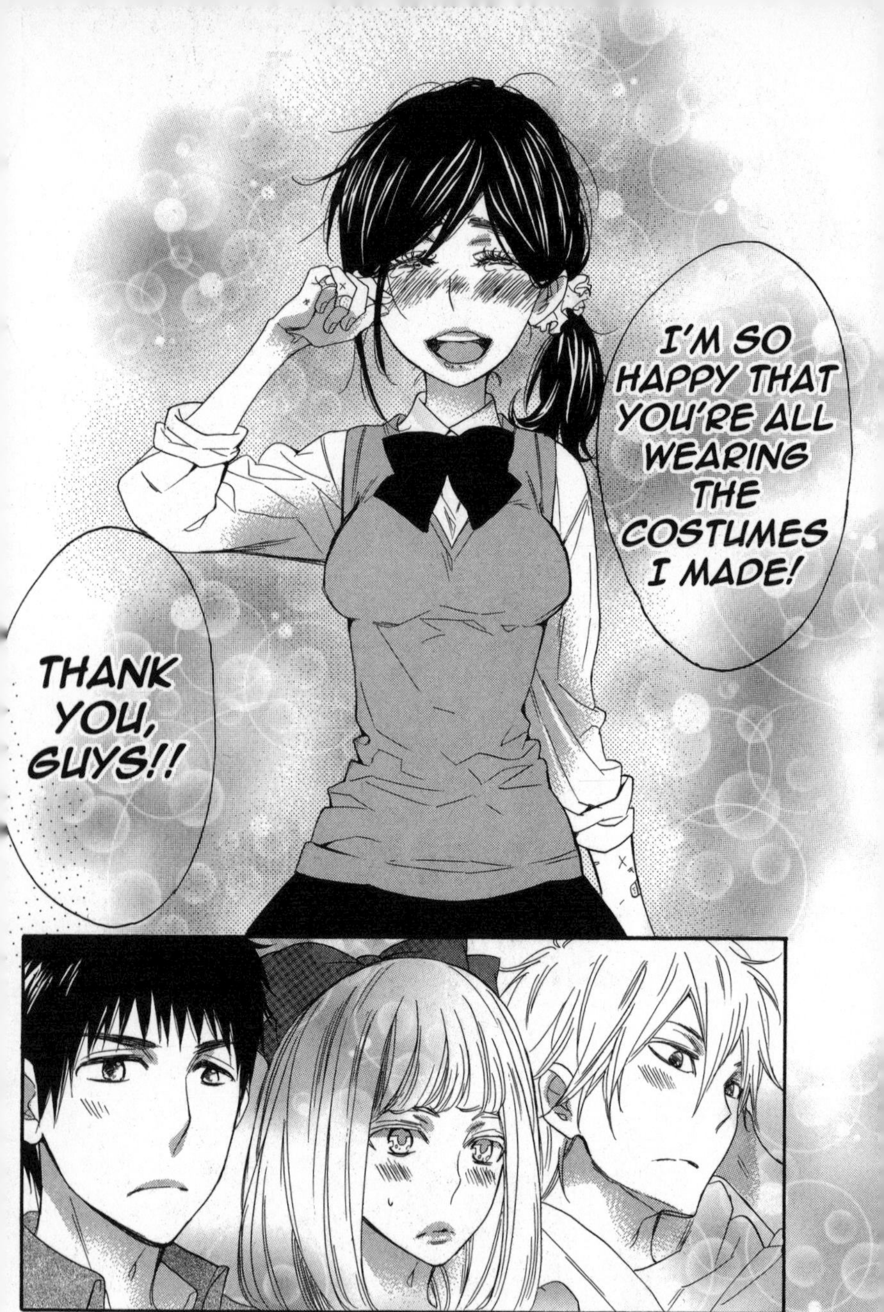
I'M SO HAPPY THAT YOU'RE ALL WEARING THE COSTUMES I MADE!
THANK YOU, GUYS!!

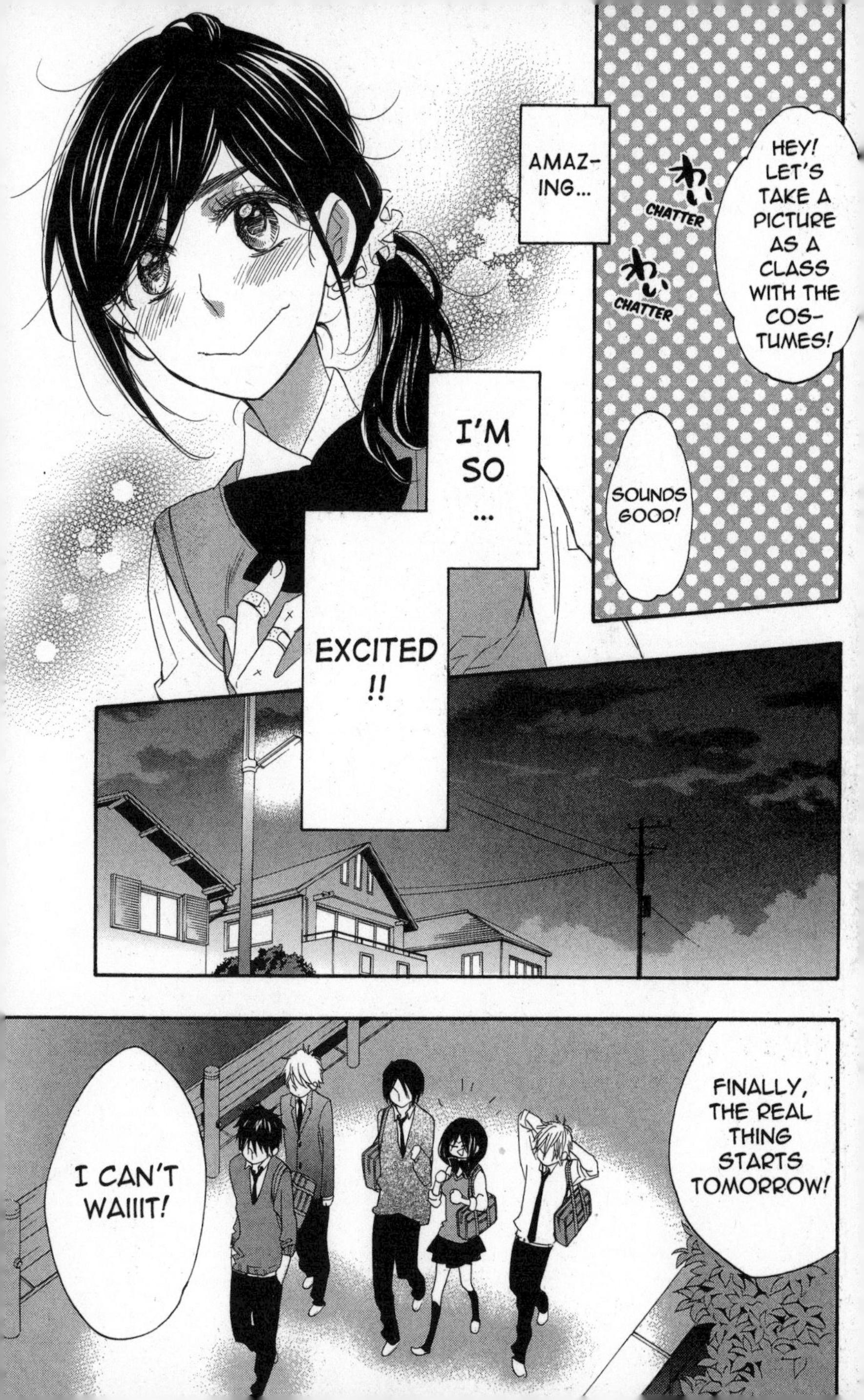
HEY! LET'S TAKE A PICTURE AS A CLASS WITH THE COS-TUMES!
わい CHATTER
わい CHATTER
SOUNDS GOOD!
AMAZ-ING...
I'M SO ...
EXCITED !!
FINALLY, THE REAL THING STARTS TOMORROW!
I CAN'T WAIIIT!

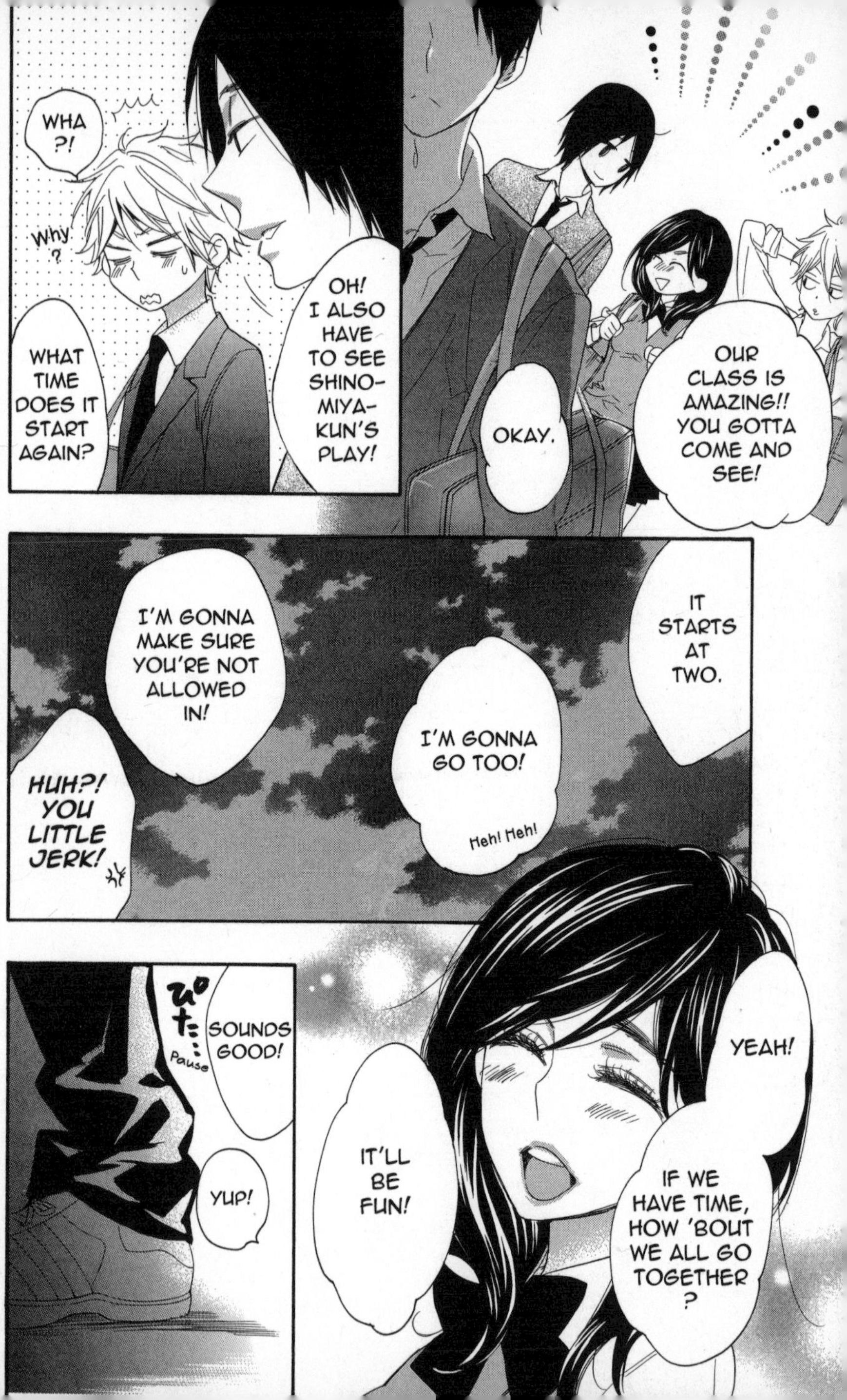
OUR CLASS IS AMAZING!! YOU GOTTA COME AND SEE!
OKAY.
OH! I ALSO HAVE TO SEE SHINO-MIYA-KUN'S PLAY!
WHA ?!
Why ?
WHAT TIME DOES IT START AGAIN?
IT STARTS AT TWO.
I'M GONNA GO TOO!
Heh! Heh!
I'M GONNA MAKE SURE YOU'RE NOT ALLOWED IN!
HUH?! YOU LITTLE JERK!
YEAH!
IF WE HAVE TIME, HOW 'BOUT WE ALL GO TOGETHER ?
IT'LL BE FUN!
SOUNDS GOOD!
ぴた…
Pause
YUP!

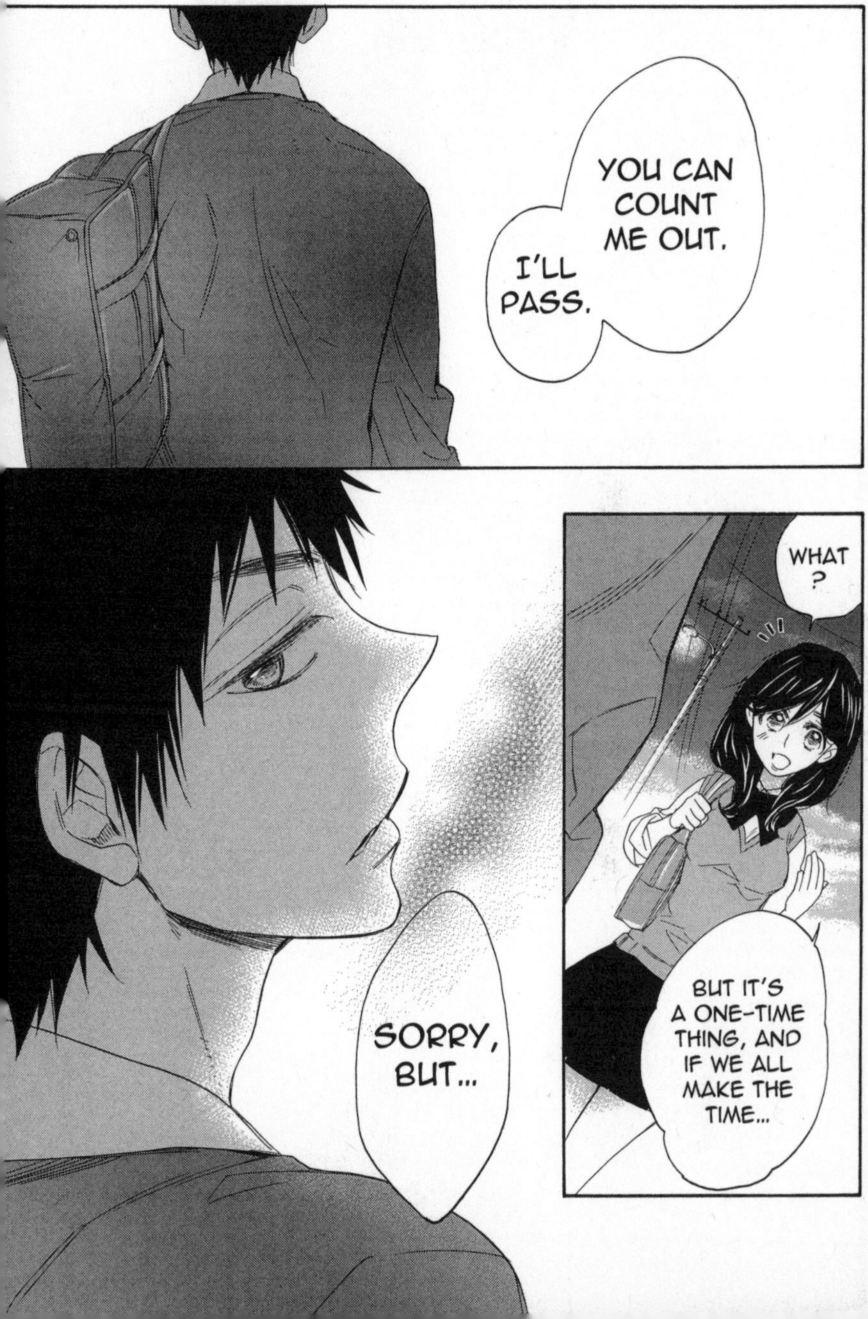
YOU CAN COUNT ME OUT.
I'LL PASS.
WHAT?
BUT IT'S A ONE-TIME THING, AND IF WE ALL MAKE THE TIME...
SORRY, BUT...

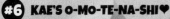
#6 KAE'S O-MO-TE-NA-SHI ❤

"I'M NOT INTERESTED IN PRETENDING WE'RE ALL 'JUST FRIENDS' ANYMORE."
IGARASHI-KUN ...?!

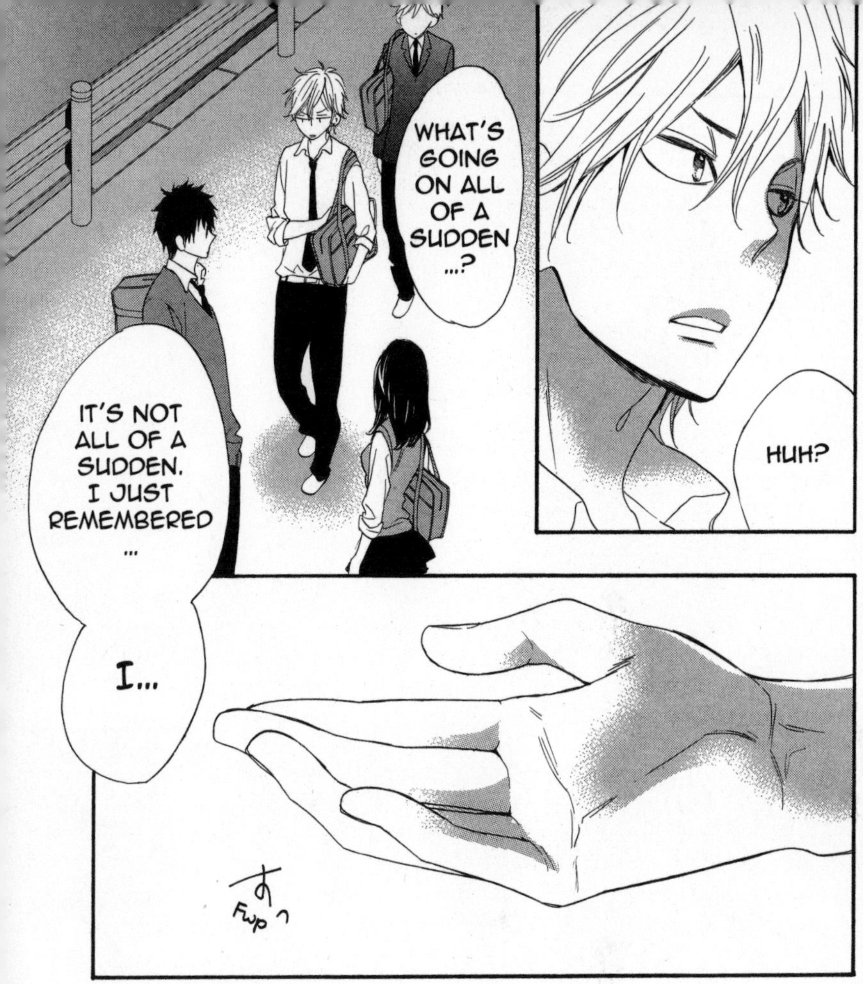
HUH?
WHAT'S GOING ON ALL OF A SUDDEN ...?
IT'S NOT ALL OF A SUDDEN. I JUST REMEMBERED ...
I...
Fwp

KiSS HiM, NOT ME!

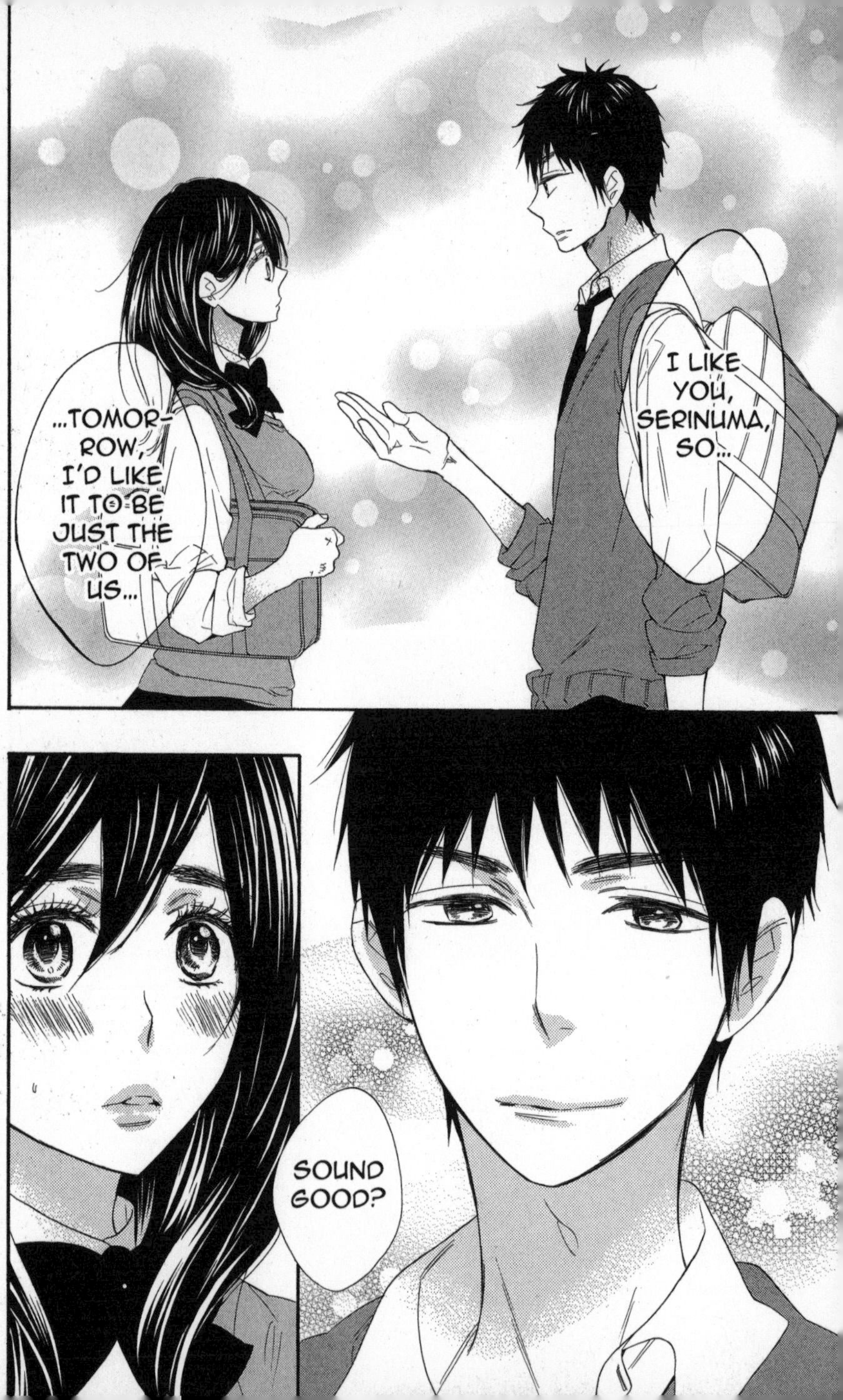
I LIKE YOU, SERINUMA, SO...
...TOMOR-ROW, I'D LIKE IT TO BE JUST THE TWO OF US...
SOUND GOOD?

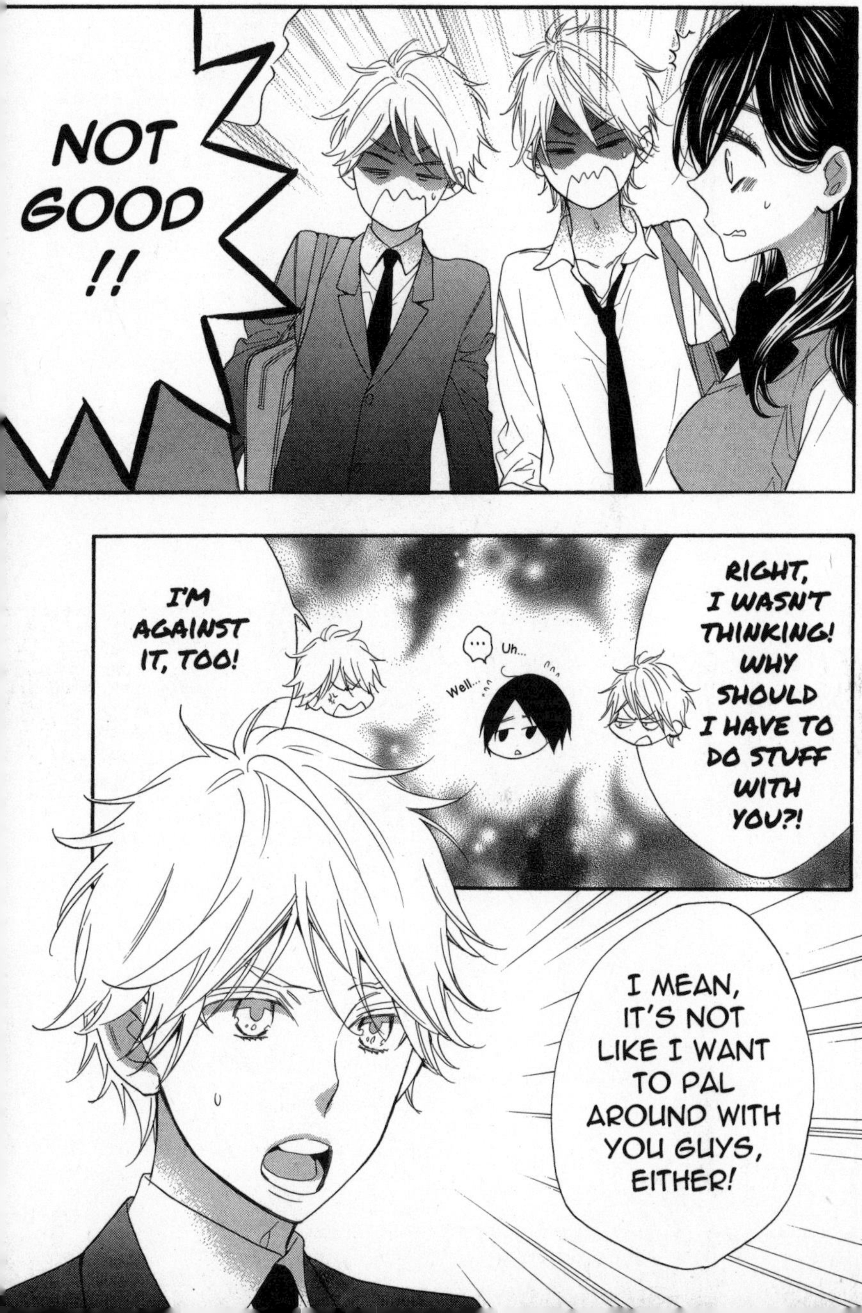
NOT GOOD!!
RIGHT, I WASN'T THINKING! WHY SHOULD I HAVE TO DO STUFF WITH YOU?!
...
Uh...
Well...
I'M AGAINST IT, TOO!
I MEAN, IT'S NOT LIKE I WANT TO PAL AROUND WITH YOU GUYS, EITHER!

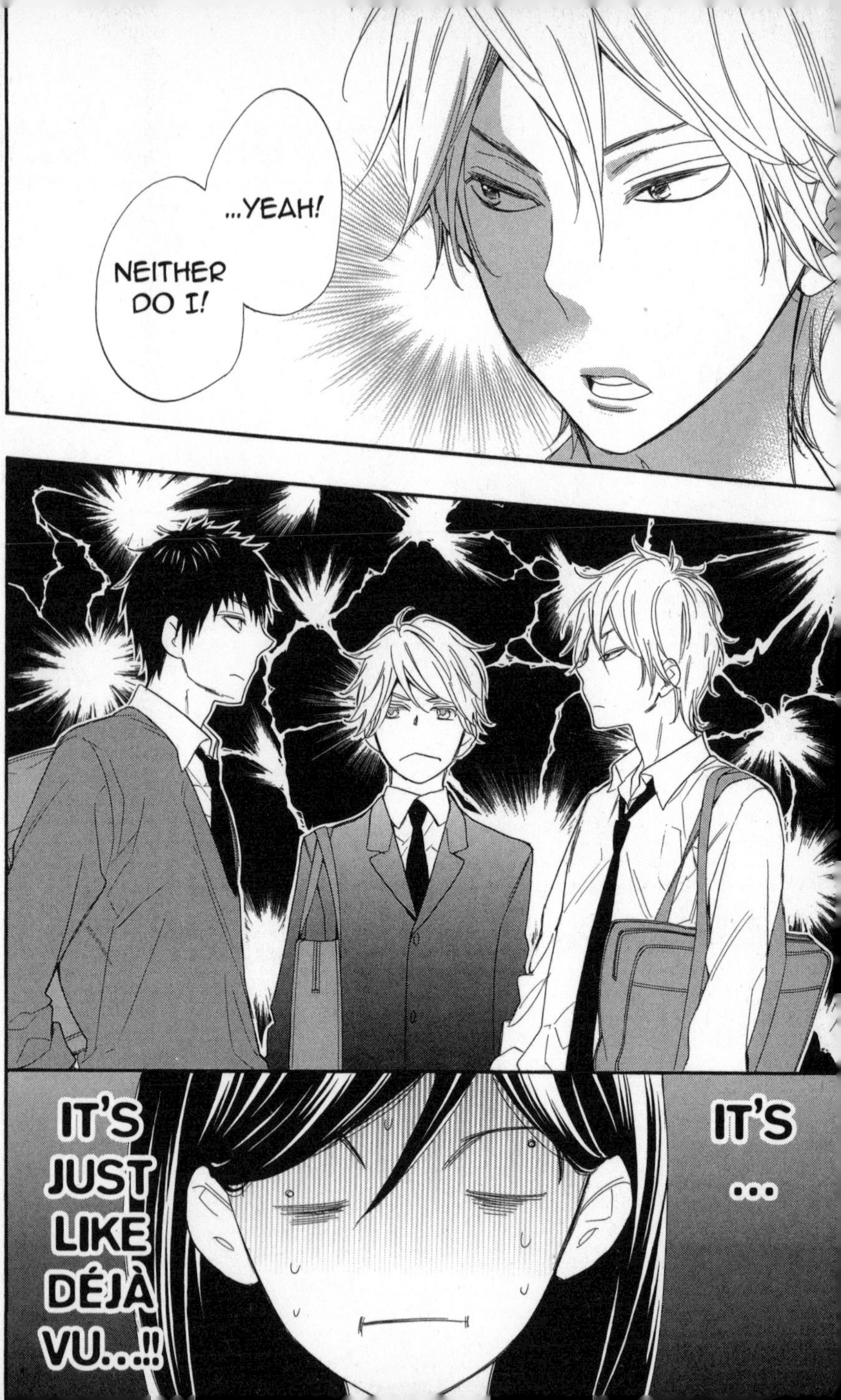
...YEAH! NEITHER DO I!
IT'S ...
IT'S JUST LIKE DÉJÀ VU...!!

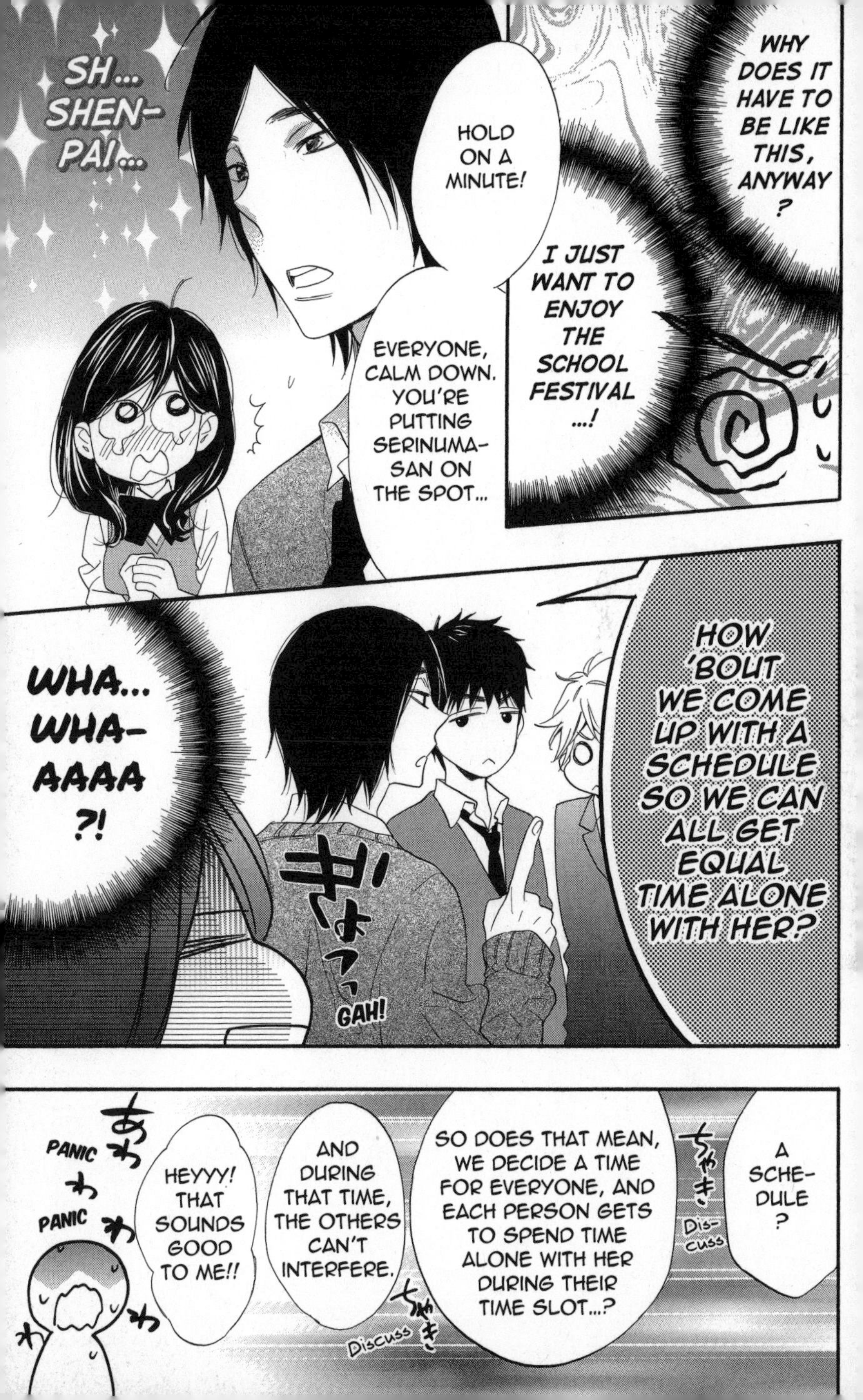
WHY DOES IT HAVE TO BE LIKE THIS, ANYWAY?
I JUST WANT TO ENJOY THE SCHOOL FESTIVAL ...!
HOLD ON A MINUTE!
EVERYONE, CALM DOWN. YOU'RE PUTTING SERINUMA-SAN ON THE SPOT...
SH... SHEN-PAI...
HOW 'BOUT WE COME UP WITH A SCHEDULE SO WE CAN ALL GET EQUAL TIME ALONE WITH HER?
WHA... WHA-AAAA?!
GAH!
A SCHE-DULE?
DIS-CUSS
SO DOES THAT MEAN, WE DECIDE A TIME FOR EVERYONE, AND EACH PERSON GETS TO SPEND TIME ALONE WITH HER DURING THEIR TIME SLOT...?
AND DURING THAT TIME, THE OTHERS CAN'T INTERFERE.
DISCUSS
HEYYY! THAT SOUNDS GOOD TO ME!!
PANIC
PANIC

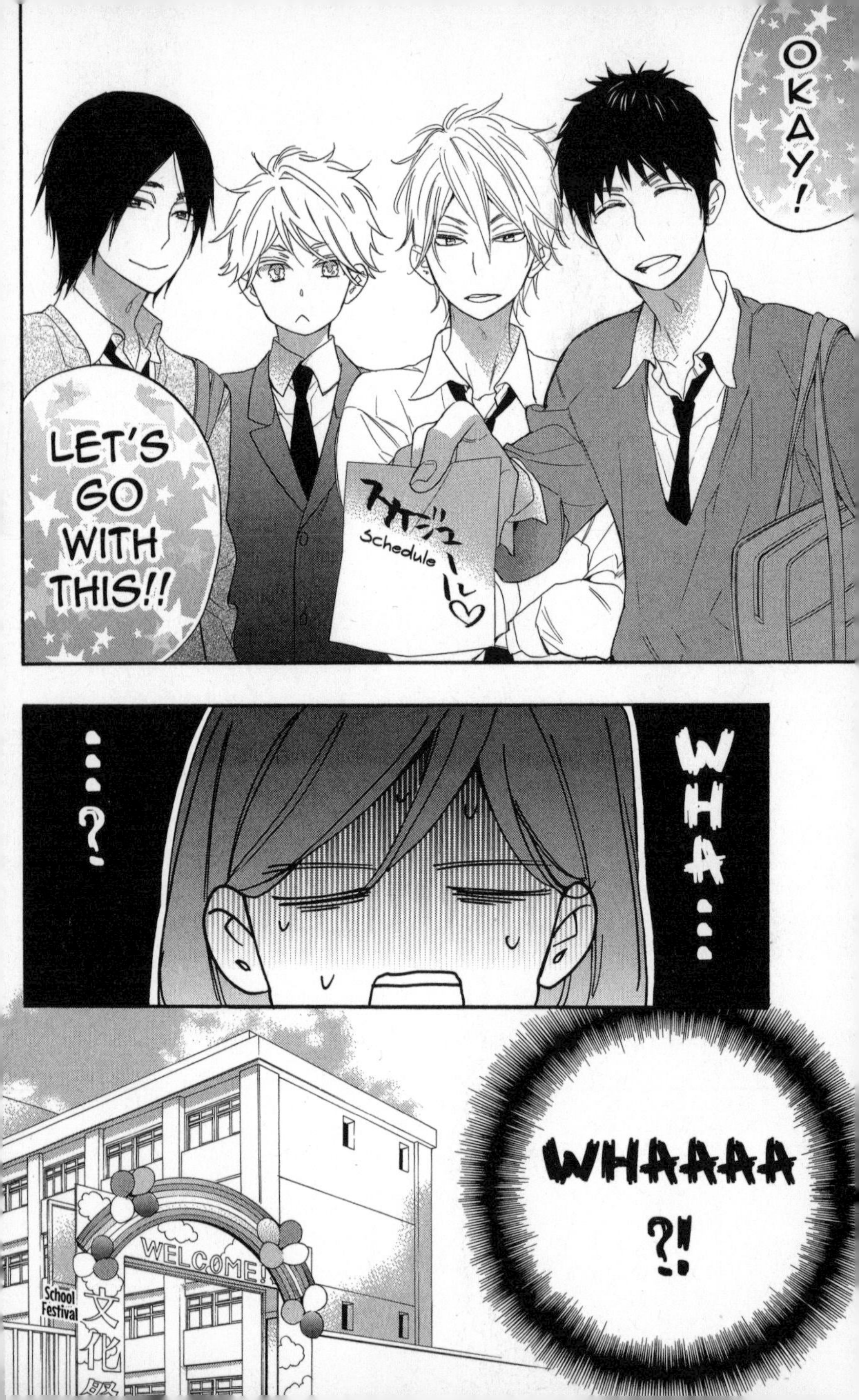
OKAY!
LET'S GO WITH THIS!!
Schedule
WHA...
...?
WHAAAA ?!!
WELCOME!
School Festival
文化祭

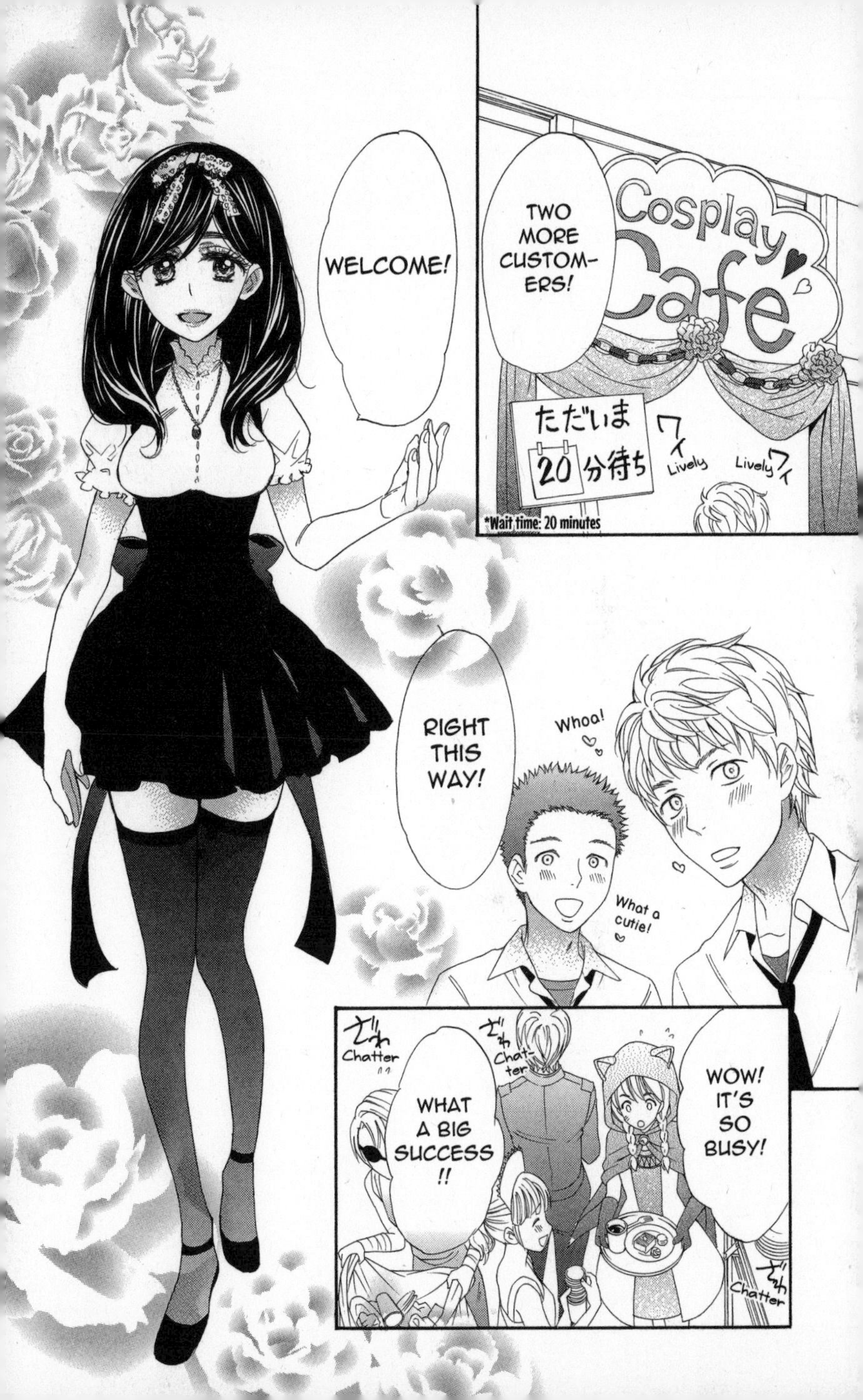

TWO MORE CUSTOMERS!
Cosplay Cafe
ただいま 20 分待ち
*Wait time: 20 minutes
ワイ Lively
ワイ Lively
WELCOME!
RIGHT THIS WAY!
Whoa!
What a cutie!
WOW! IT'S SO BUSY!
WHAT A BIG SUCCESS!!
ざわ Chatter
ざわ Chatter
ざわ Chatter

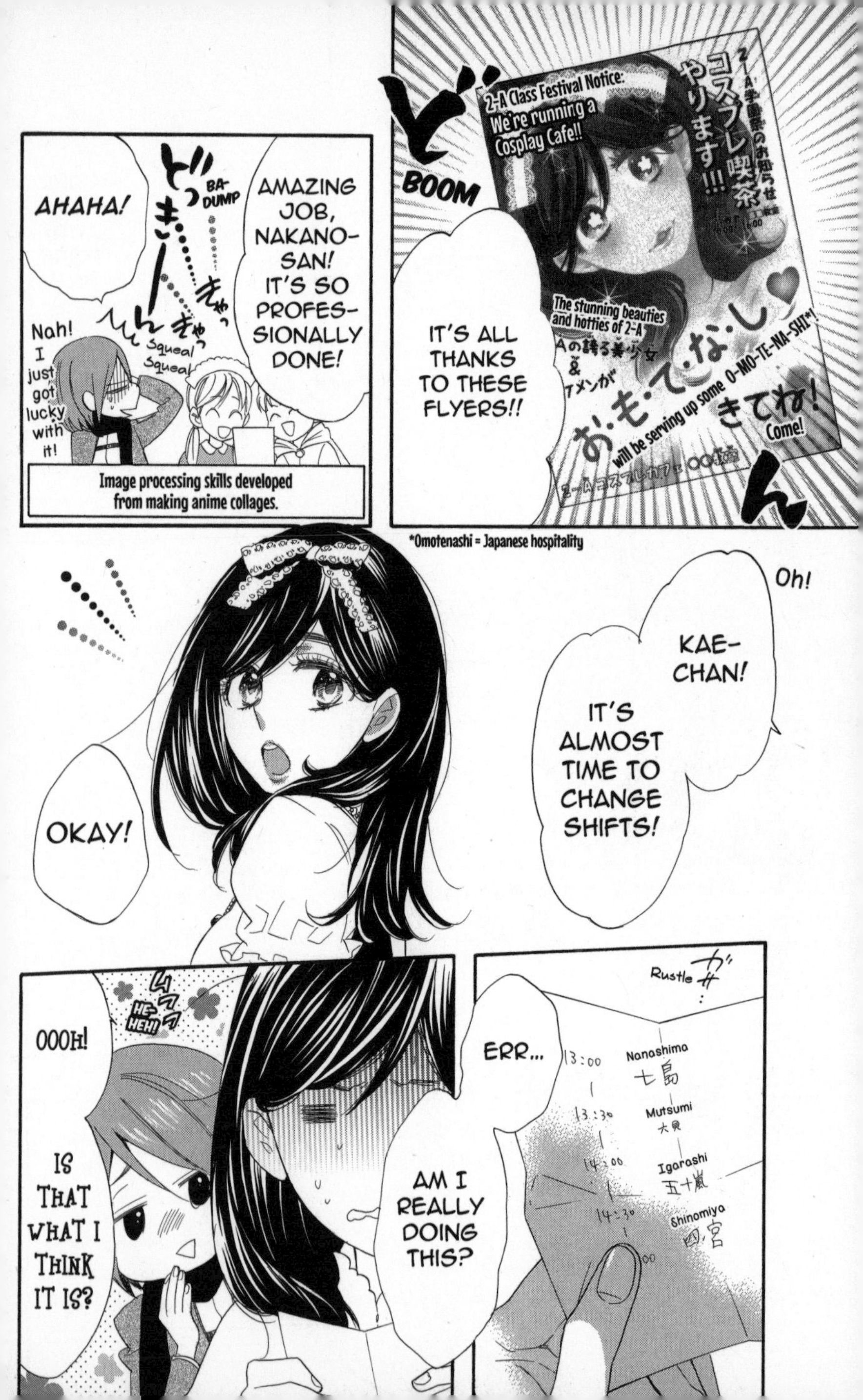
BOOM
2-A学園祭のお知らせ
コスプレ喫茶やります!!!
2-A Class Festival Notice: We're running a Cosplay Cafe!!
Aの誇る美少女&イケメンが
The stunning beauties and hotties of 2-A
お・も・て・な・し
will be serving up some O-MO-TE-NA-SHI*!
きてね!
Come!
IT'S ALL THANKS TO THESE FLYERS!!
AMAZING JOB, NAKANO-SAN! IT'S SO PROFESSIONALLY DONE!
BA-DUMP
AHAHA!
Squeal Squeal
Nah! I just got lucky with it!
Image processing skills developed from making anime collages.
Oh!
KAE-CHAN!
IT'S ALMOST TIME TO CHANGE SHIFTS!
OKAY!
Rustle
ERR...
13:00 Nanashima 七島
13:30 Mutsumi 六見
14:00 Igarashi 五十嵐
14:30 Shinomiya 四宮
AM I REALLY DOING THIS?
HE-HEH!
OOOH!
IS THAT WHAT I THINK IT IS?
*Omotenashi = Japanese hospitality

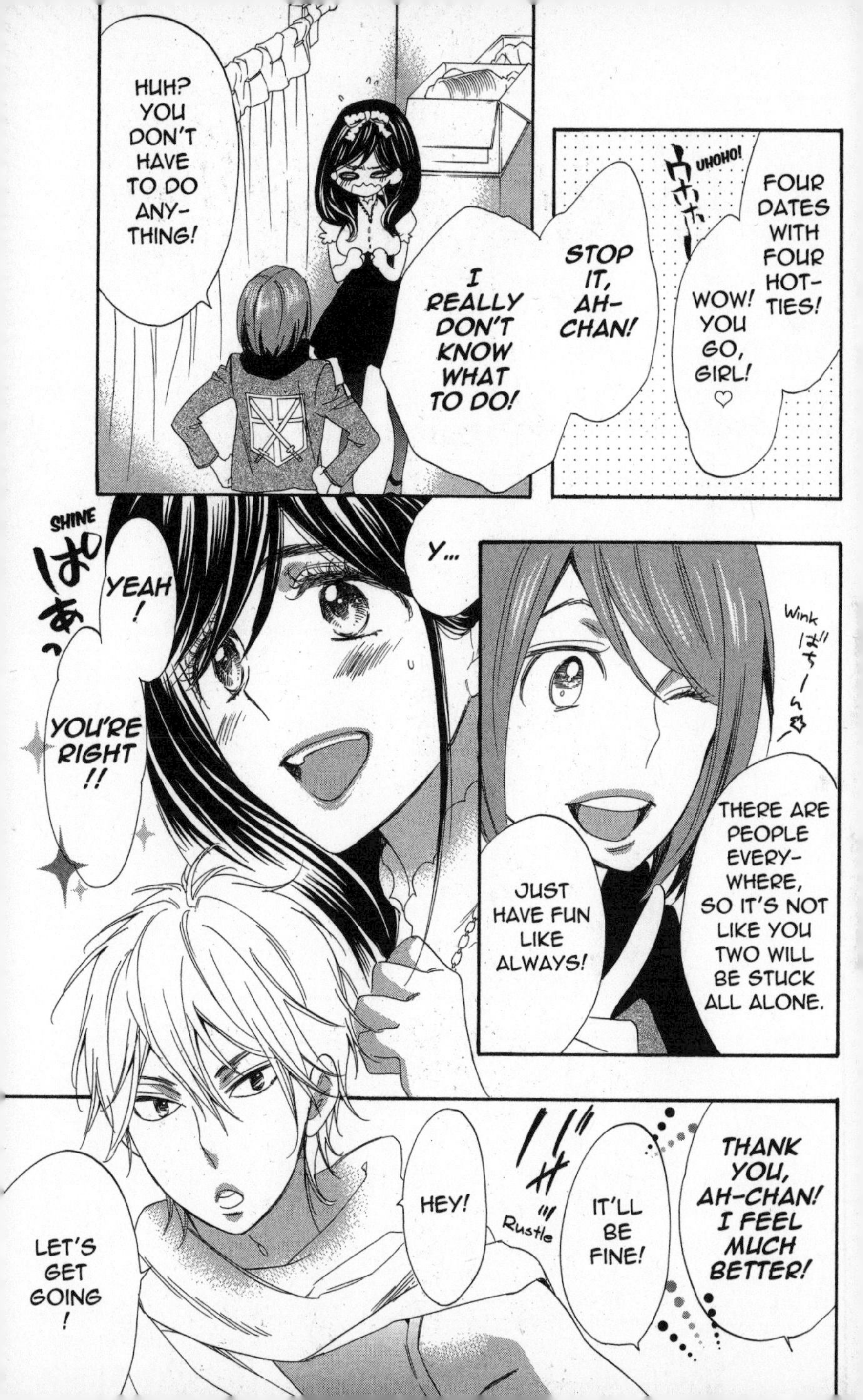
UHOHO!
FOUR DATES WITH FOUR HOT-TIES!
WOW! YOU GO, GIRL! ♡
STOP IT, AH-CHAN!
I REALLY DON'T KNOW WHAT TO DO!
HUH? YOU DON'T HAVE TO DO ANY-THING!
Wink
THERE ARE PEOPLE EVERY-WHERE, SO IT'S NOT LIKE YOU TWO WILL BE STUCK ALL ALONE.
JUST HAVE FUN LIKE ALWAYS!
Y...
SHINE
YEAH!
YOU'RE RIGHT!!
THANK YOU, AH-CHAN! I FEEL MUCH BETTER!
IT'LL BE FINE!
Rustle
HEY!
LET'S GET GOING!

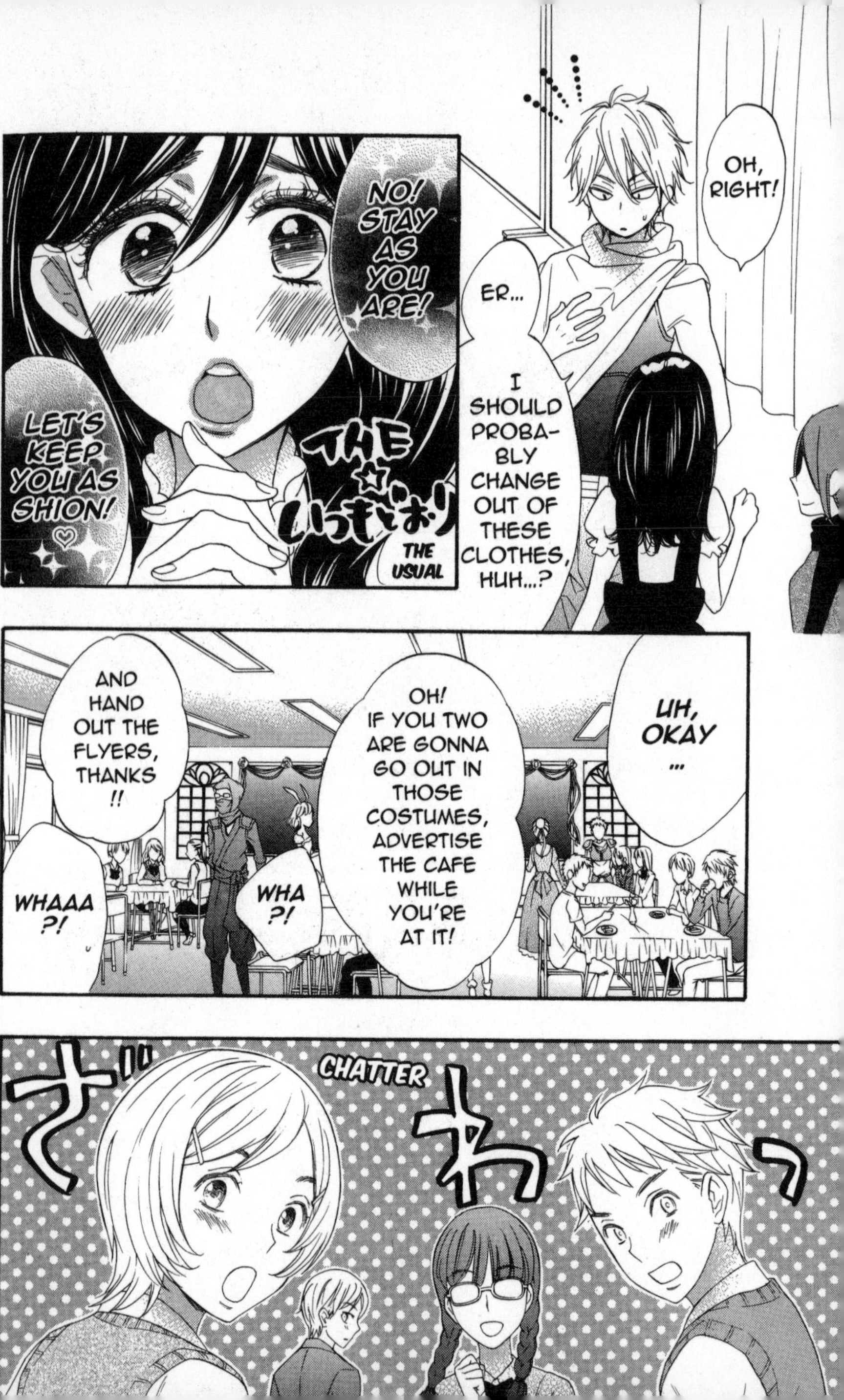
OH, RIGHT!
ER...
I SHOULD PROBA-BLY CHANGE OUT OF THESE CLOTHES, HUH...?
NO! STAY AS YOU ARE!
LET'S KEEP YOU AS SHION! ♡
THE ☆ いつもどおり
THE USUAL
UH, OKAY ...
OH! IF YOU TWO ARE GONNA GO OUT IN THOSE COSTUMES, ADVERTISE THE CAFE WHILE YOU'RE AT IT!
AND HAND OUT THE FLYERS, THANKS !!
WHA ?!
WHAAA ?!
ざわっ
CHATTER

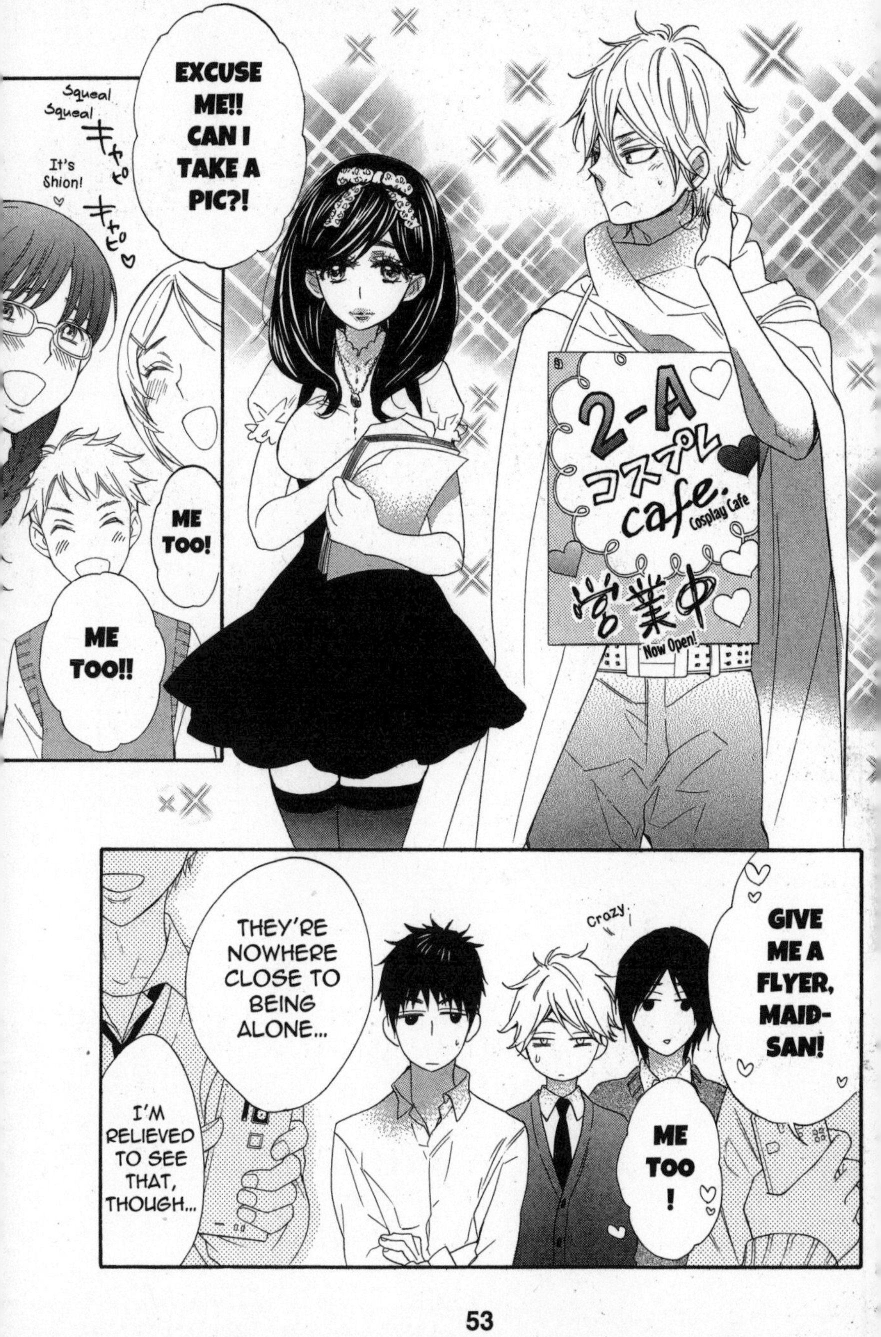
2-A
コスプレ
cafe.
Cosplay Cafe
営業中
Now Open!
EXCUSE ME!! CAN I TAKE A PIC?!
Squeal Squeal
キャピ キャピ
It's Shion!
ME TOO!
ME TOO!!
GIVE ME A FLYER, MAID-SAN!
ME TOO !
Crazy
THEY'RE NOWHERE CLOSE TO BEING ALONE...
I'M RELIEVED TO SEE THAT, THOUGH...

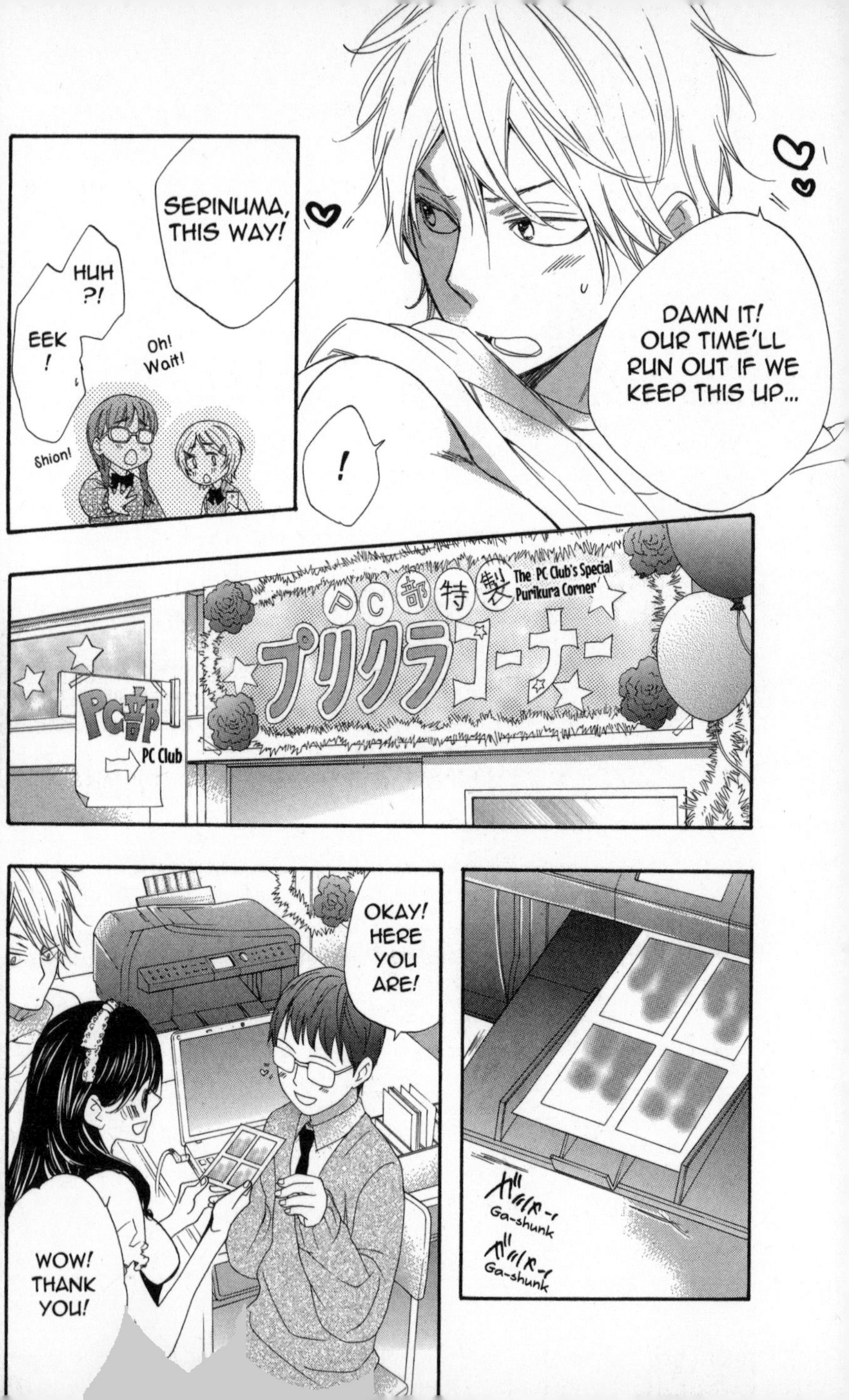
DAMN IT! OUR TIME'LL RUN OUT IF WE KEEP THIS UP...
!
SERINUMA, THIS WAY!
HUH?!
Oh! Wait!
EEK!
Shion!
PC部特製
The PC Club's Special Purikura Corner
プリクラコーナー
PC部
PC Club
Ga-shunk
Ga-shunk
OKAY! HERE YOU ARE!
WOW! THANK YOU!

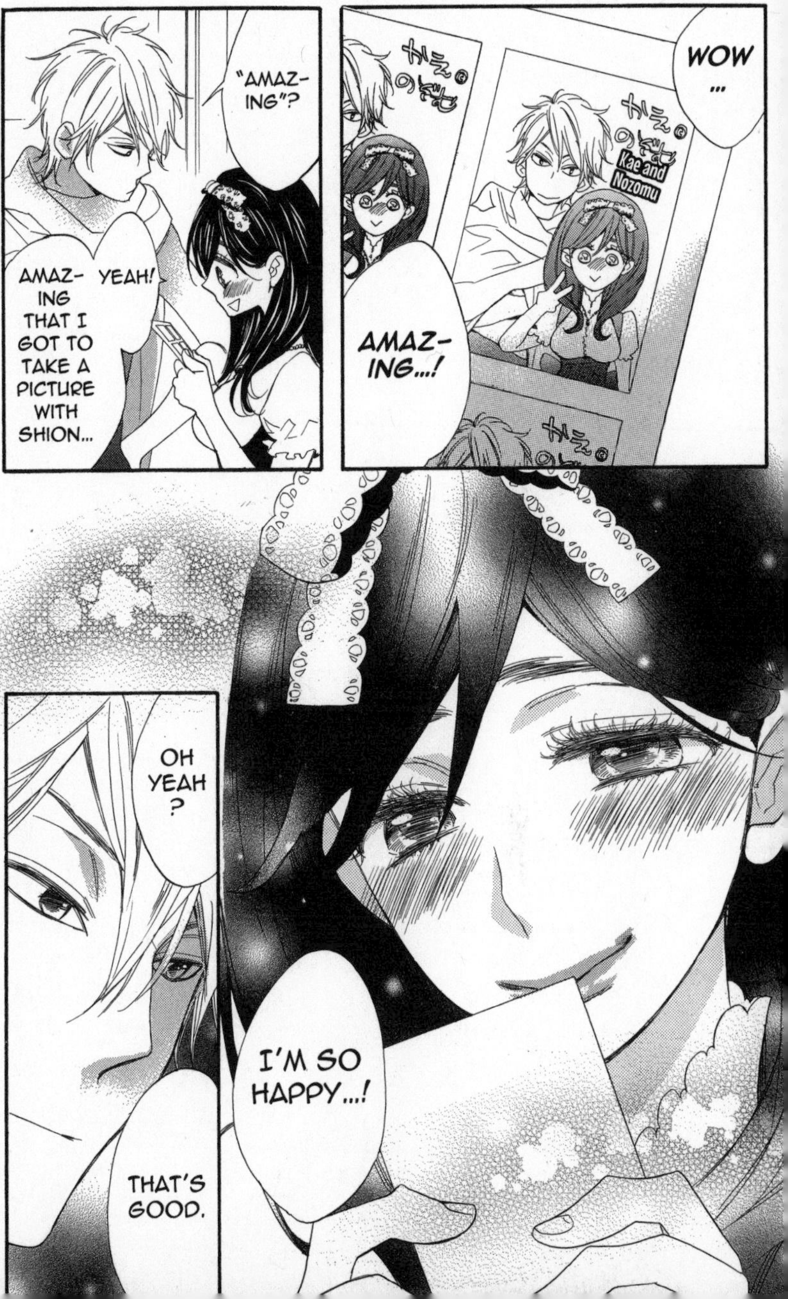
WOW ...
Kae and Nozomu
AMAZ-ING...!
"AMAZ-ING"?
YEAH!
AMAZ-ING THAT I GOT TO TAKE A PICTURE WITH SHION...
I'M SO HAPPY...!
OH YEAH?
THAT'S GOOD.

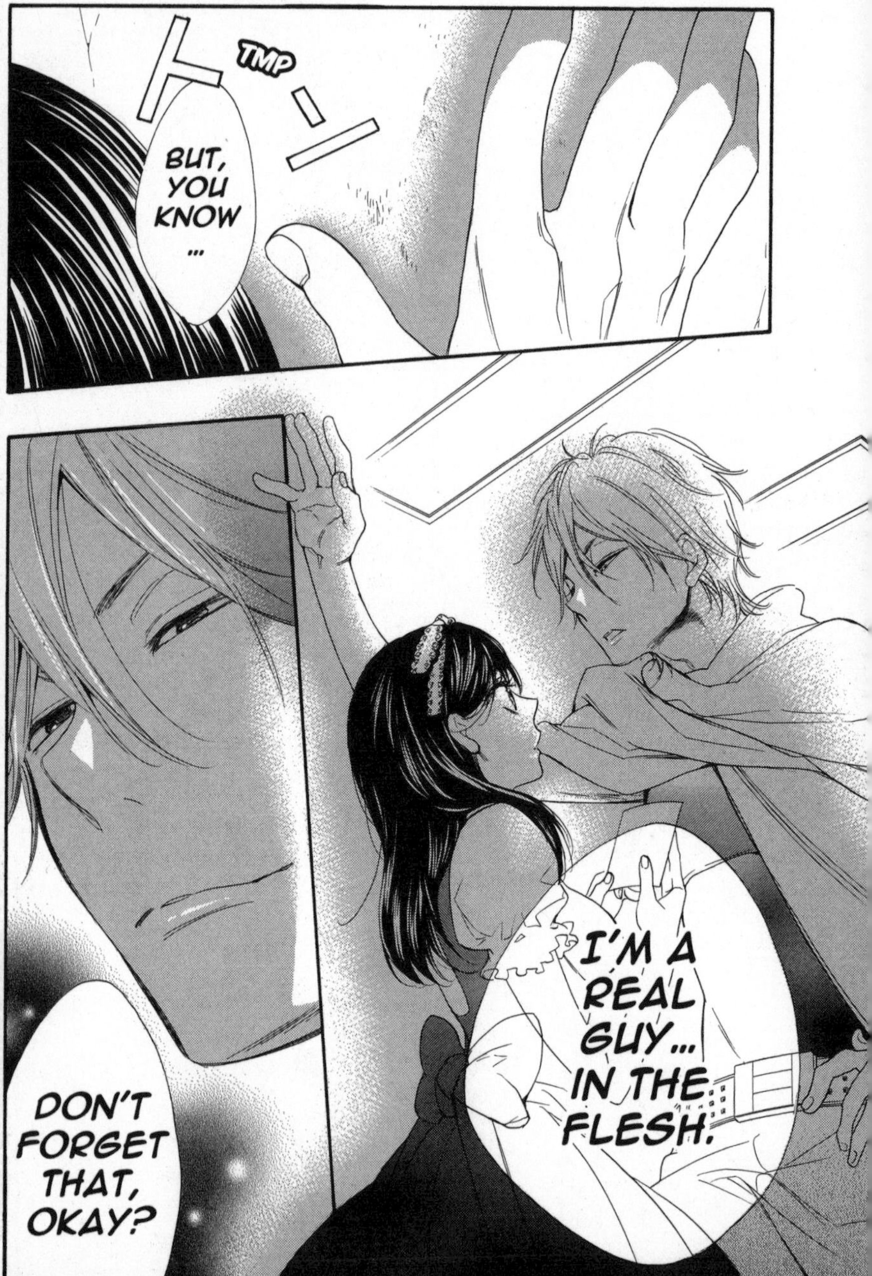
TMP
BUT, YOU KNOW ...
I'M A REAL GUY... IN THE FLESH.
DON'T FORGET THAT, OKAY?

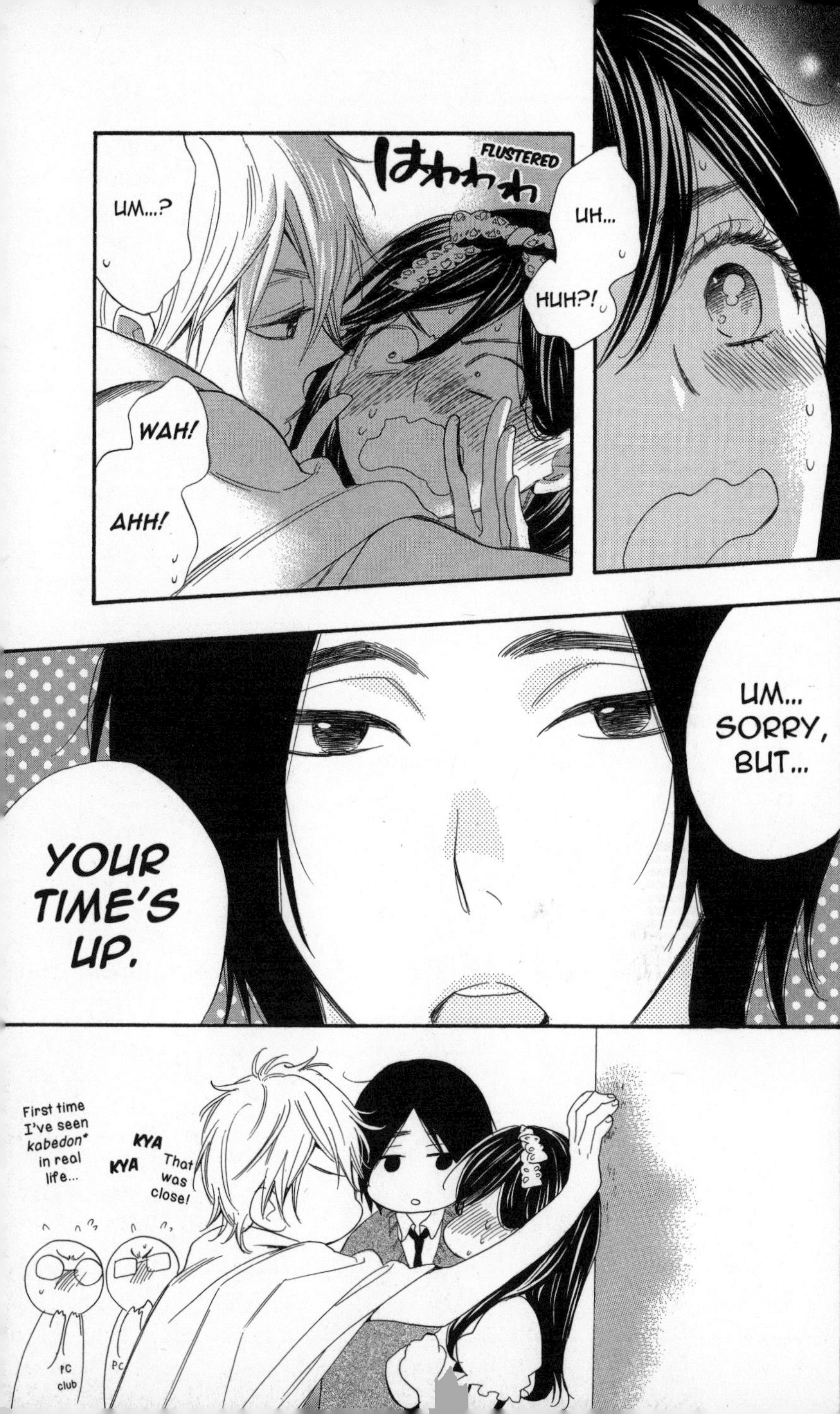
UH...
HUH?!
はわわわ
FLUSTERED
UM...?
WAH!
AHH!
UM... SORRY, BUT...
YOUR TIME'S UP.
KYA
KYA
That was close!
First time I've seen kabedon* in real life...
PC club
PC

*Kabedon = The art of a guy backing a girl up against a wall.

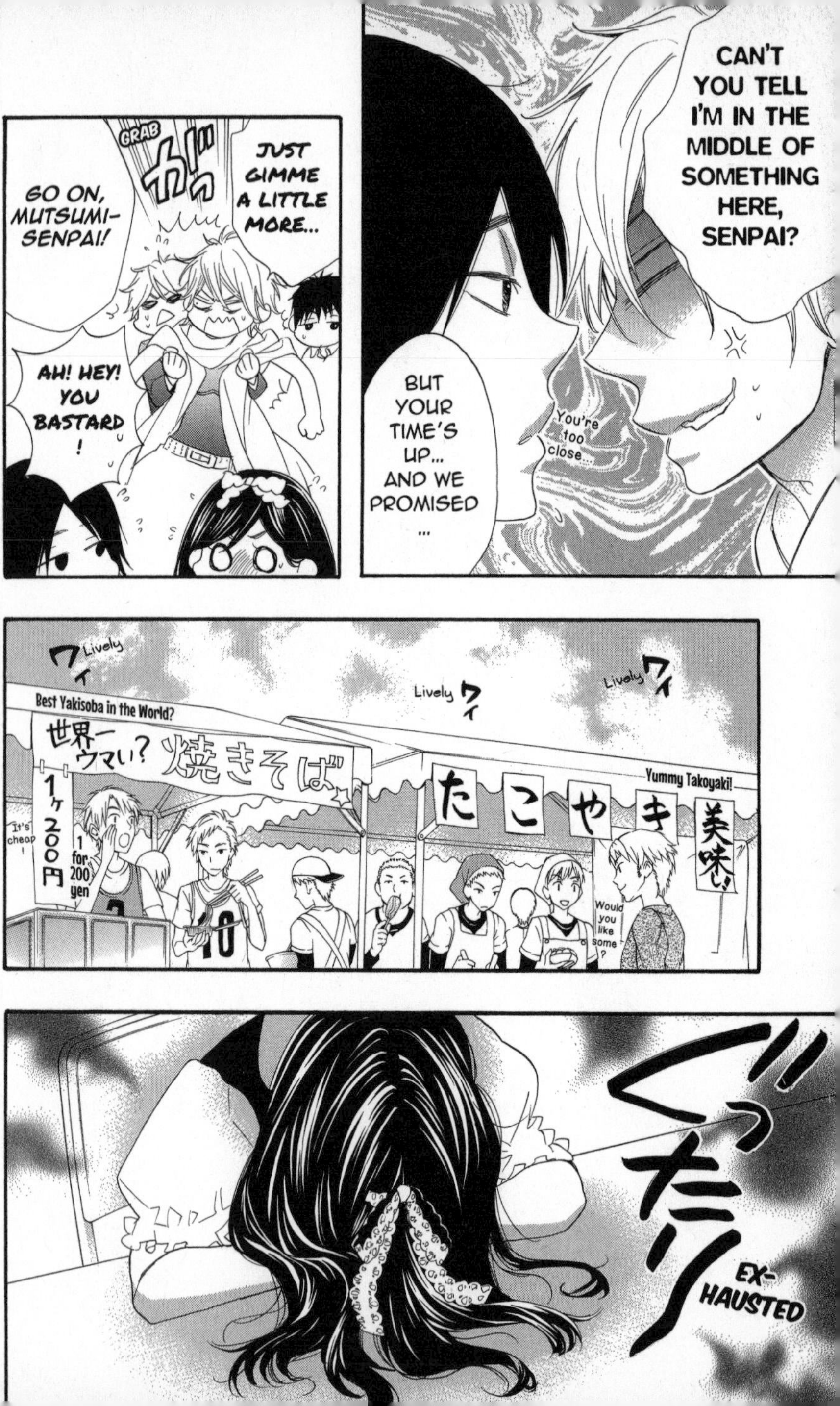
CAN'T YOU TELL I'M IN THE MIDDLE OF SOMETHING HERE, SENPAI?
BUT YOUR TIME'S UP... AND WE PROMISED...
You're too close...
GRAB
JUST GIMME A LITTLE MORE...
GO ON, MUTSUMI-SENPAI!
AH! HEY! YOU BASTARD!
Lively
Lively
Lively
Best Yakisoba in the World?
世界一ウマい？焼きそば
1ヶ200円
1 for 200 yen
It's cheap!
たこやき
美味し！
Yummy Takoyaki!
Would you like some?
EX-HAUSTED

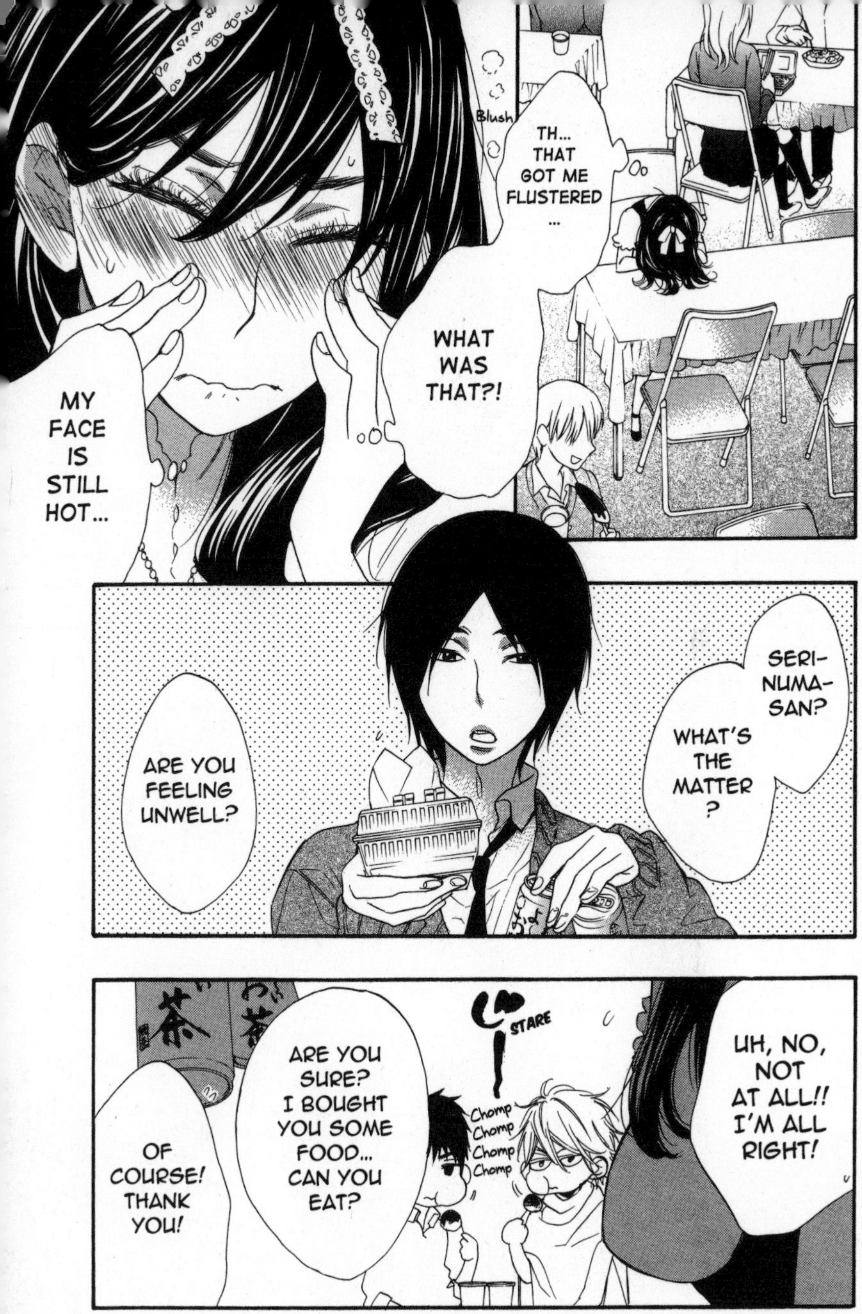
Blush
TH... THAT GOT ME FLUSTERED ...
WHAT WAS THAT?!
MY FACE IS STILL HOT...
SERI-NUMA-SAN?
WHAT'S THE MATTER ?
ARE YOU FEELING UNWELL?
UH, NO, NOT AT ALL!! I'M ALL RIGHT!
STARE
Chomp Chomp Chomp Chomp
ARE YOU SURE? I BOUGHT YOU SOME FOOD... CAN YOU EAT?
OF COURSE! THANK YOU!

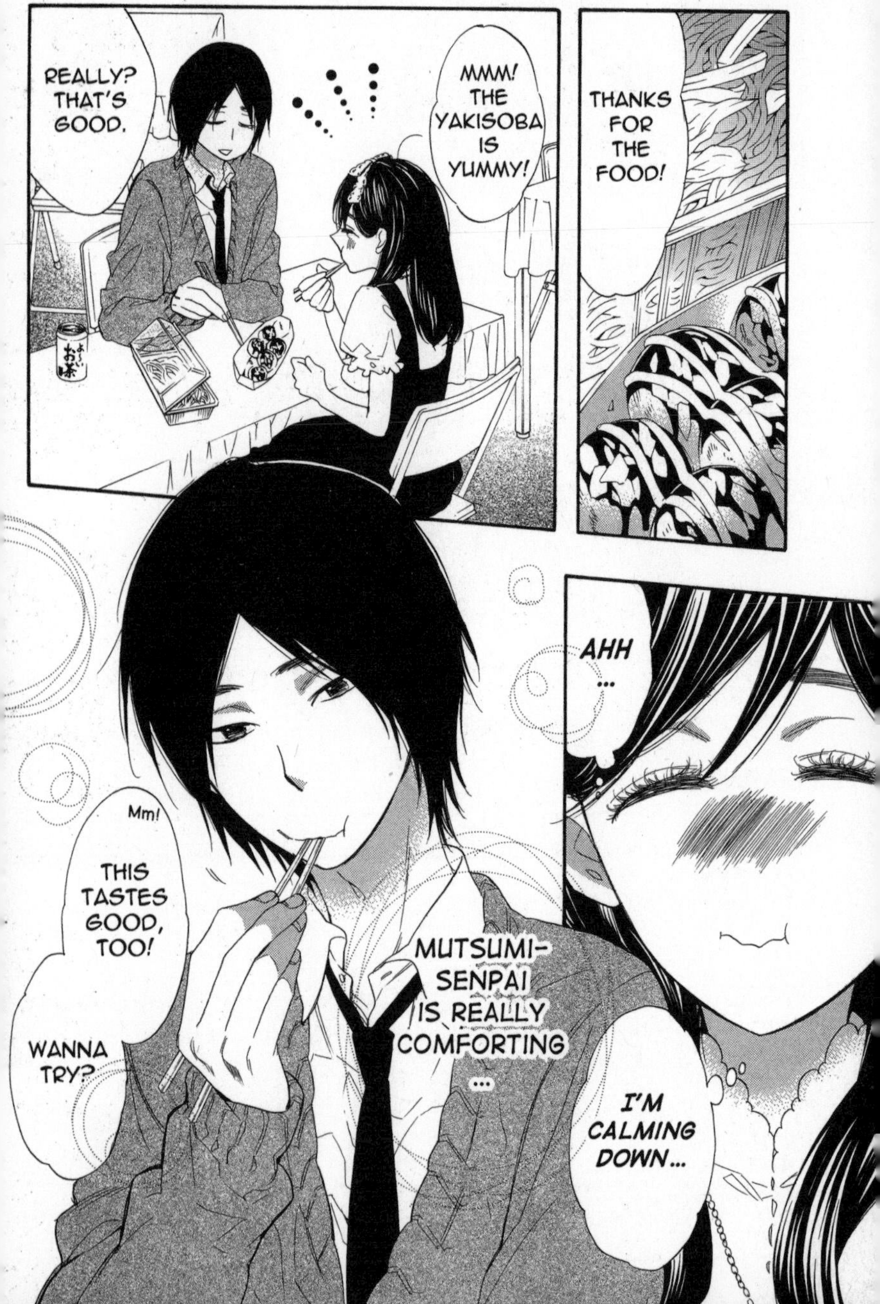
THANKS FOR THE FOOD!
MMM! THE YAKISOBA IS YUMMY!
REALLY? THAT'S GOOD.
AHH ...
I'M CALMING DOWN...
Mm!
THIS TASTES GOOD, TOO!
MUTSUMI-SENPAI IS REALLY COMFORTING ...
WANNA TRY?

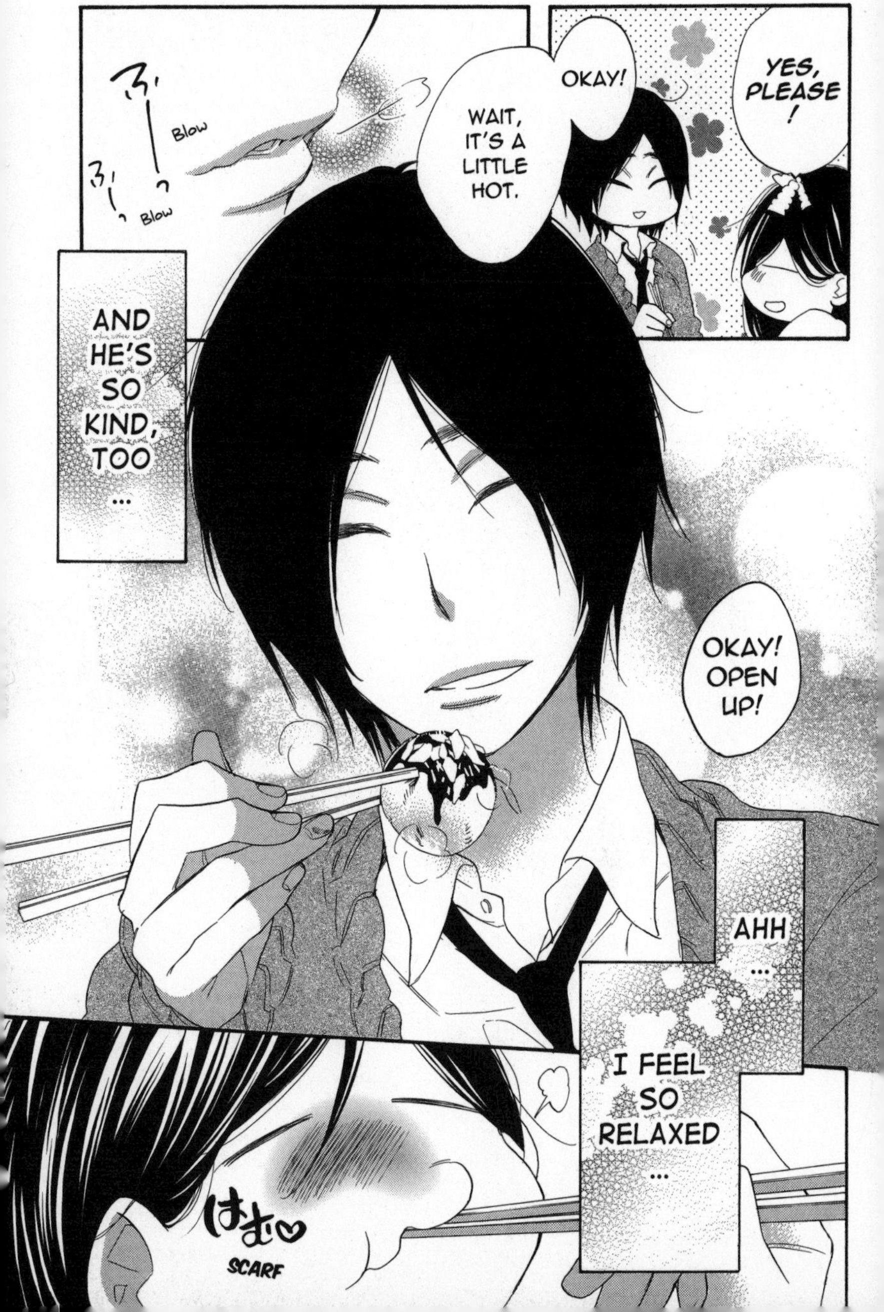
YES, PLEASE!
OKAY!
WAIT, IT'S A LITTLE HOT.
ふー Blow
ふー Blow
OKAY! OPEN UP!
AND HE'S SO KIND, TOO...
AHH...
I FEEL SO RELAXED...
はむ♡
SCARF

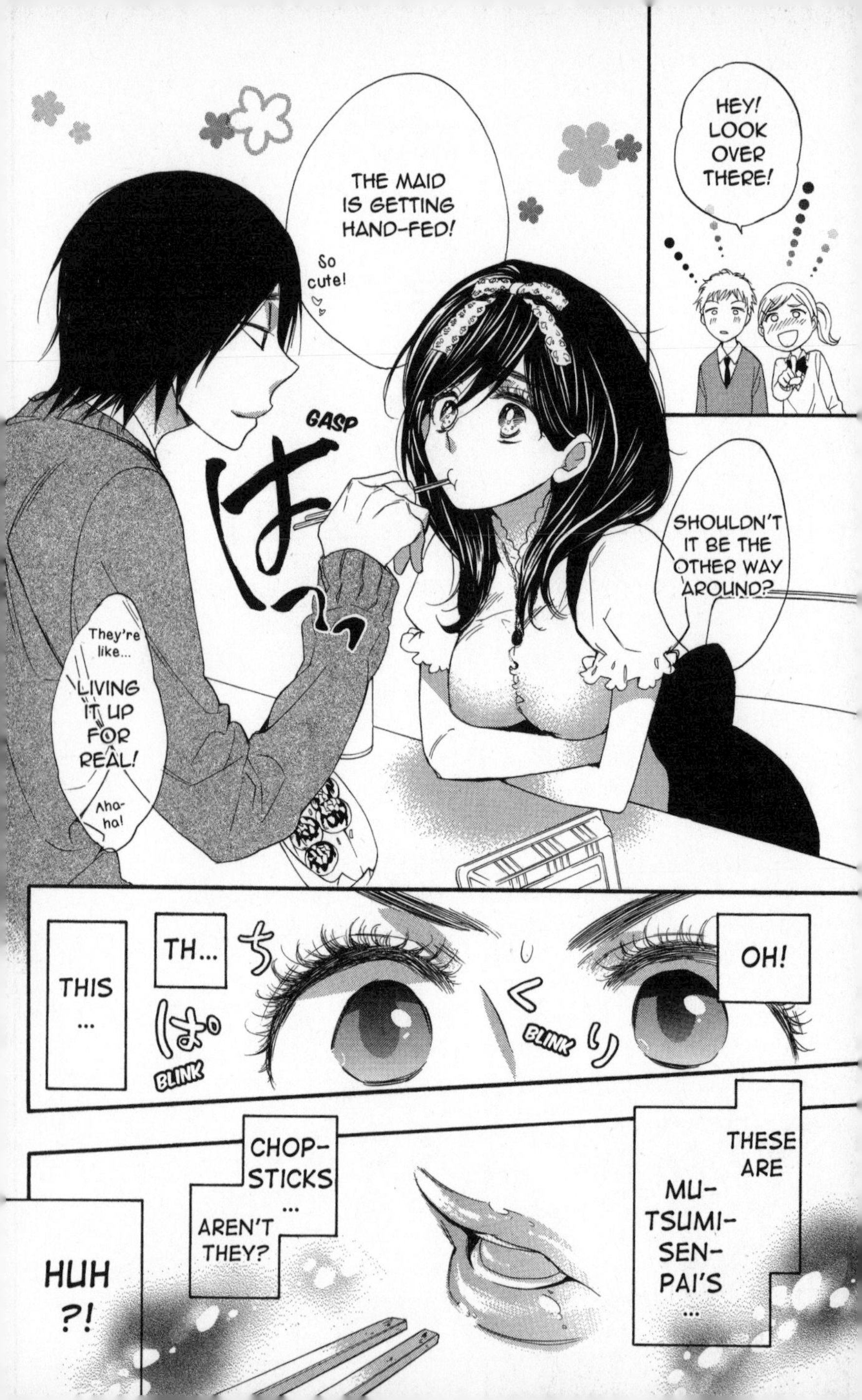
HEY! LOOK OVER THERE!
THE MAID IS GETTING HAND-FED!
So cute!
GASP
はっ
SHOULDN'T IT BE THE OTHER WAY AROUND?
They're like... LIVING IT UP FOR REAL!
Aha-ha!
OH!
BLINK
TH...
BLINK
THIS ...
THESE ARE MUTSUMI-SENPAI'S ...
CHOPSTICKS ...
AREN'T THEY?
HUH ?!

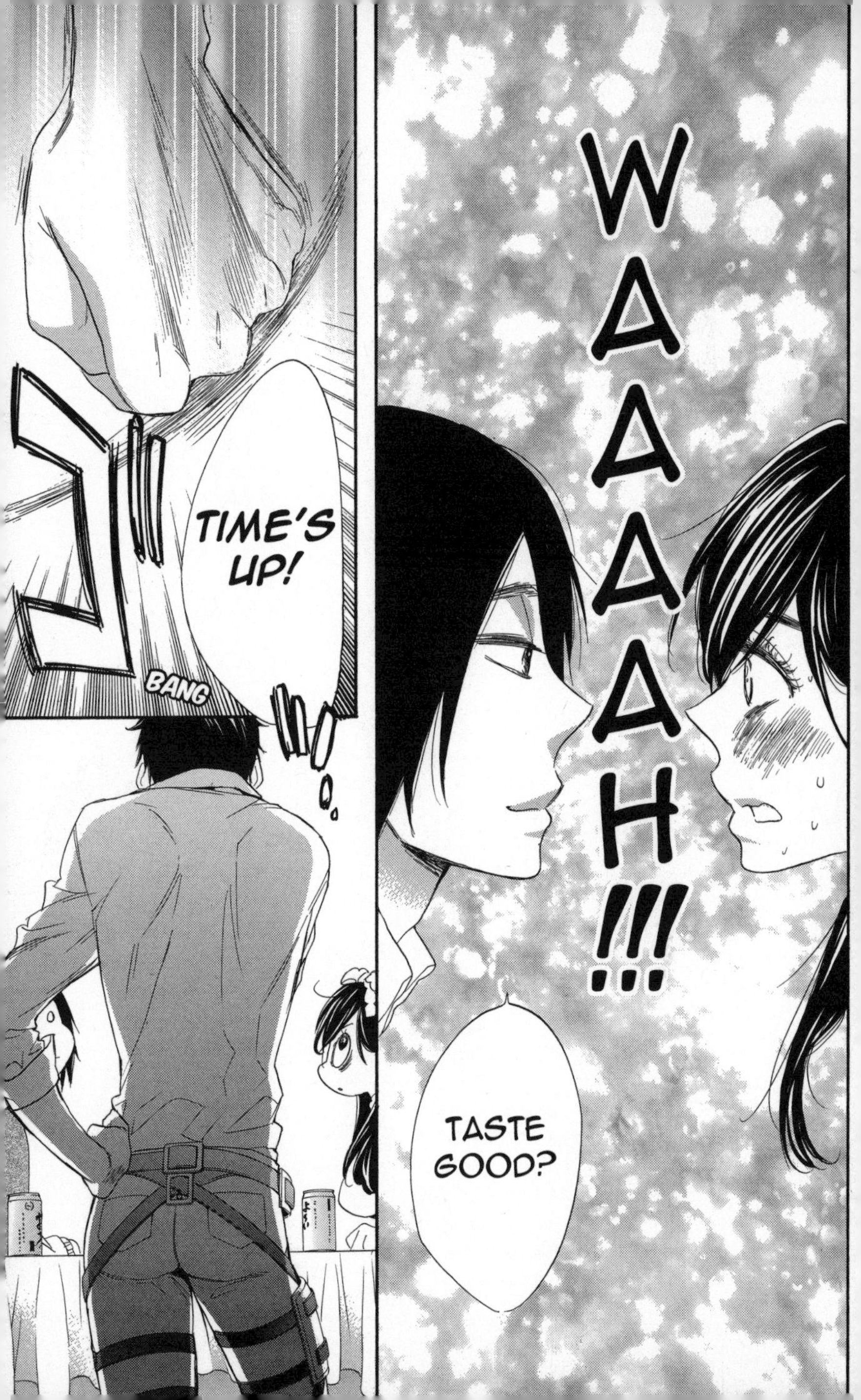
WAAAAH!!!
TASTE GOOD?
TIME'S UP!
BANG

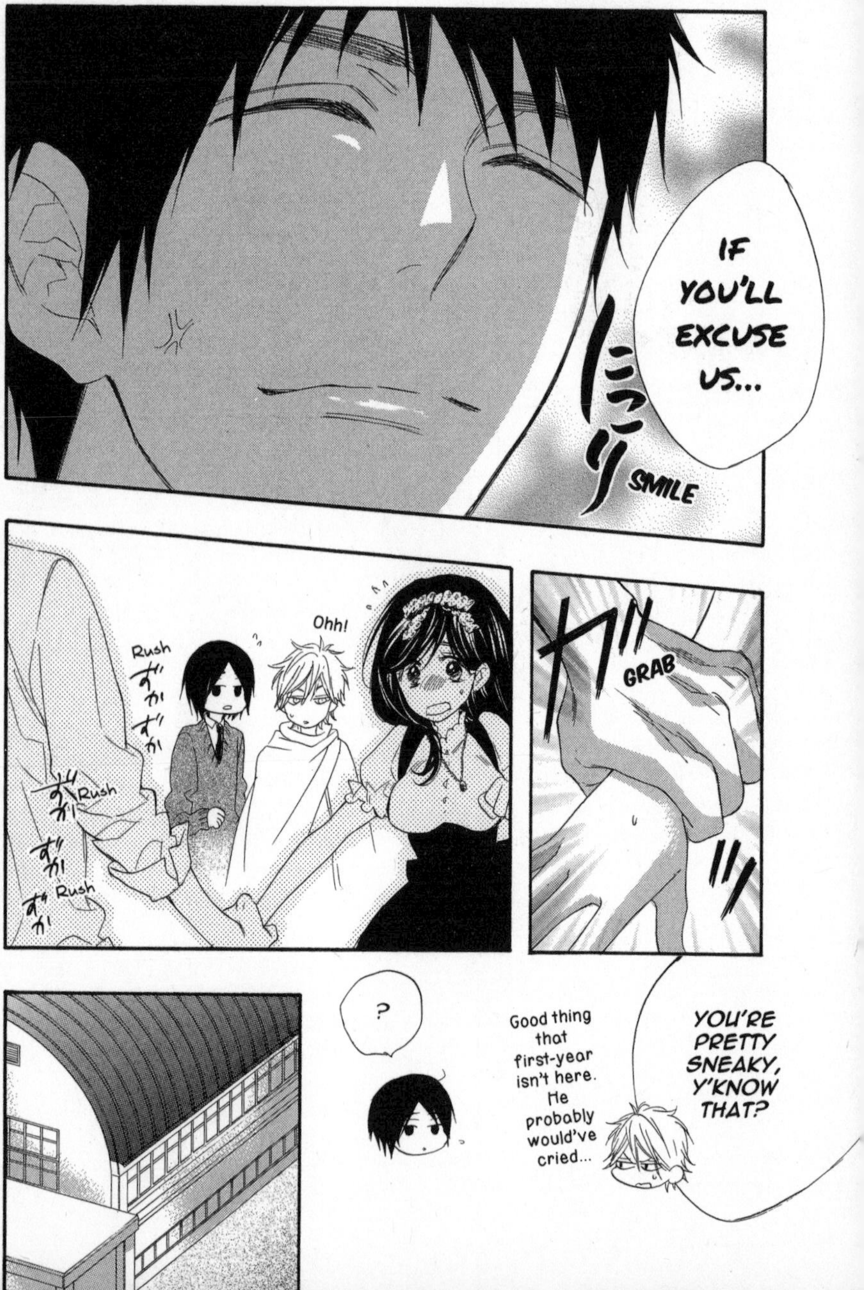
IF YOU'LL EXCUSE US...
にこり
SMILE
ガッ
GRAB
Ohh!
Rush
ずかずか
Rush
ずかずか
Rush
ずかずか
YOU'RE PRETTY SNEAKY, Y'KNOW THAT?
Good thing that first-year isn't here. He probably would've cried...
?

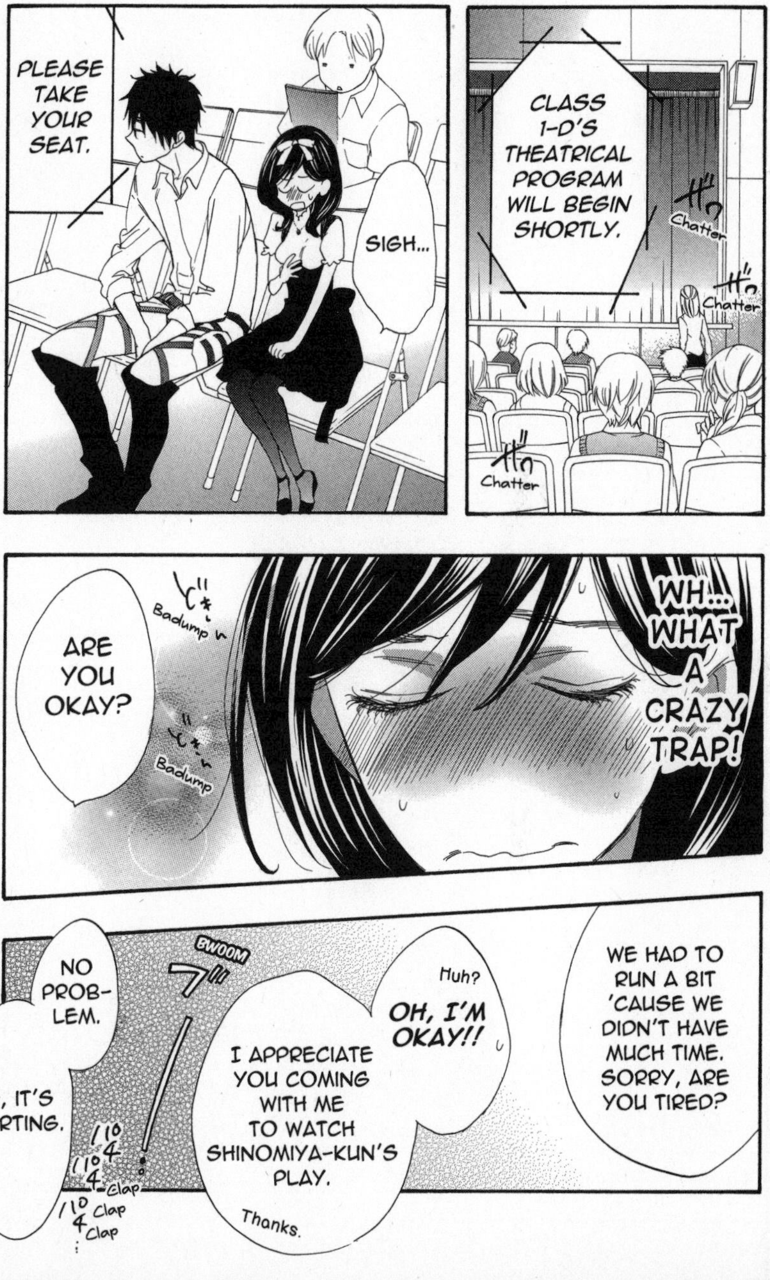
CLASS 1-D'S THEATRICAL PROGRAM WILL BEGIN SHORTLY.
Chatter
Chatter
Chatter
PLEASE TAKE YOUR SEAT.
SIGH...
WH... WHAT A CRAZY TRAP!
Badump
ARE YOU OKAY?
Badump
WE HAD TO RUN A BIT 'CAUSE WE DIDN'T HAVE MUCH TIME. SORRY, ARE YOU TIRED?
Huh?
OH, I'M OKAY!!
BWOOM
I APPRECIATE YOU COMING WITH ME TO WATCH SHINOMIYA-KUN'S PLAY.
Thanks.
NO PROBLEM.
OH, IT'S STARTING.
Clap
Clap
Clap

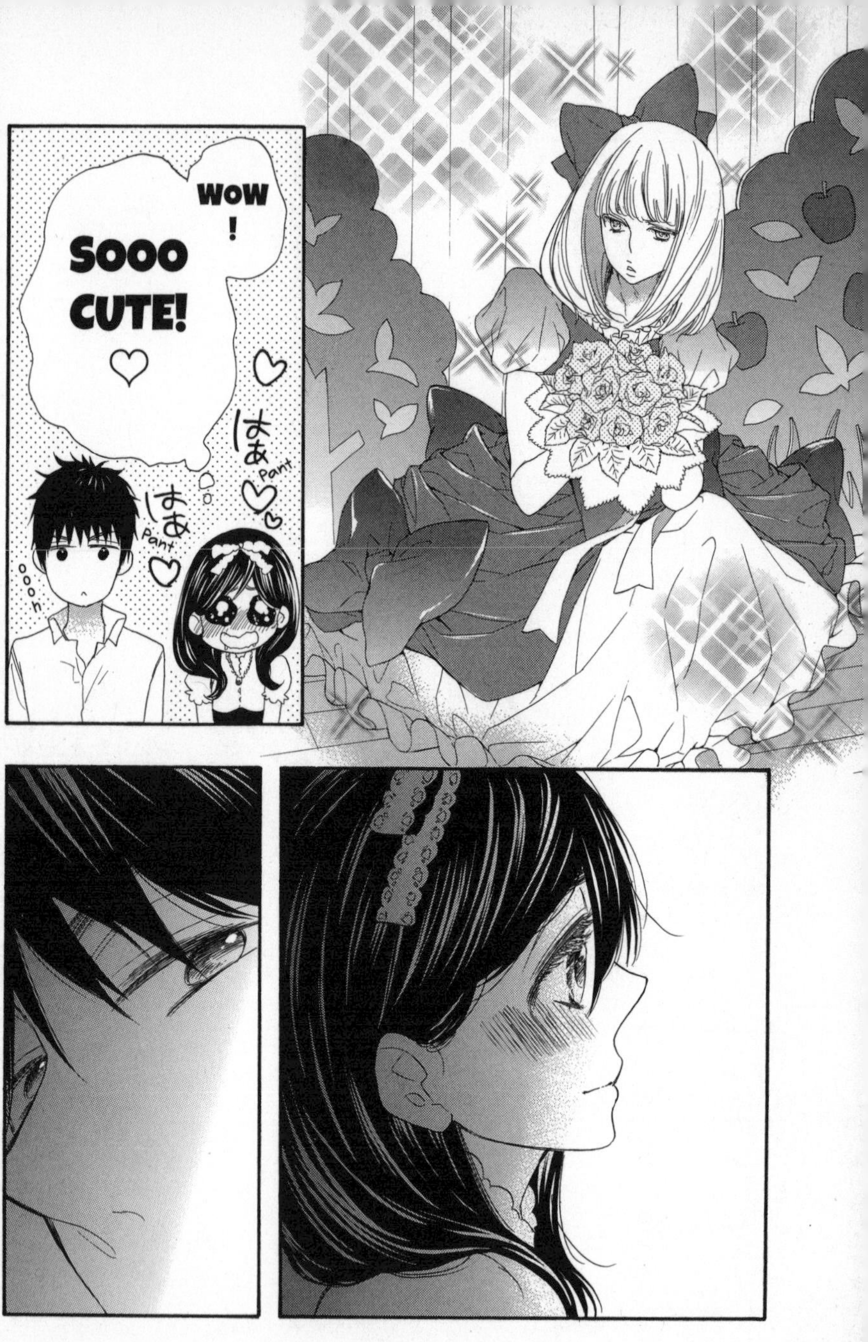
WOW! SOOO CUTE! ♡
はあ Pant
はあ Pant
oooh

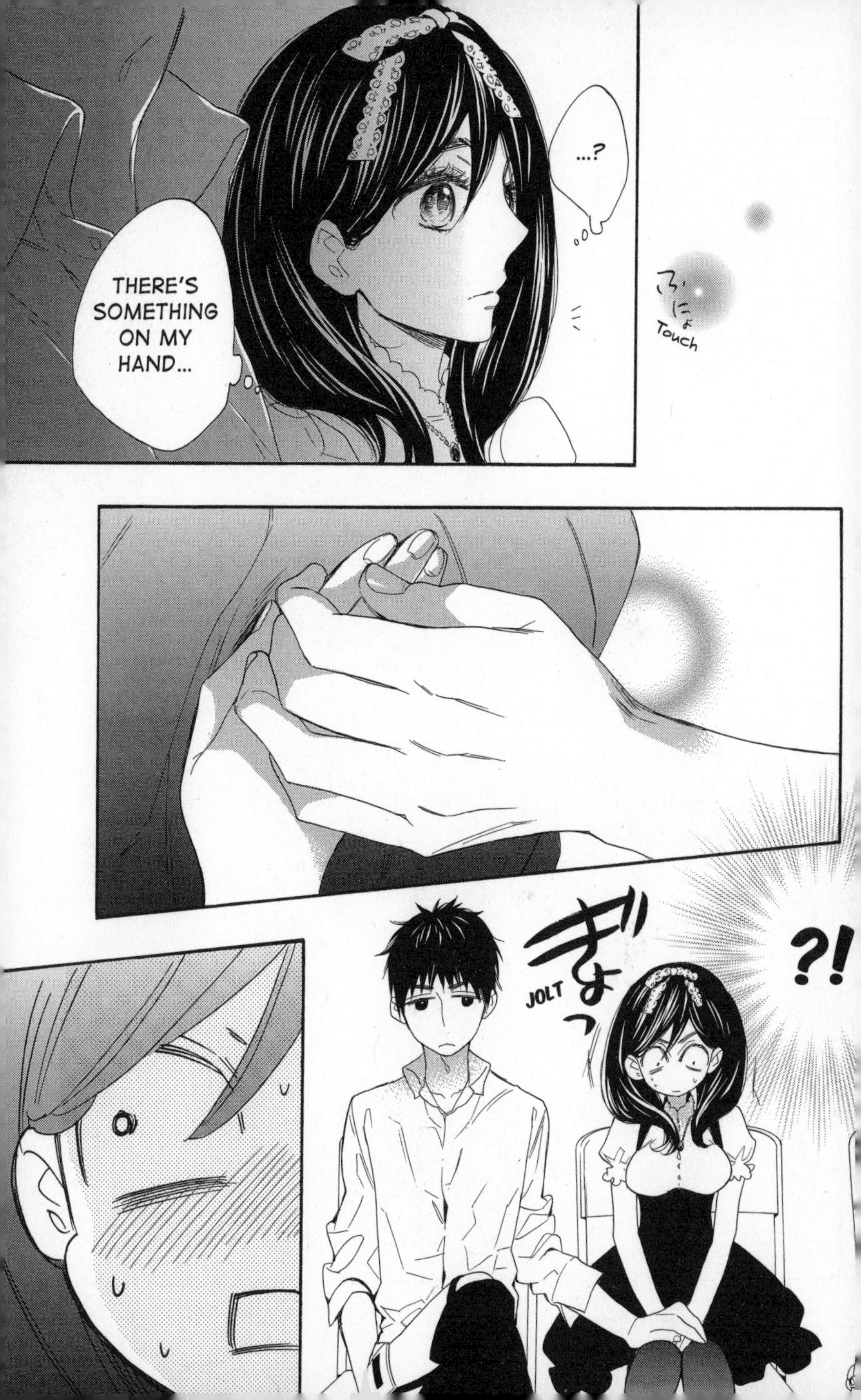
ふにょ
Touch
...?
THERE'S SOMETHING ON MY HAND...
?!
ぎょっ
JOLT

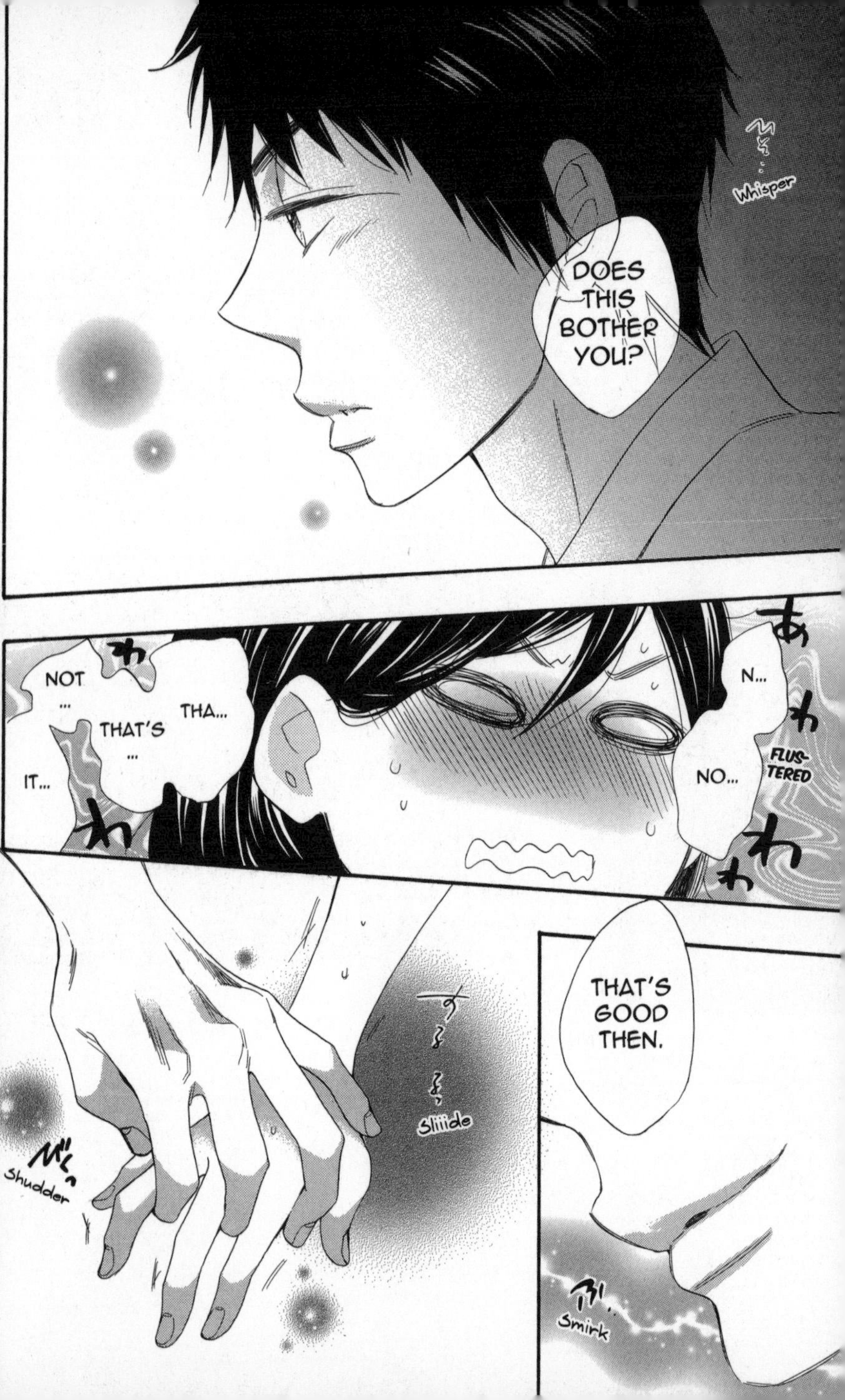
Whisper
DOES THIS BOTHER YOU?
N...
FLUSTERED
NO...
THA...
THAT'S ...
NOT ...
IT...
THAT'S GOOD THEN.
Smirk
Sliiide
Shudder

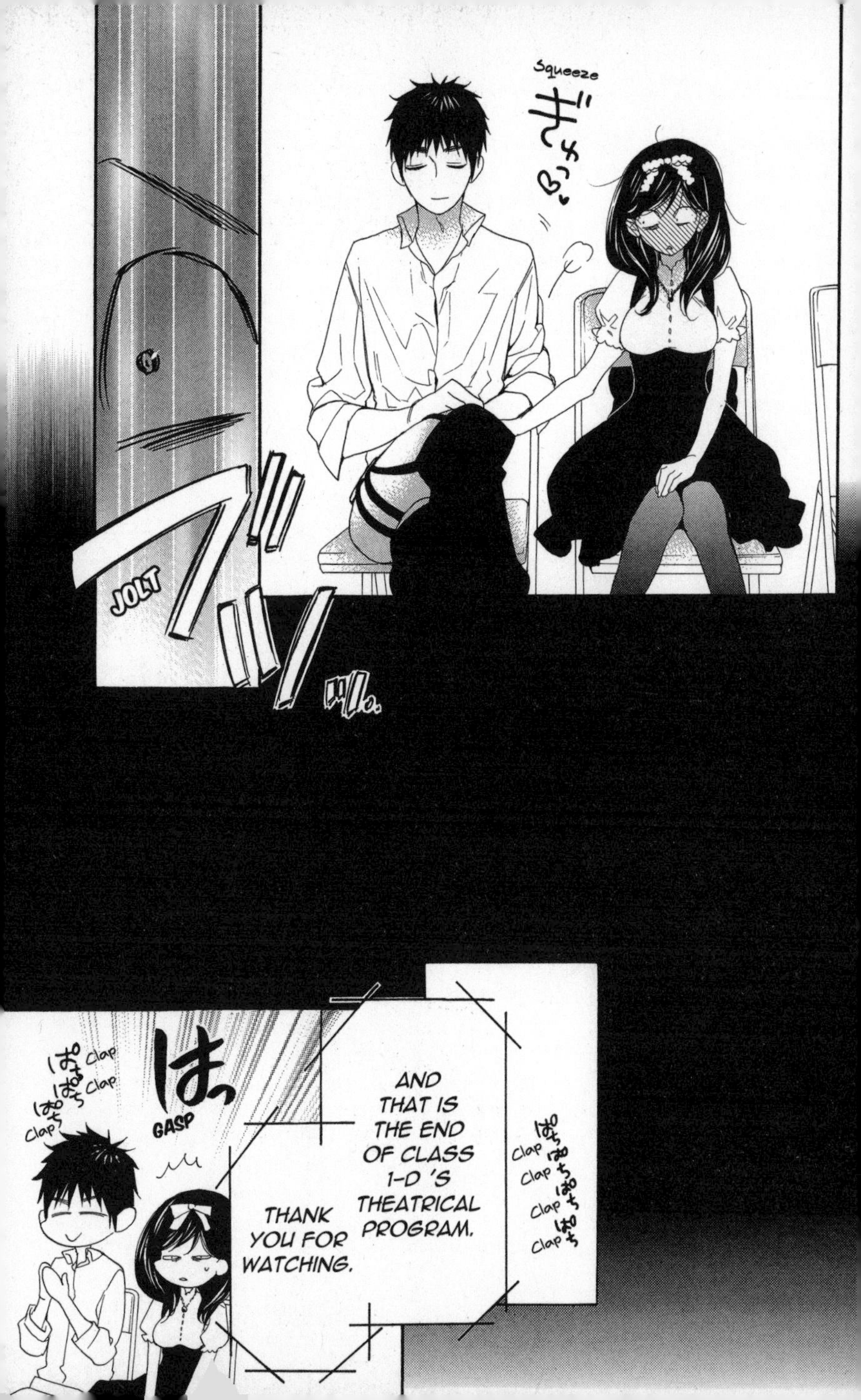
Squeeze
ぎゅっ
JOLT
ぱち Clap
ぱち Clap
ぱち Clap
ぱち Clap
AND THAT IS THE END OF CLASS 1-D'S THEATRICAL PROGRAM.
THANK YOU FOR WATCHING.
は
GASP
ぱち Clap
ぱち Clap
ぱち Clap

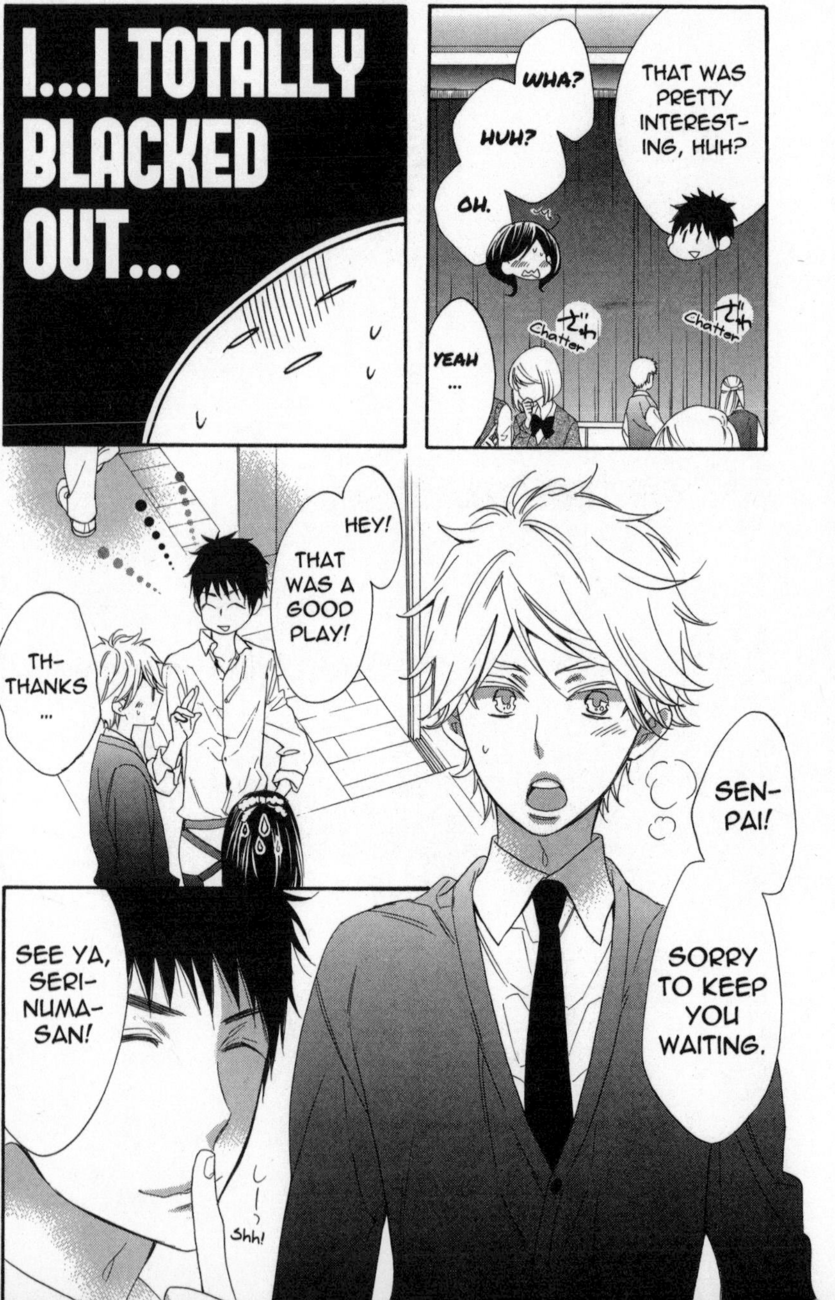
THAT WAS PRETTY INTERESTING, HUH?
WHA?
HUH?
OH.
Chatter
Chatter
YEAH...
I...I TOTALLY BLACKED OUT...
SEN-PAI!
SORRY TO KEEP YOU WAITING.
HEY!
THAT WAS A GOOD PLAY!
TH-THANKS...
SEE YA, SERI-NUMA-SAN!
Shh!

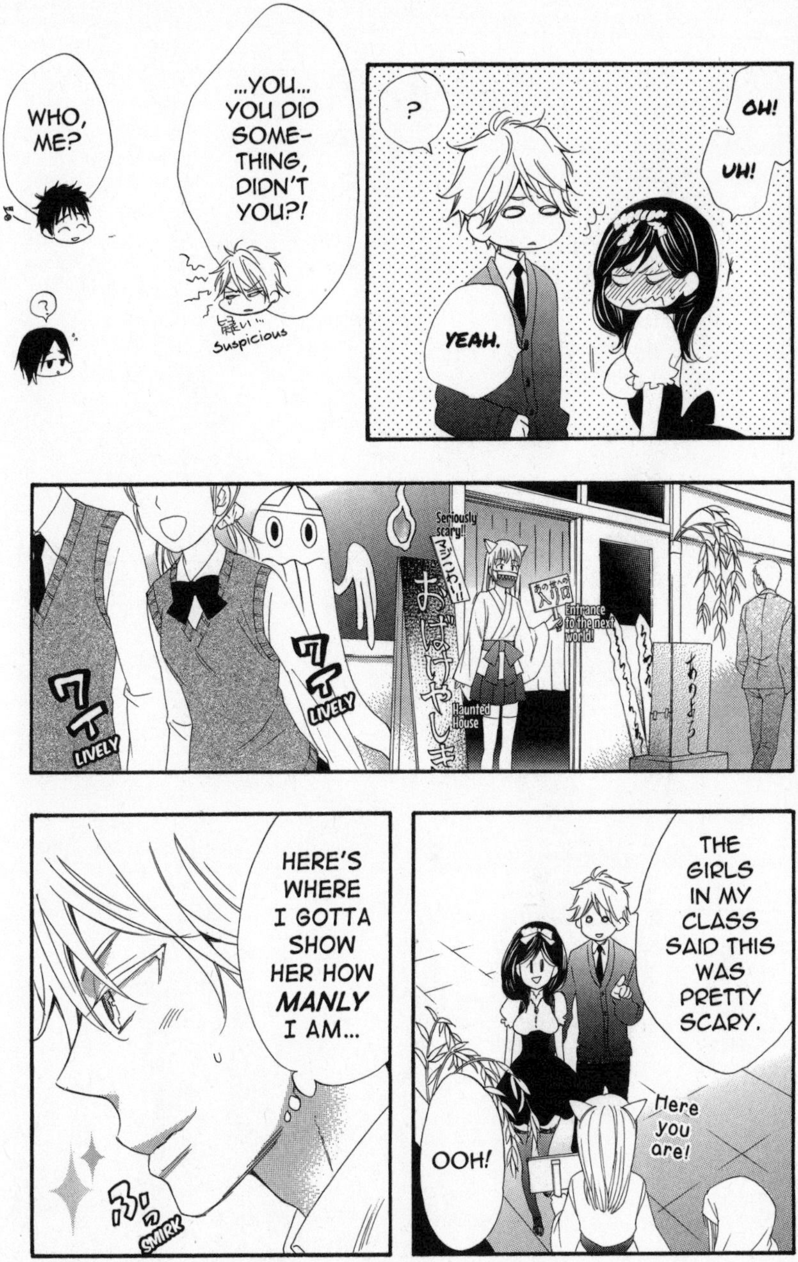
OH!
UH!
?
YEAH.
...YOU... YOU DID SOME-THING, DIDN'T YOU?!
Suspicious
WHO, ME?
Seriously scary!!
Entrance to the next world!
Haunted House
LIVELY
LIVELY
THE GIRLS IN MY CLASS SAID THIS WAS PRETTY SCARY.
Here you are!
OOH!
HERE'S WHERE I GOTTA SHOW HER HOW MANLY I AM...
SMIRK

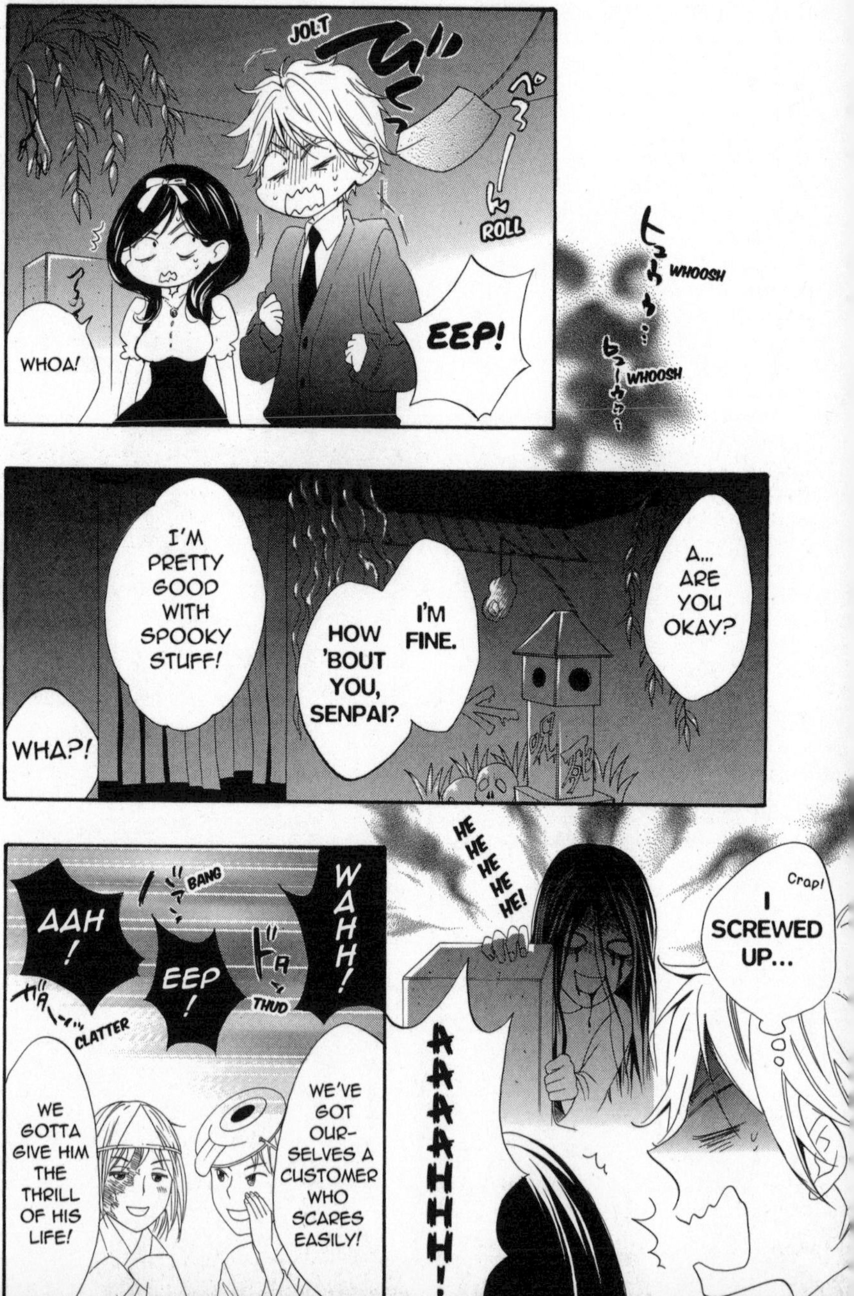
WHOOSH
WHOOSH
JOLT
ROLL
EEP!
WHOA!
A... ARE YOU OKAY?
I'M FINE.
HOW 'BOUT YOU, SENPAI?
I'M PRETTY GOOD WITH SPOOKY STUFF!
WHA?!
Crap!
I SCREWED UP...
HE HE HE HE HE!
AAAAAAHHH!
WAHH!
THUD
EEP!
BANG
AAH!
CLATTER
WE'VE GOT OURSELVES A CUSTOMER WHO SCARES EASILY!
WE GOTTA GIVE HIM THE THRILL OF HIS LIFE!

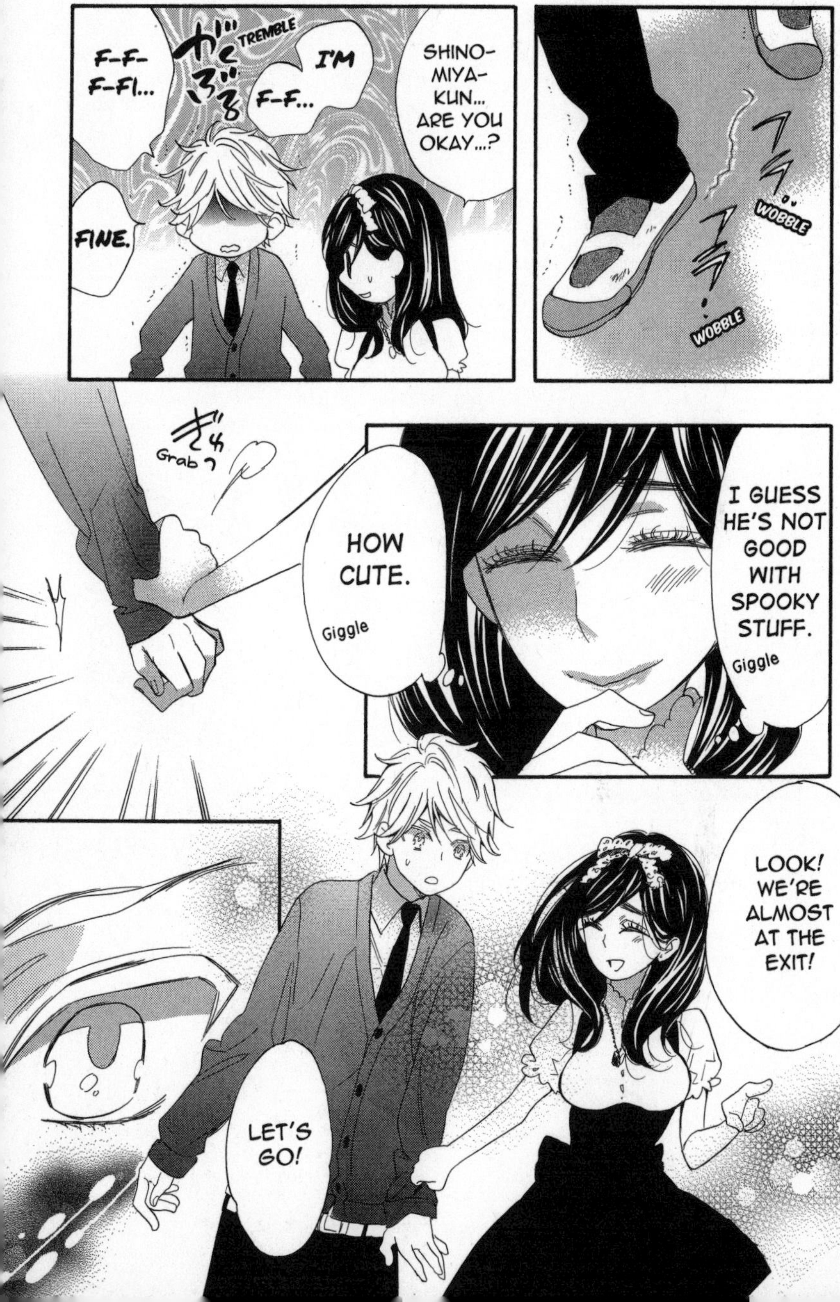
WOBBLE
WOBBLE
SHINO-MIYA-KUN... ARE YOU OKAY...?
I'M F-F...
TREMBLE
F-F-F-FI...
FINE.
I GUESS HE'S NOT GOOD WITH SPOOKY STUFF.
Giggle
HOW CUTE.
Giggle
Grab
LOOK! WE'RE ALMOST AT THE EXIT!
LET'S GO!

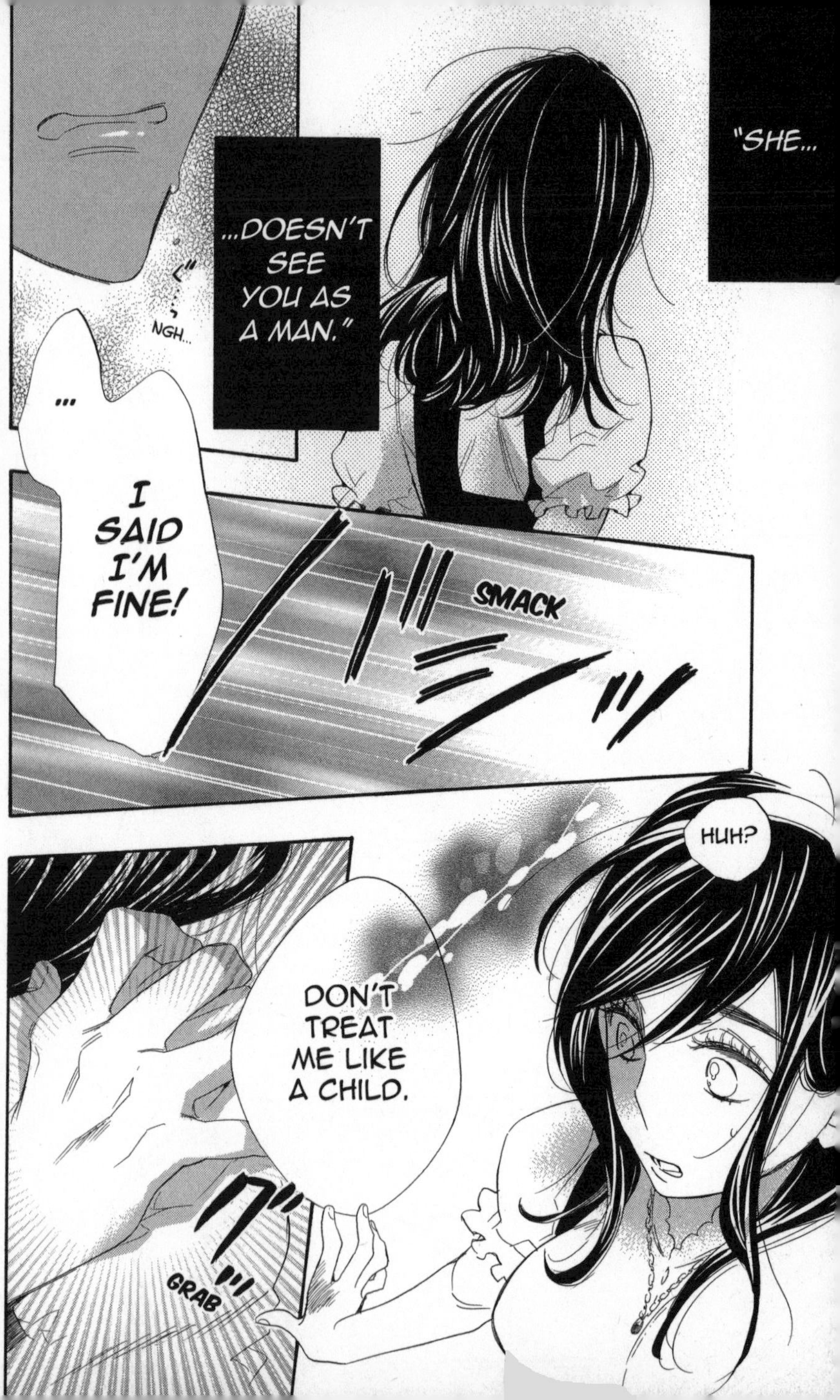
"SHE...
...DOESN'T SEE YOU AS A MAN."
NGH...
...
I SAID I'M FINE!
SMACK
HUH?
DON'T TREAT ME LIKE A CHILD.
GRAB

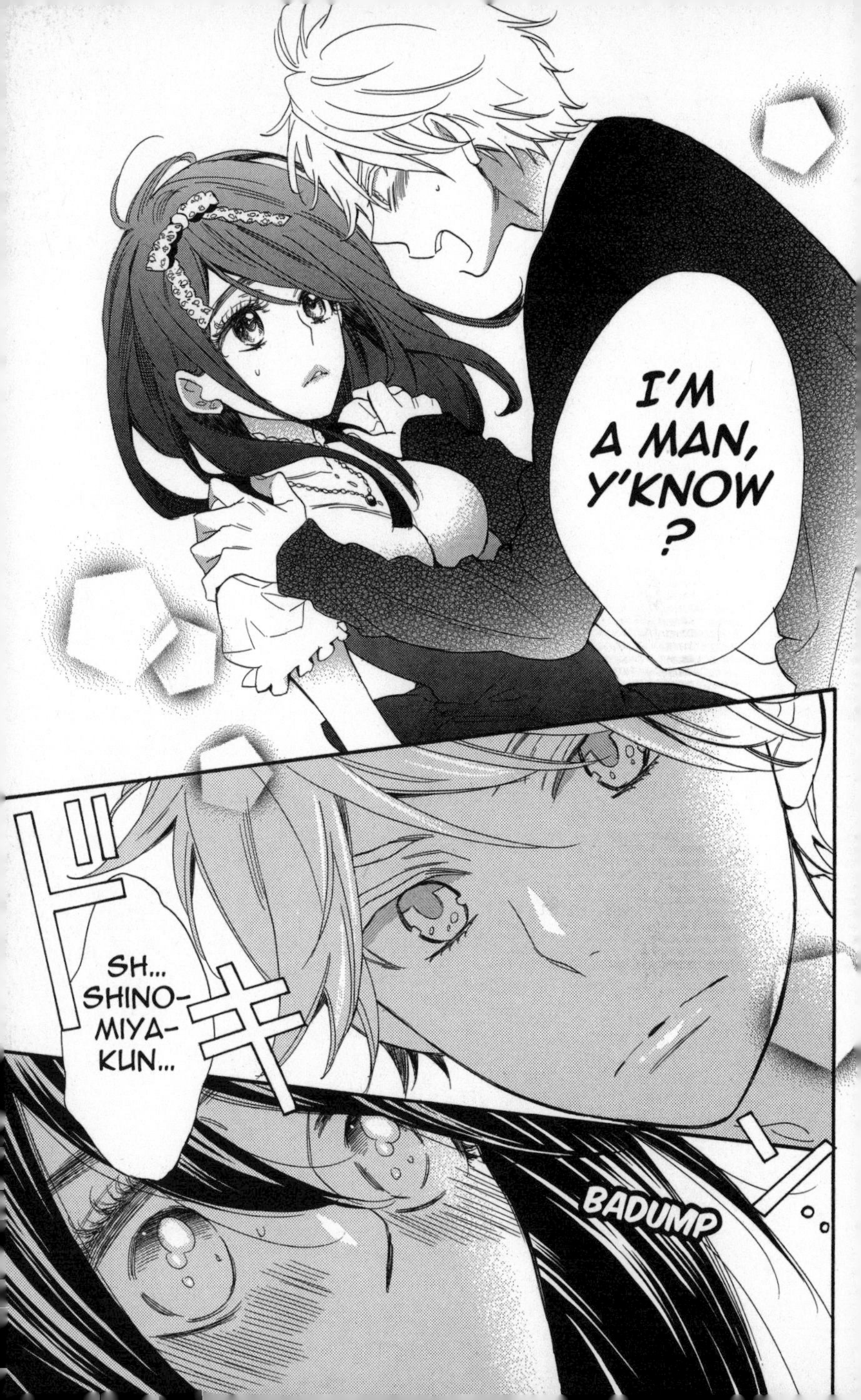
I'M A MAN, Y'KNOW?
BADUMP
SH... SHINO-MIYA-KUN...

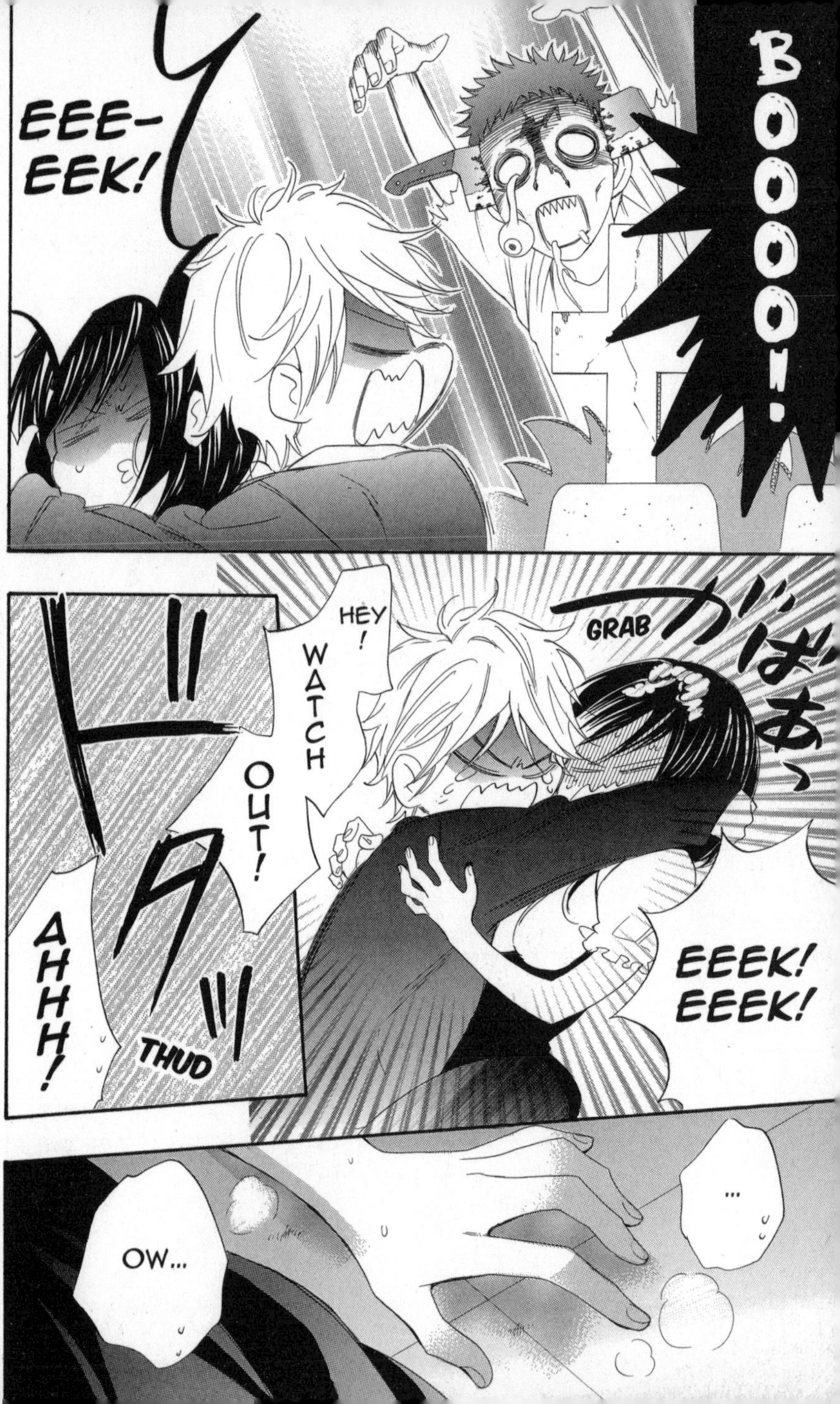
BOOOOOM!
EEE-
EEK!
GRAB
HEY!
WATCH
OUT!
EEEK!
EEEK!
THUD
AHHH!
...
OW...

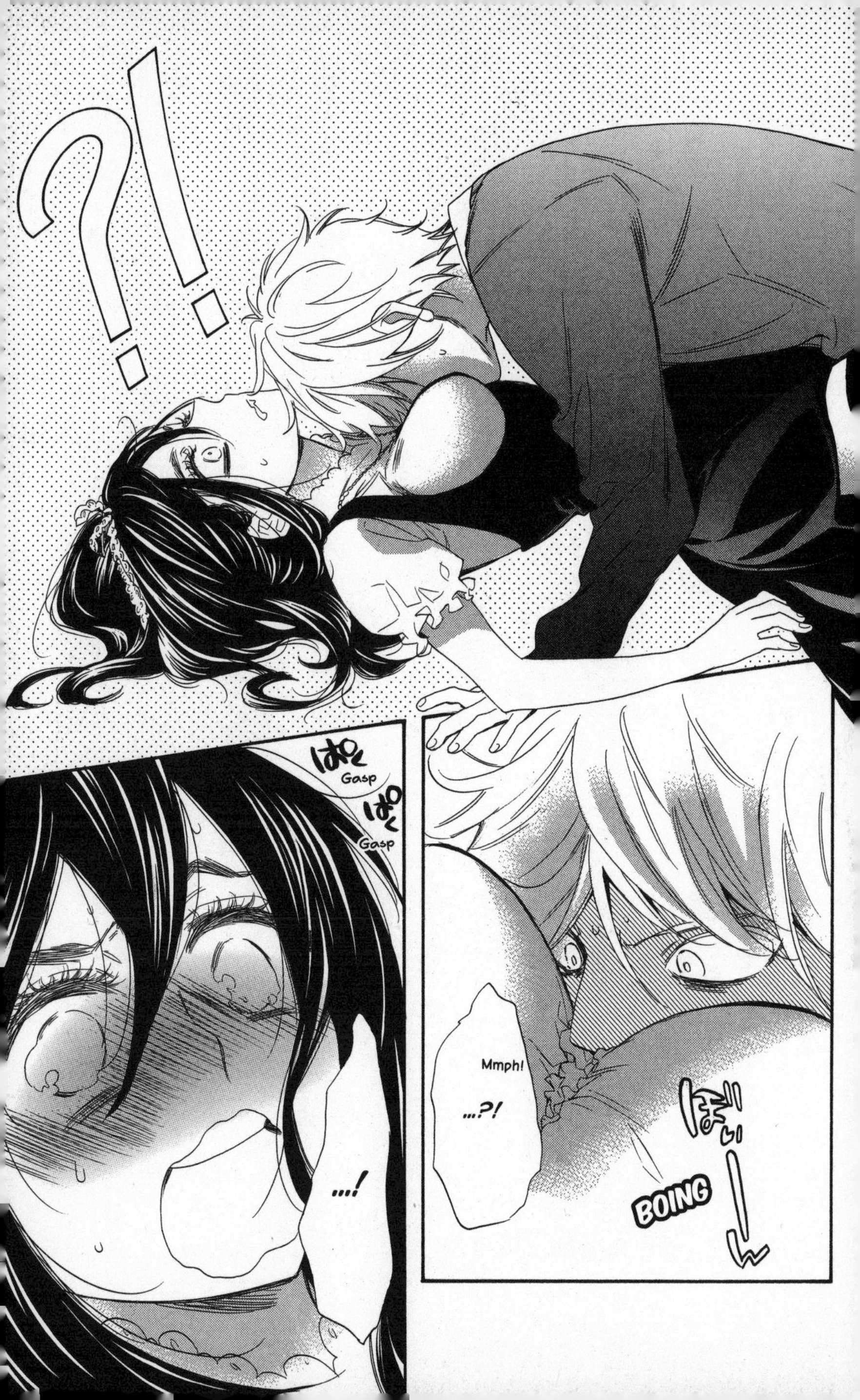
?!
Mmph!
...?!
BOING
Gasp
Gasp
...!

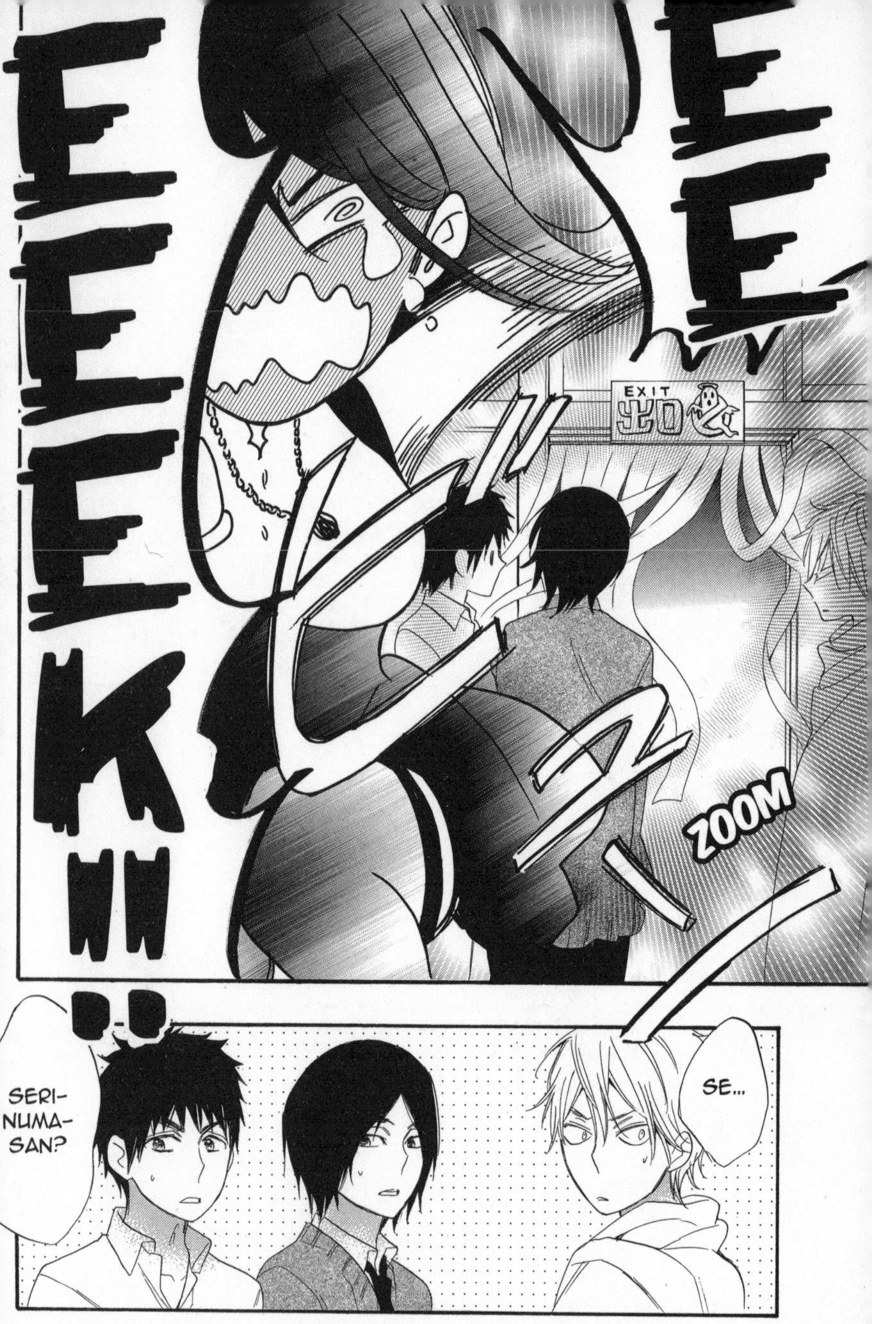
EEEEEEEEEEEK!!!
EXIT
ZOOM
SE...
SERI-
NUMA-
SAN?

KISS HIM, NOT ME!

#7 WHERE SHE BELONGS

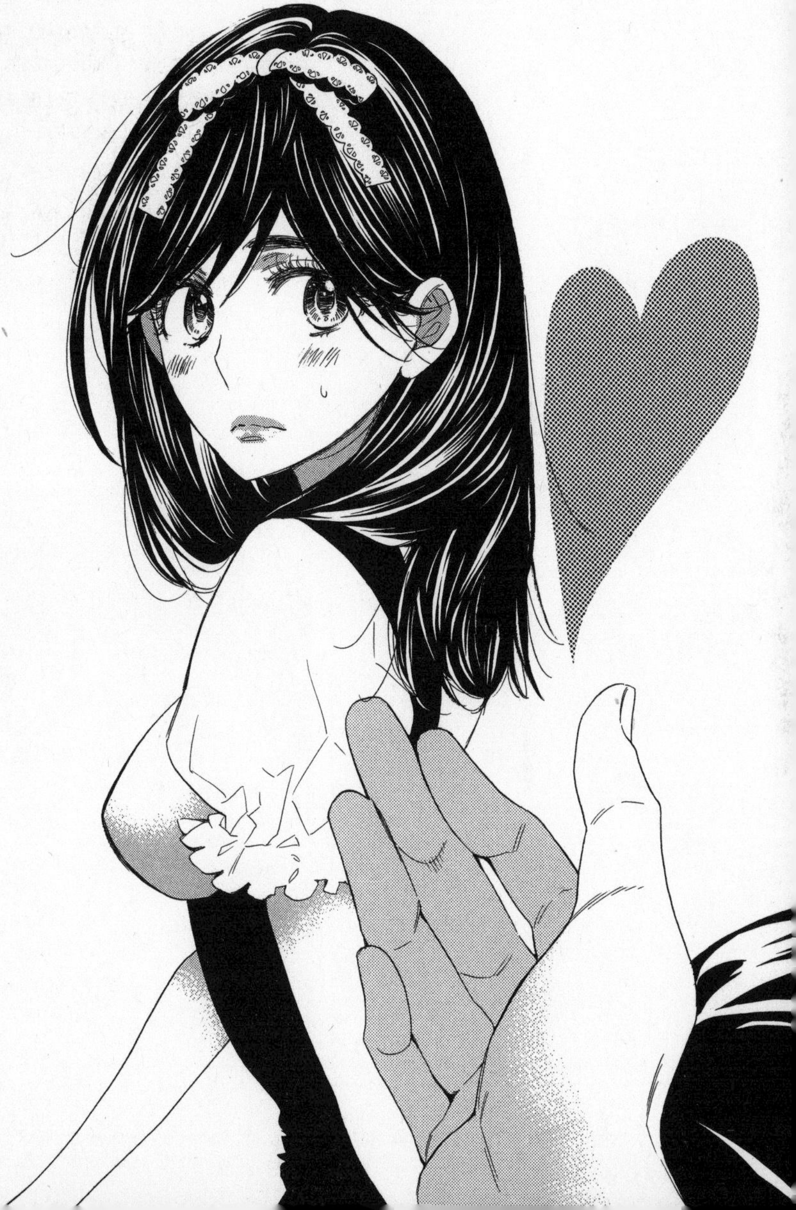

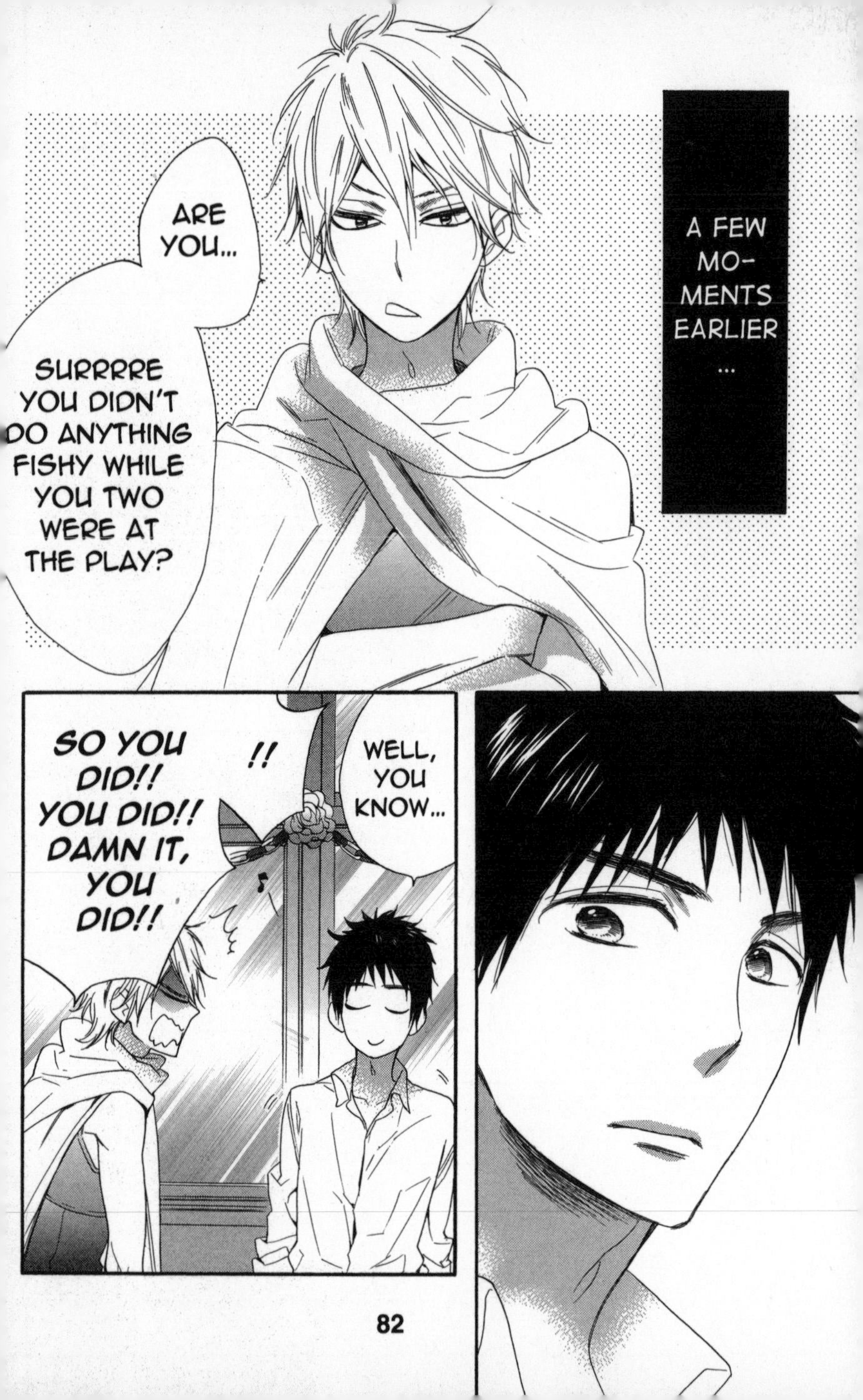
A FEW MO-MENTS EARLIER...
ARE YOU...
SURRRRE YOU DIDN'T DO ANYTHING FISHY WHILE YOU TWO WERE AT THE PLAY?
WELL, YOU KNOW...
!!
SO YOU DID!! YOU DID!! DAMN IT, YOU DID!!

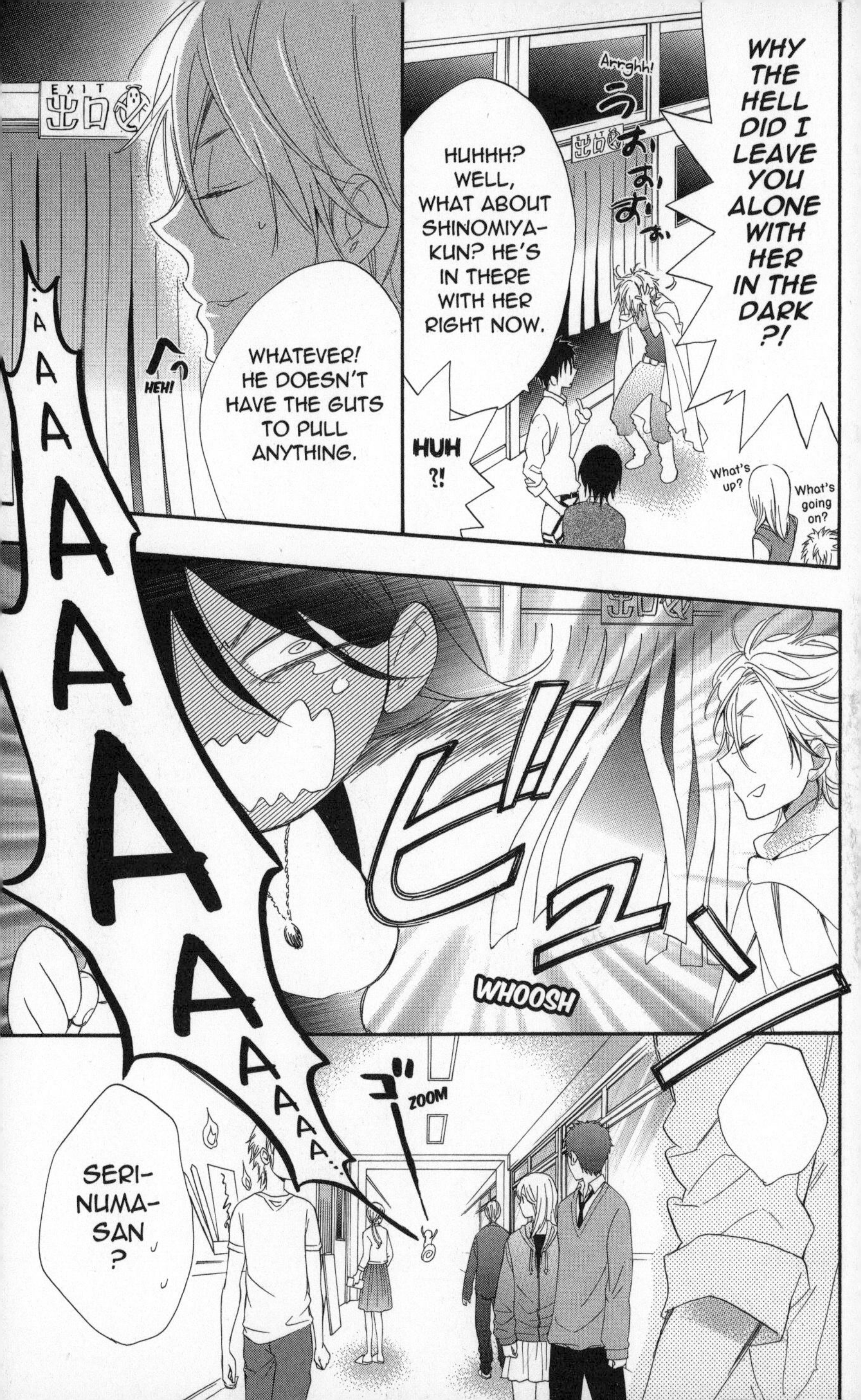
WHY THE HELL DID I LEAVE YOU ALONE WITH HER IN THE DARK?!
Arrghh!
HUHHH? WELL, WHAT ABOUT SHINOMIYA-KUN? HE'S IN THERE WITH HER RIGHT NOW.
HUH?!
What's up?
What's going on?
WHATEVER! HE DOESN'T HAVE THE GUTS TO PULL ANYTHING.
HEH!
...AAAAAAAAAAAA...
WHOOSH
ZOOM
SERI-NUMA-SAN?

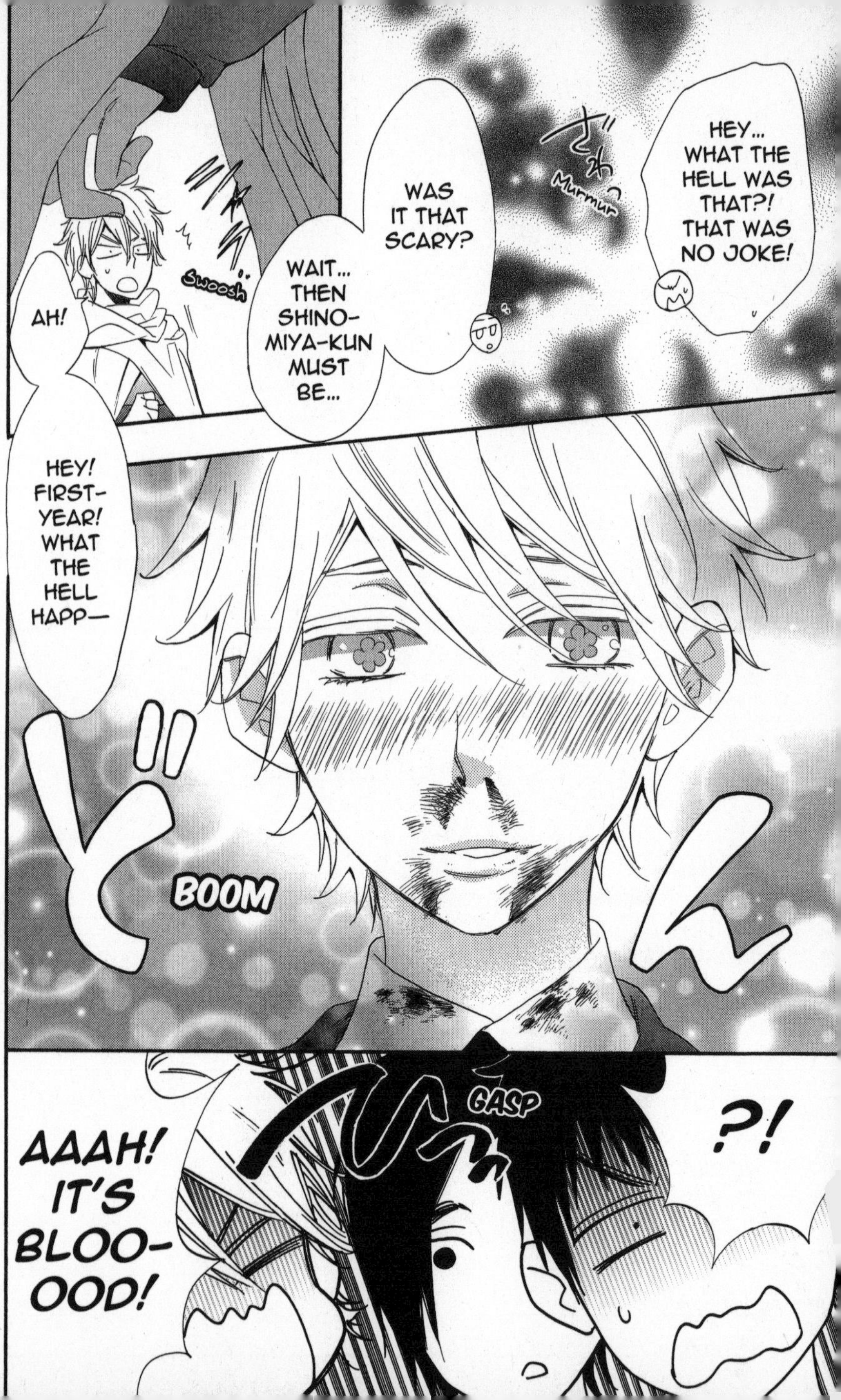
HEY... WHAT THE HELL WAS THAT?! THAT WAS NO JOKE!
Murmur
WAS IT THAT SCARY?
WAIT... THEN SHINOMIYA-KUN MUST BE...
Swoosh
AH!
HEY! FIRST-YEAR! WHAT THE HELL HAPP—
BOOM
?!
GASP
AAAH! IT'S BLOO-OOD!

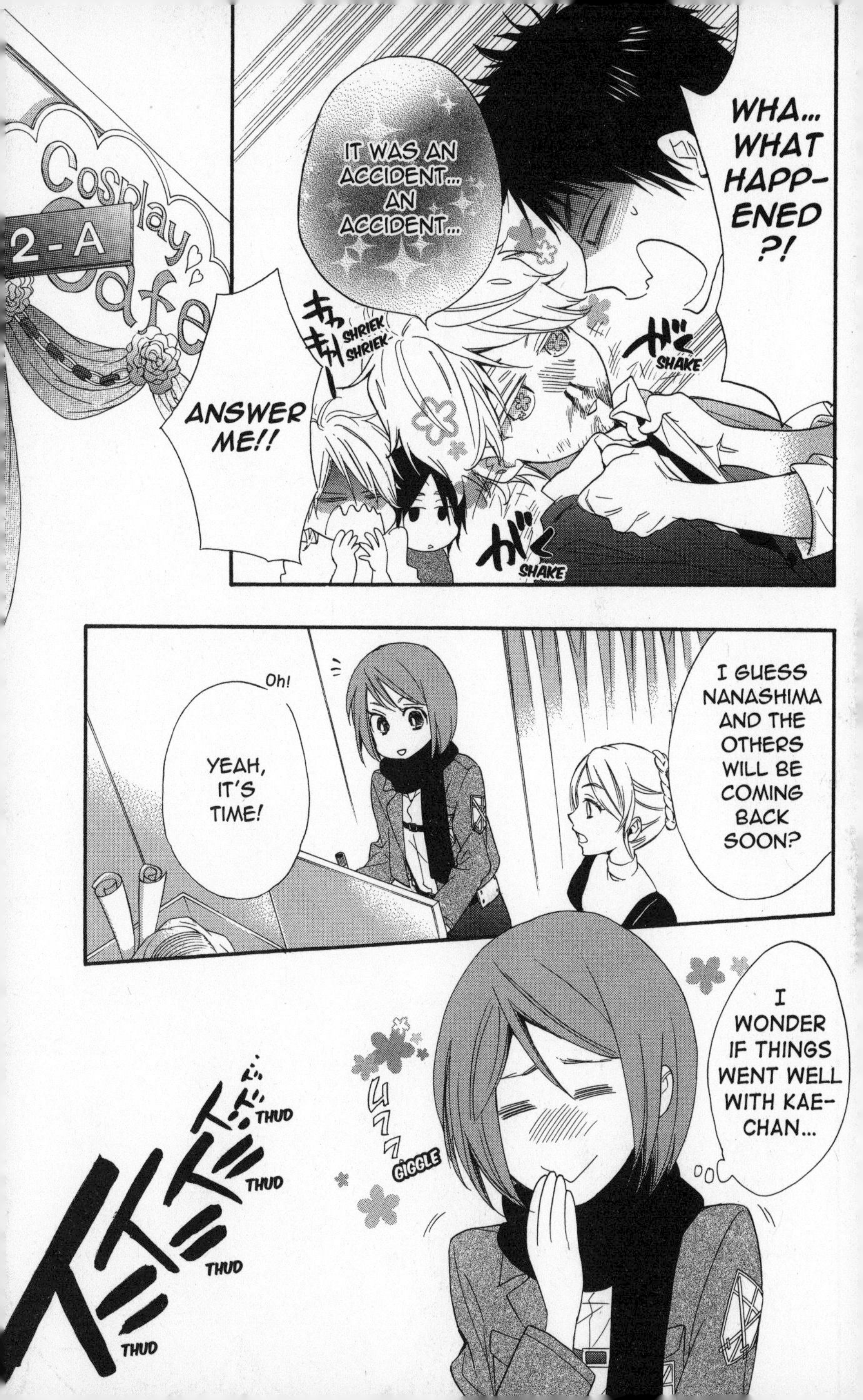
WHA... WHAT HAPP-ENED ?!
IT WAS AN ACCIDENT... AN ACCIDENT...
がく
SHAKE
SHRIEK SHRIEK
ANSWER ME!!
がく
SHAKE
Cosplay Cafe
2-A
I GUESS NANASHIMA AND THE OTHERS WILL BE COMING BACK SOON?
Oh!
YEAH, IT'S TIME!
I WONDER IF THINGS WENT WELL WITH KAE-CHAN...
ムフフ
GIGGLE
THUD
THUD
THUD
THUD

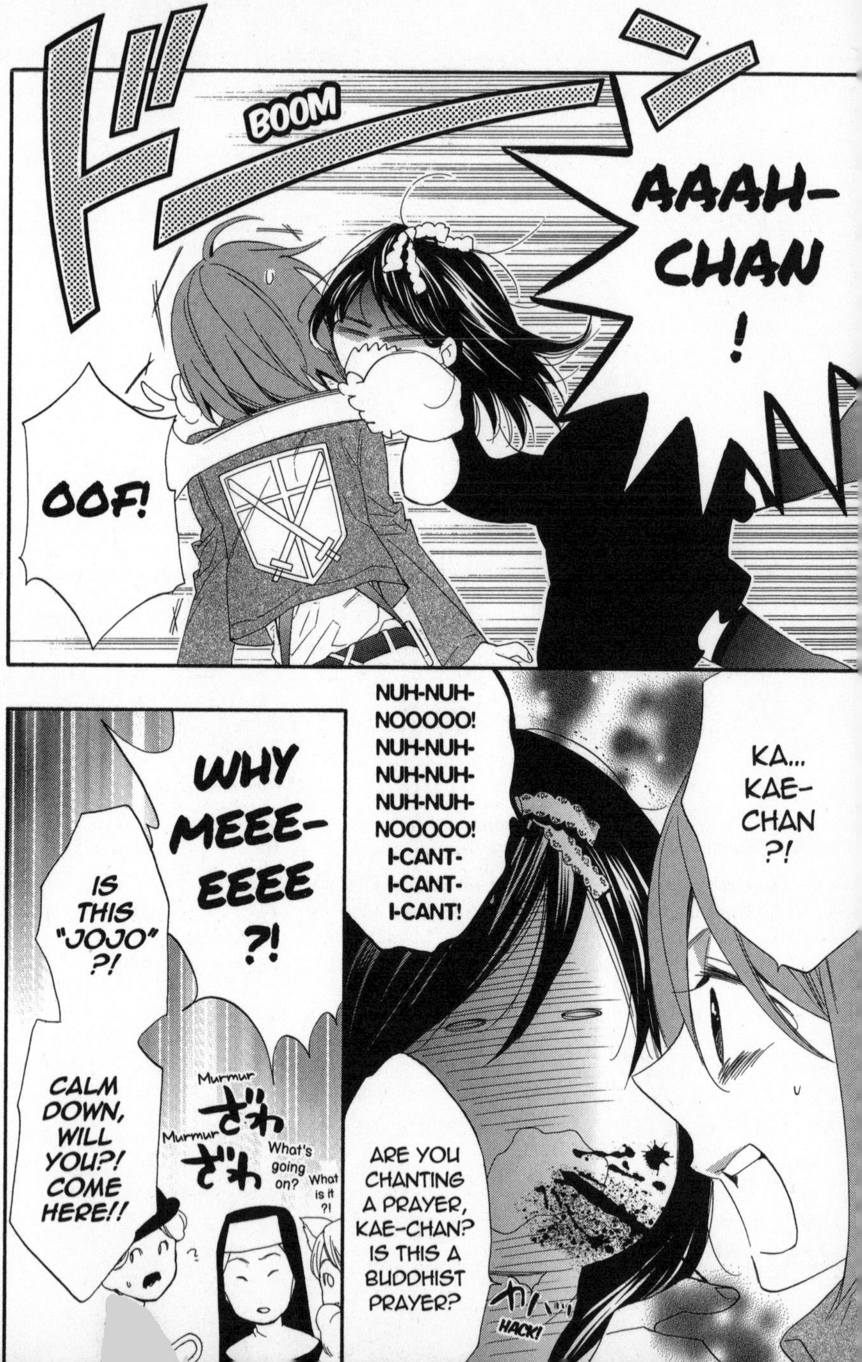

ドーン
BOOM
AAAH-CHAN!
OOF!
KA... KAE-CHAN?!
NUH-NUH-NOOOOO! NUH-NUH-NUH-NUH-NUH-NUH-NOOOOO! I-CANT-I-CANT-I-CANT!
ARE YOU CHANTING A PRAYER, KAE-CHAN? IS THIS A BUDDHIST PRAYER?
HACK!
WHY MEEEE-EEEE?!
IS THIS "JOJO"?!
CALM DOWN, WILL YOU?! COME HERE!!
Murmur
ざわ
Murmur
ざわ
What's going on?
What is it?!

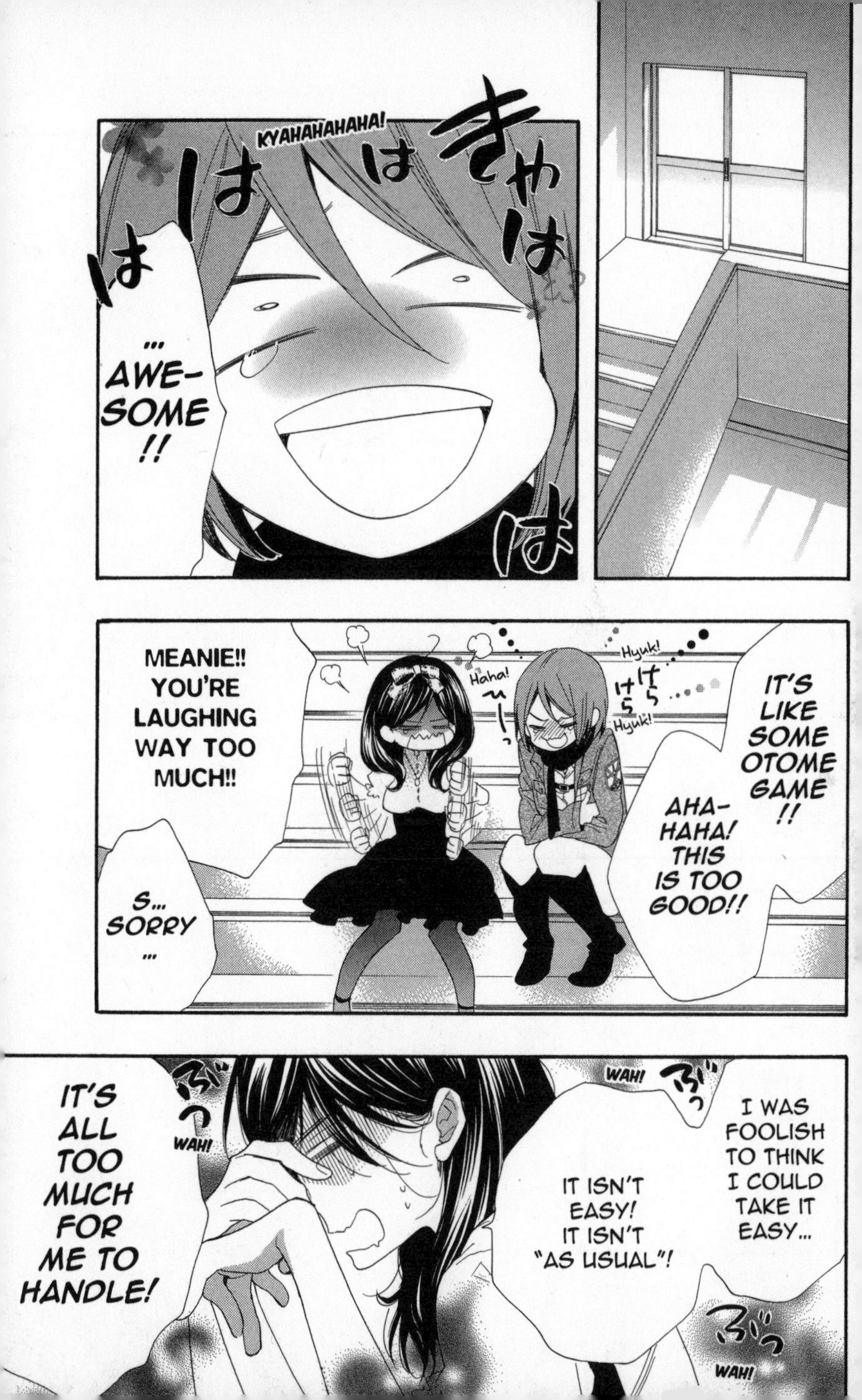
きゃははははは
KYAHAHAHAHA!
...AWESOME!!
IT'S LIKE SOME OTOME GAME!!
Hyuk!
けらけら
Hyuk!
AHA-HAHA! THIS IS TOO GOOD!!
Haha!
ひー
MEANIE!! YOU'RE LAUGHING WAY TOO MUCH!!
S... SORRY...
I WAS FOOLISH TO THINK I COULD TAKE IT EASY...
ぶっ
WAH!
IT ISN'T EASY! IT ISN'T "AS USUAL"!
ぶっ
WAH!
IT'S ALL TOO MUCH FOR ME TO HANDLE!
ぶっ
WAH!

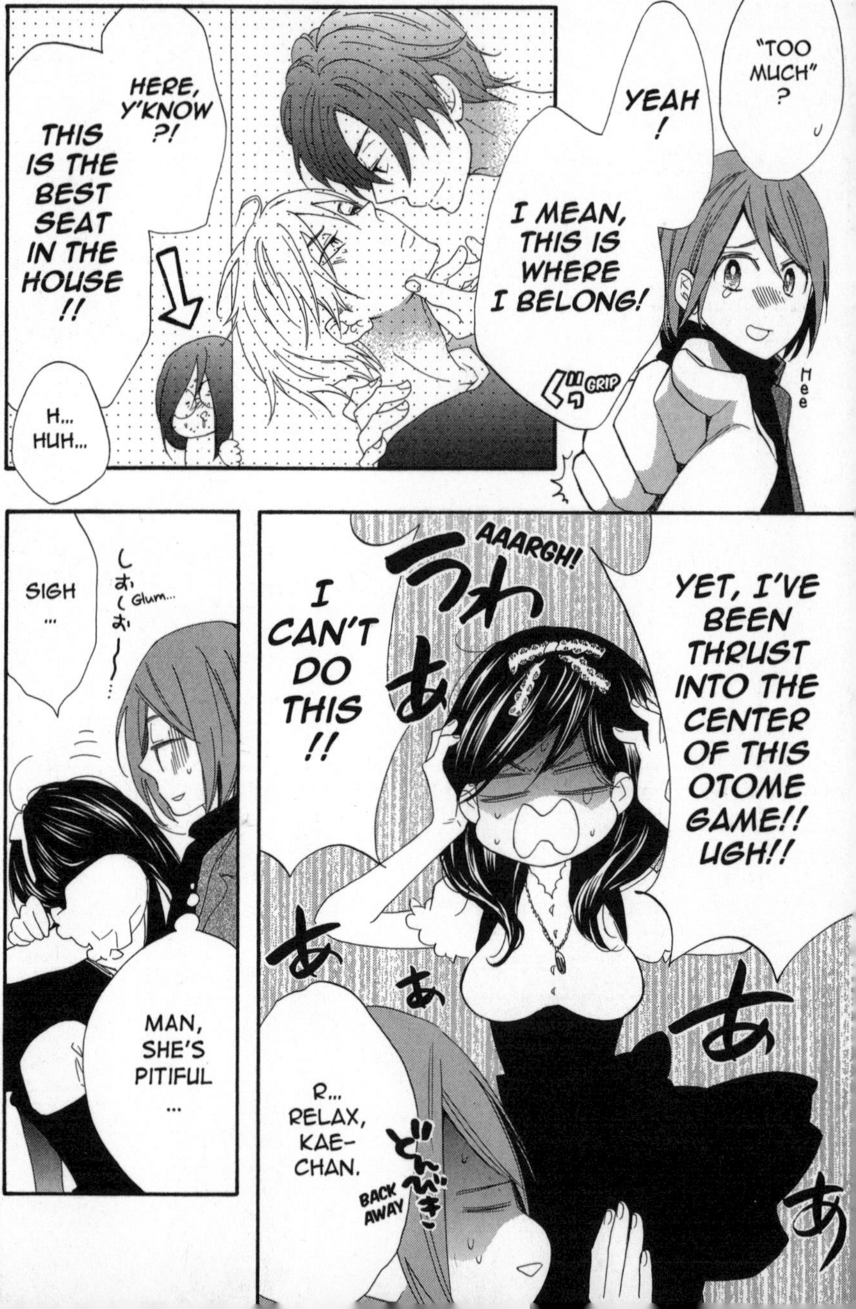
"TOO MUCH"?
YEAH!
I MEAN, THIS IS WHERE I BELONG!
ぐっ GRIP
Mee
HERE, Y'KNOW?!
THIS IS THE BEST SEAT IN THE HOUSE!!
H... HUH...
うわあ AAARGH!
YET, I'VE BEEN THRUST INTO THE CENTER OF THIS OTOME GAME!! UGH!!
I CAN'T DO THIS!!
あぁあ
R... RELAX, KAE-CHAN.
どんびき BACK AWAY
SIGH...
しおしお～ Glum...
MAN, SHE'S PITIFUL...

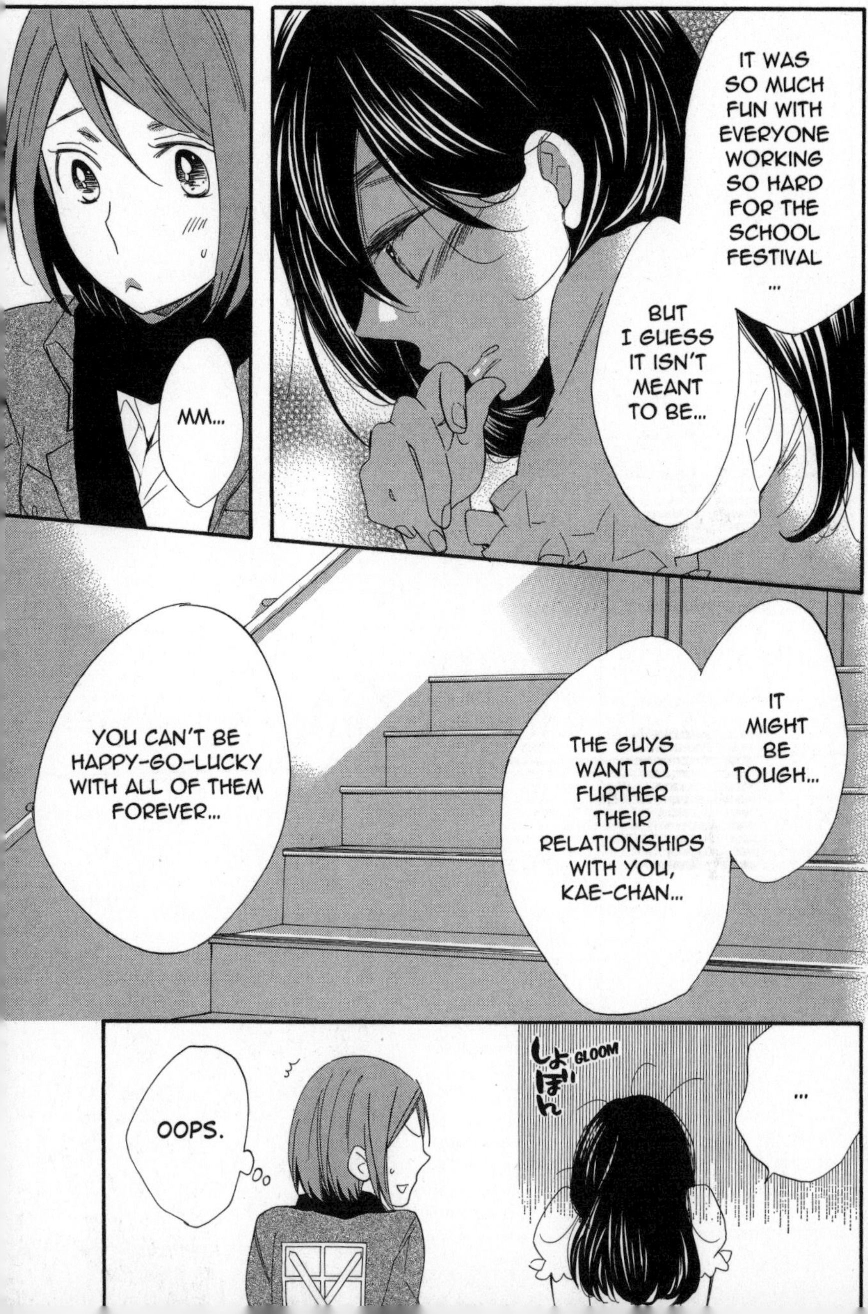
IT WAS SO MUCH FUN WITH EVERYONE WORKING SO HARD FOR THE SCHOOL FESTIVAL ...
BUT I GUESS IT ISN'T MEANT TO BE...
MM...
IT MIGHT BE TOUGH...
THE GUYS WANT TO FURTHER THEIR RELATIONSHIPS WITH YOU, KAE-CHAN...
YOU CAN'T BE HAPPY-GO-LUCKY WITH ALL OF THEM FOREVER...
...
しょぼん GLOOM
OOPS.

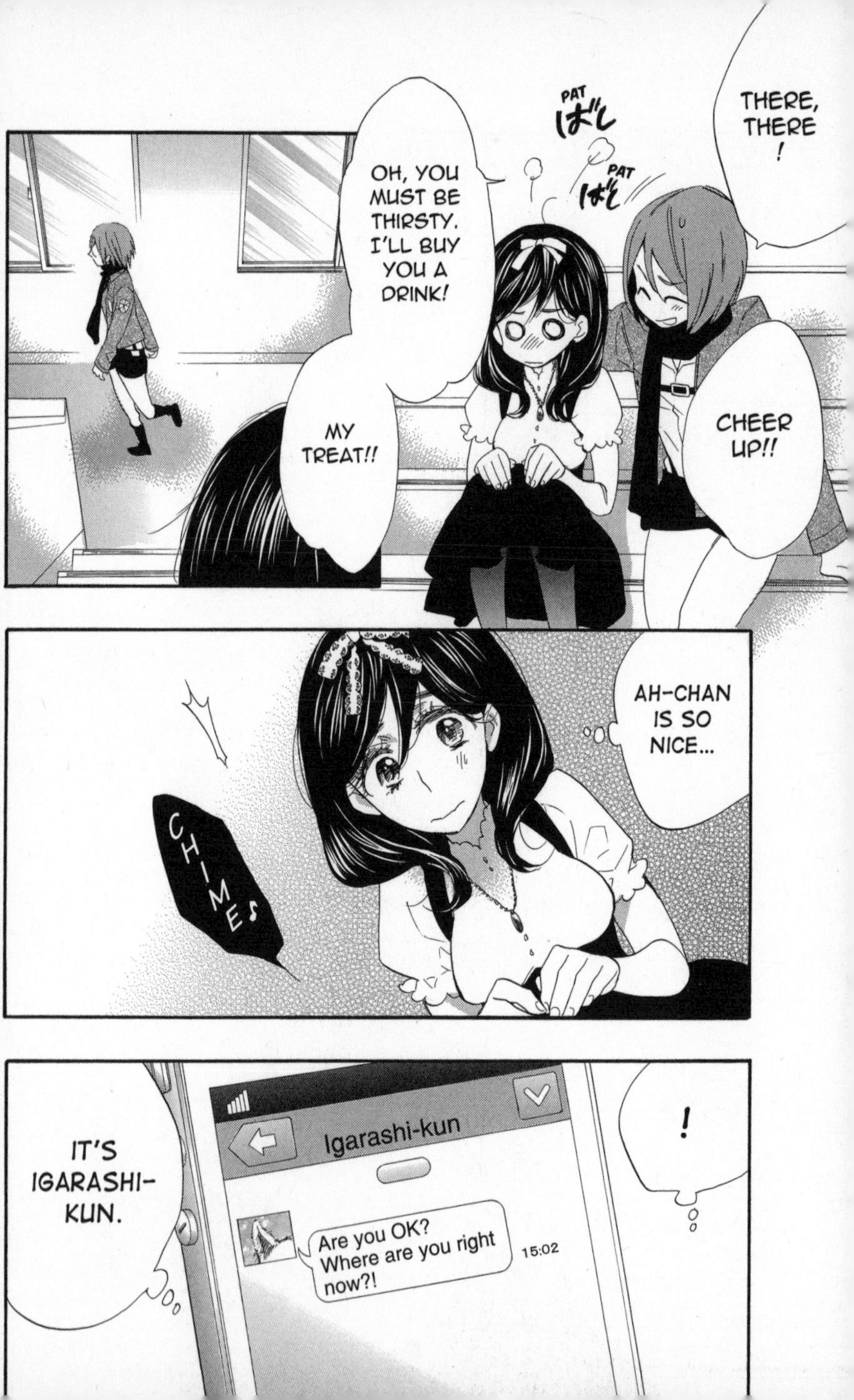
THERE, THERE!
PAT ぱし
PAT ぱし
CHEER UP!!
OH, YOU MUST BE THIRSTY. I'LL BUY YOU A DRINK!
MY TREAT!!
AH-CHAN IS SO NICE...
CHIME♪
!
Igarashi-kun
Are you OK? Where are you right now?!
15:02
IT'S IGARASHI-KUN.

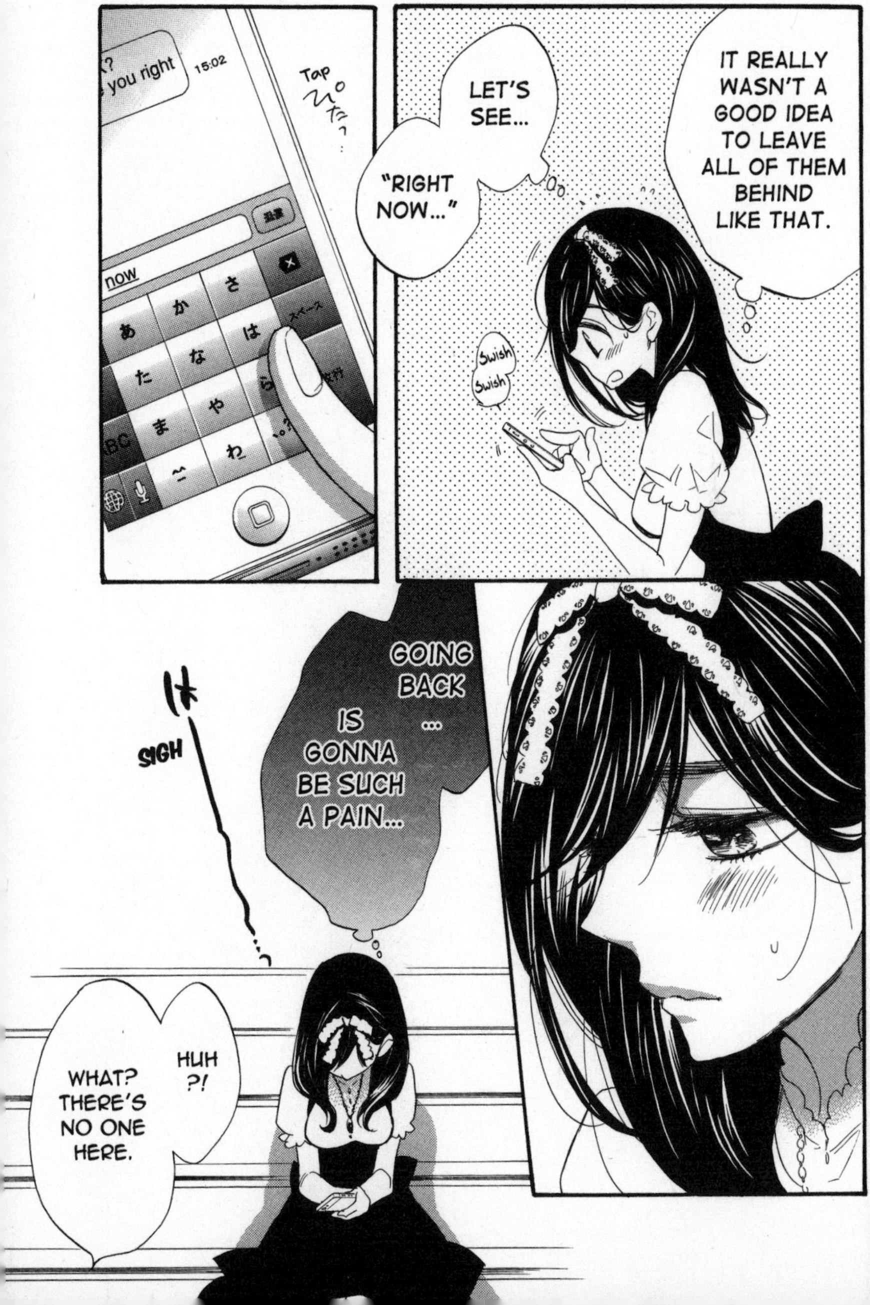
IT REALLY WASN'T A GOOD IDEA TO LEAVE ALL OF THEM BEHIND LIKE THAT.
LET'S SEE...
"RIGHT NOW..."
Swish Swish
Tap
you right
15:02
now
GOING BACK ... IS GONNA BE SUCH A PAIN...
SIGH
HUH ?!
WHAT? THERE'S NO ONE HERE.

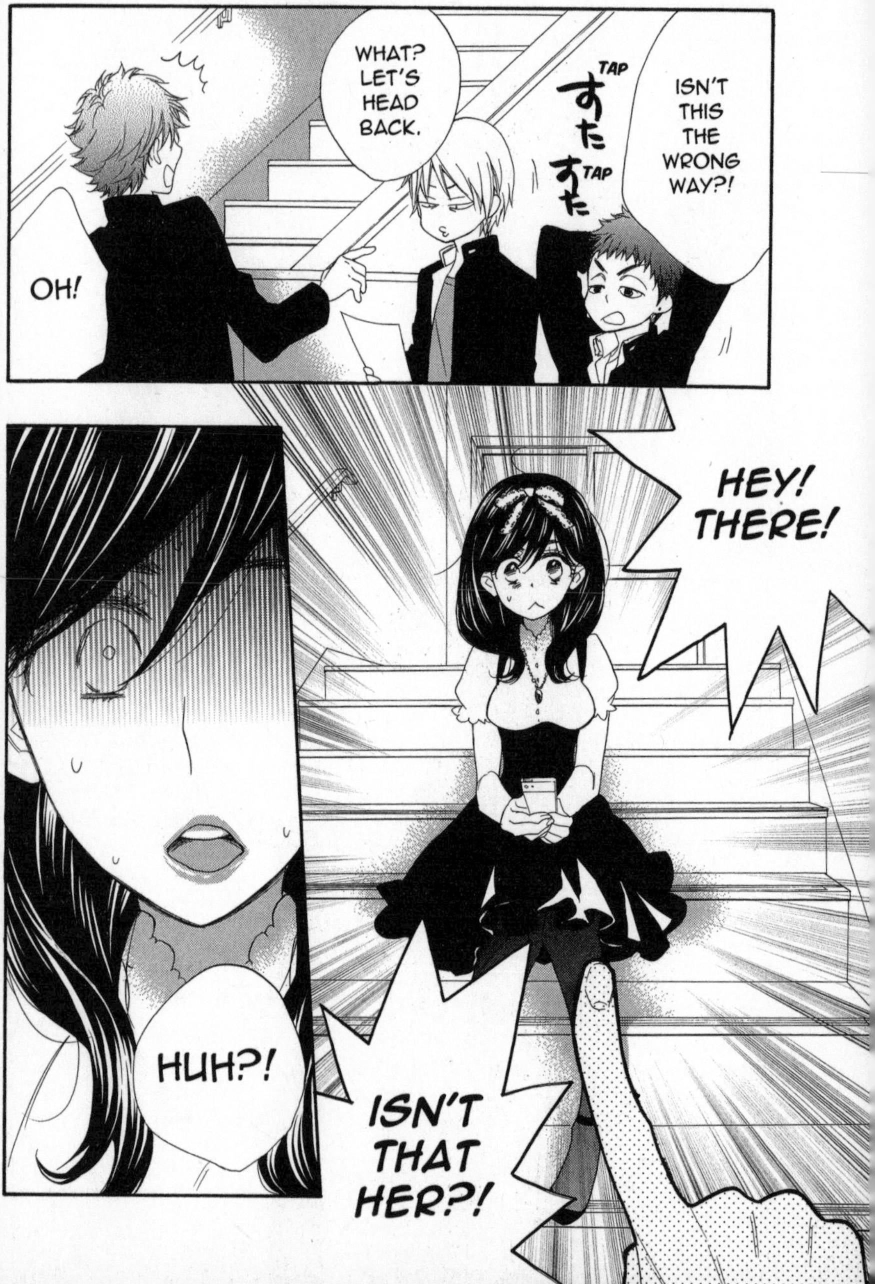
ISN'T THIS THE WRONG WAY?!
すた すた
TAP TAP
WHAT? LET'S HEAD BACK.
OH!
HEY! THERE!
ISN'T THAT HER?!
HUH?!

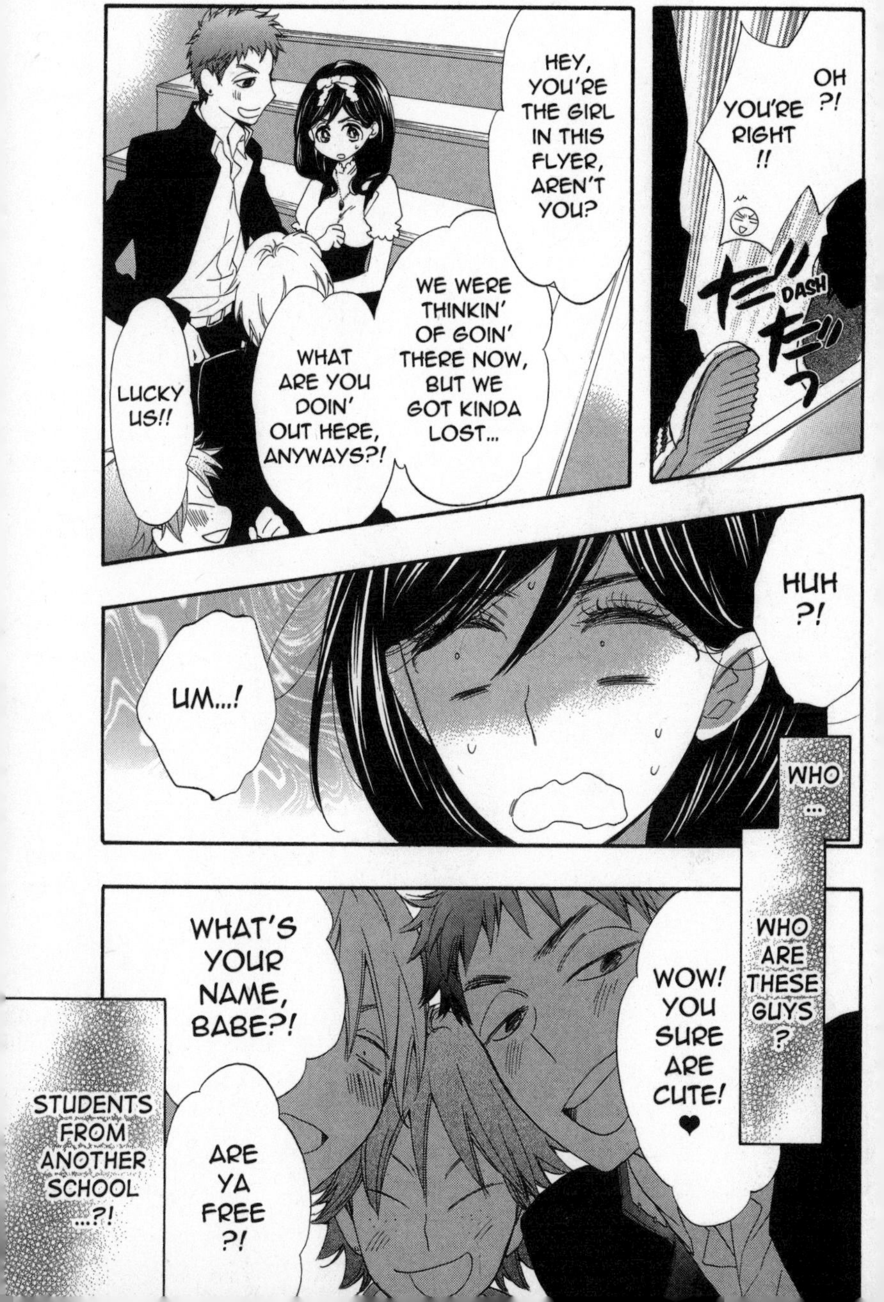
OH ?!
YOU'RE RIGHT !!
DASH
HEY, YOU'RE THE GIRL IN THIS FLYER, AREN'T YOU?
WE WERE THINKIN' OF GOIN' THERE NOW, BUT WE GOT KINDA LOST...
WHAT ARE YOU DOIN' OUT HERE, ANYWAYS?!
LUCKY US!!
HUH ?!
UM...!
WHO ...
WHO ARE THESE GUYS ?
WOW! YOU SURE ARE CUTE! ❤
WHAT'S YOUR NAME, BABE?!
ARE YA FREE ?!
STUDENTS FROM ANOTHER SCHOOL ...?!

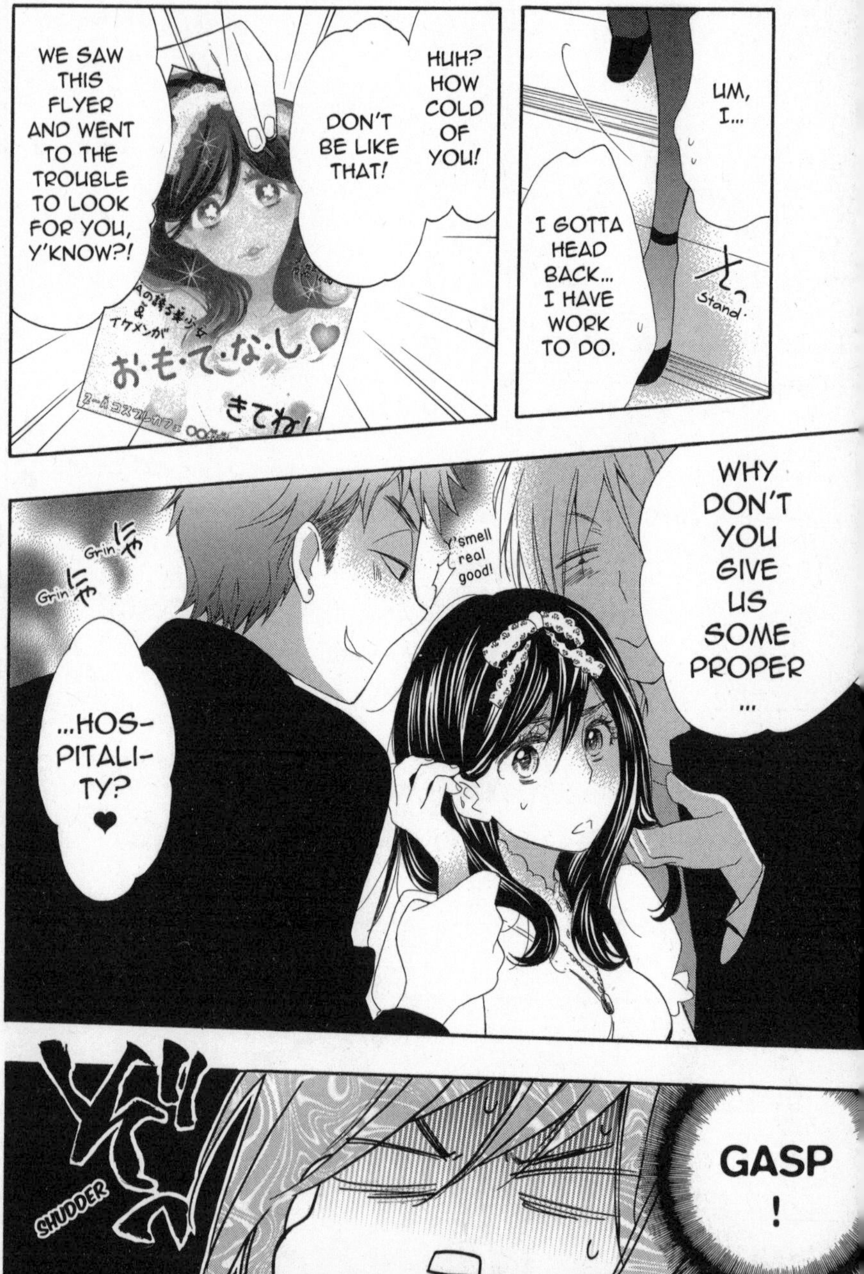

UM, I...
I GOTTA HEAD BACK... I HAVE WORK TO DO.
Stand
HUH? HOW COLD OF YOU!
DON'T BE LIKE THAT!
WE SAW THIS FLYER AND WENT TO THE TROUBLE TO LOOK FOR YOU, Y'KNOW?!
お・も・て・な・し
WHY DON'T YOU GIVE US SOME PROPER...
Y'smell real good!
Grin
Grin
...HOSPITALITY? ♥
GASP!
SHUDDER

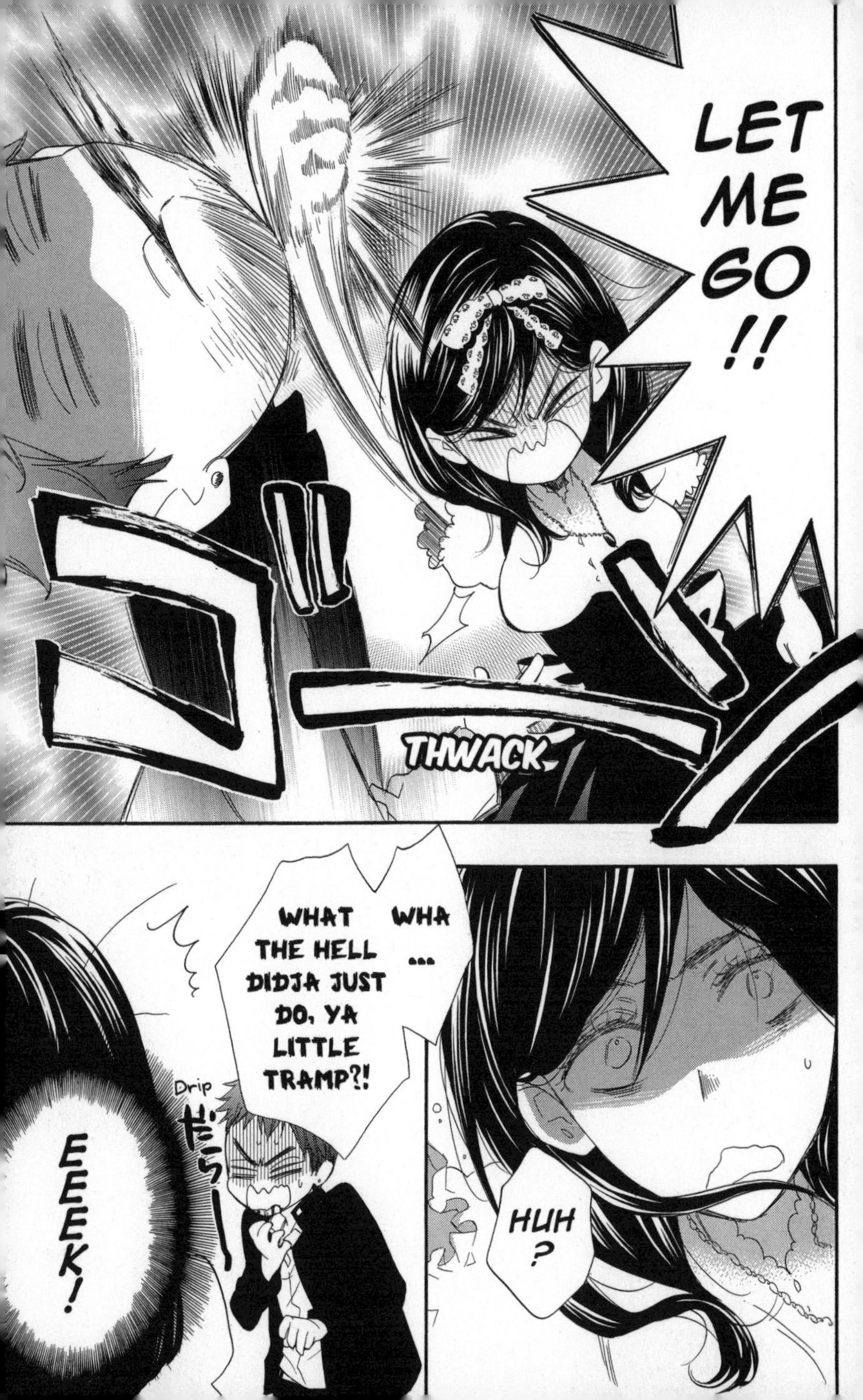

LET ME GO!!
THWACK
HUH?
WHA ...
WHAT THE HELL DIDJA JUST DO, YA LITTLE TRAMP?!
Drip
だらー
EEEK!

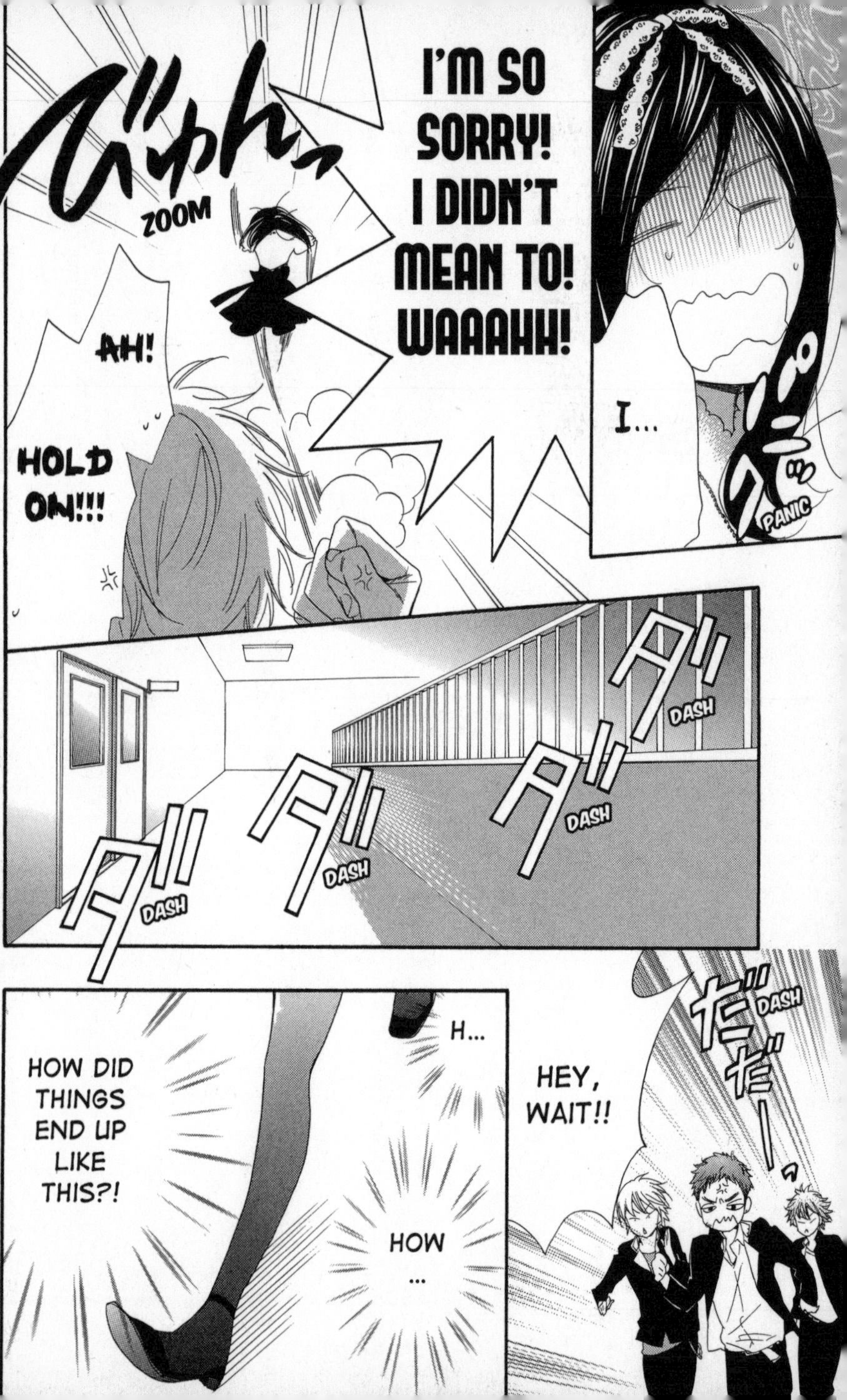
I...
PANIC
I'M SO SORRY! I DIDN'T MEAN TO! WAAAHH!
ZOOM
AH!
HOLD ON!!!
DASH
DASH
DASH
DASH
HEY, WAIT!!
DASH
H...
HOW ...
HOW DID THINGS END UP LIKE THIS?!

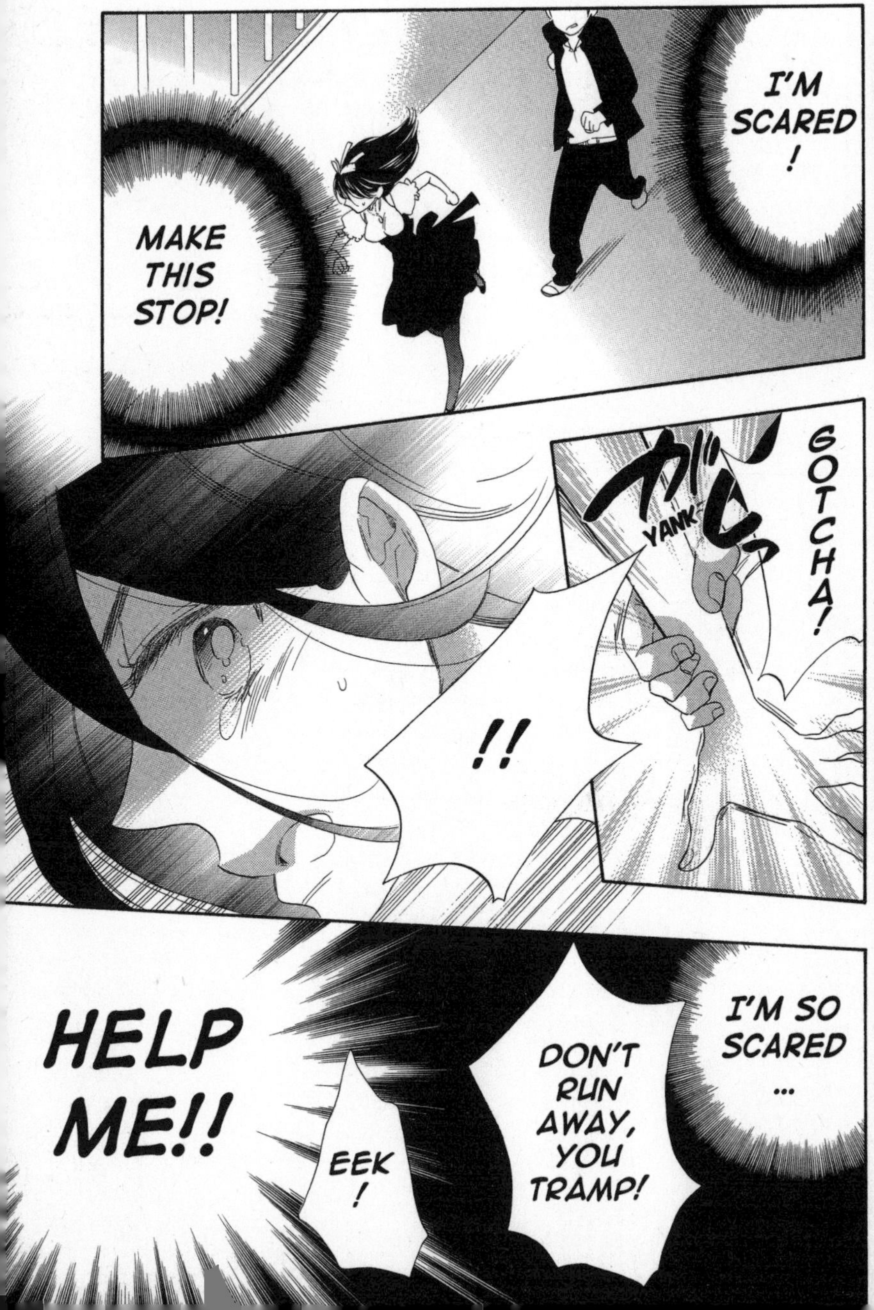
I'M SCARED!
MAKE THIS STOP!
GOTCHA!
YANK
!!
I'M SO SCARED...
DON'T RUN AWAY, YOU TRAMP!
EEK!
HELP ME!!

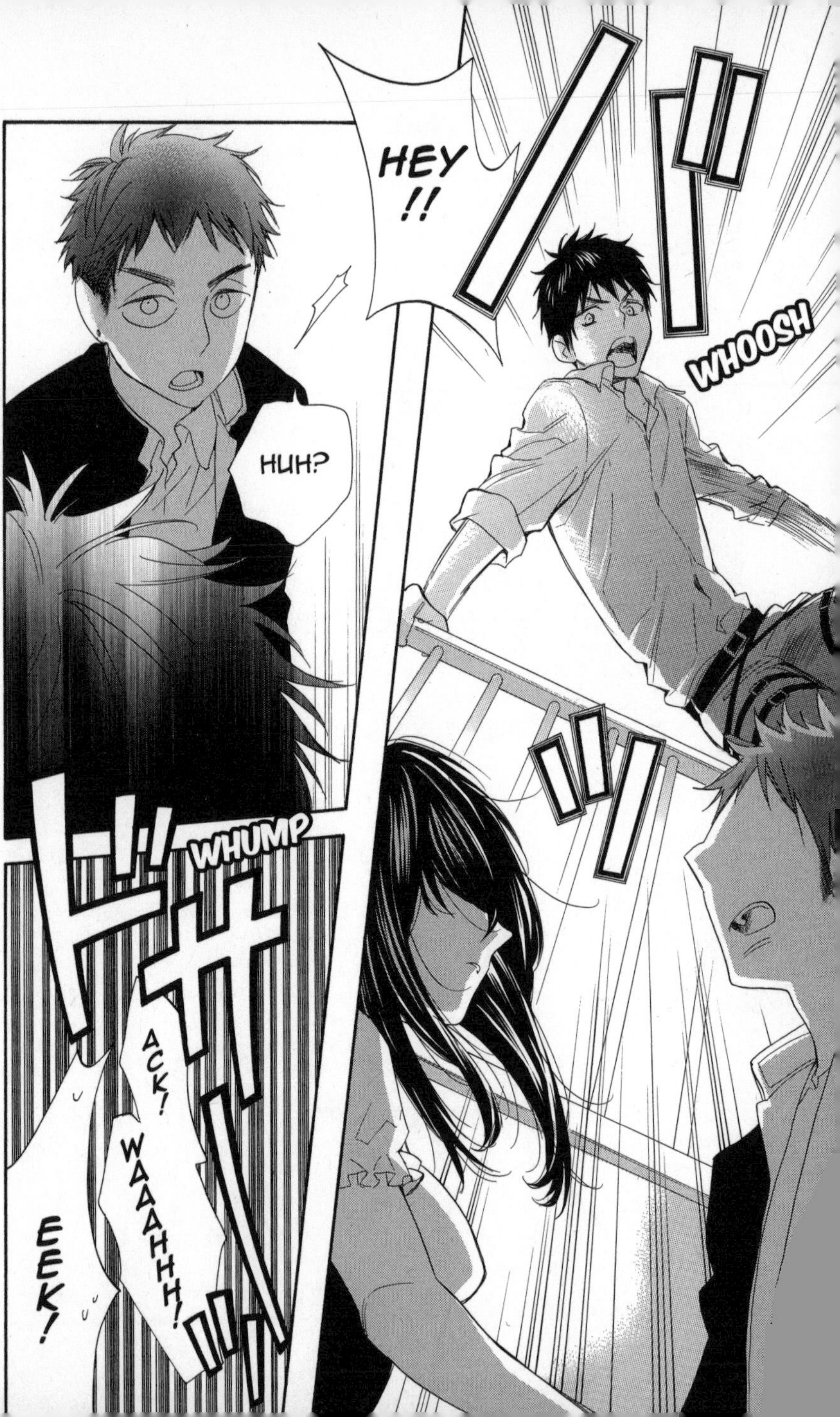
HEY !!
WHOOSH
HUH?
WHUMP
ACK!
WAAAHHH!
EEK!

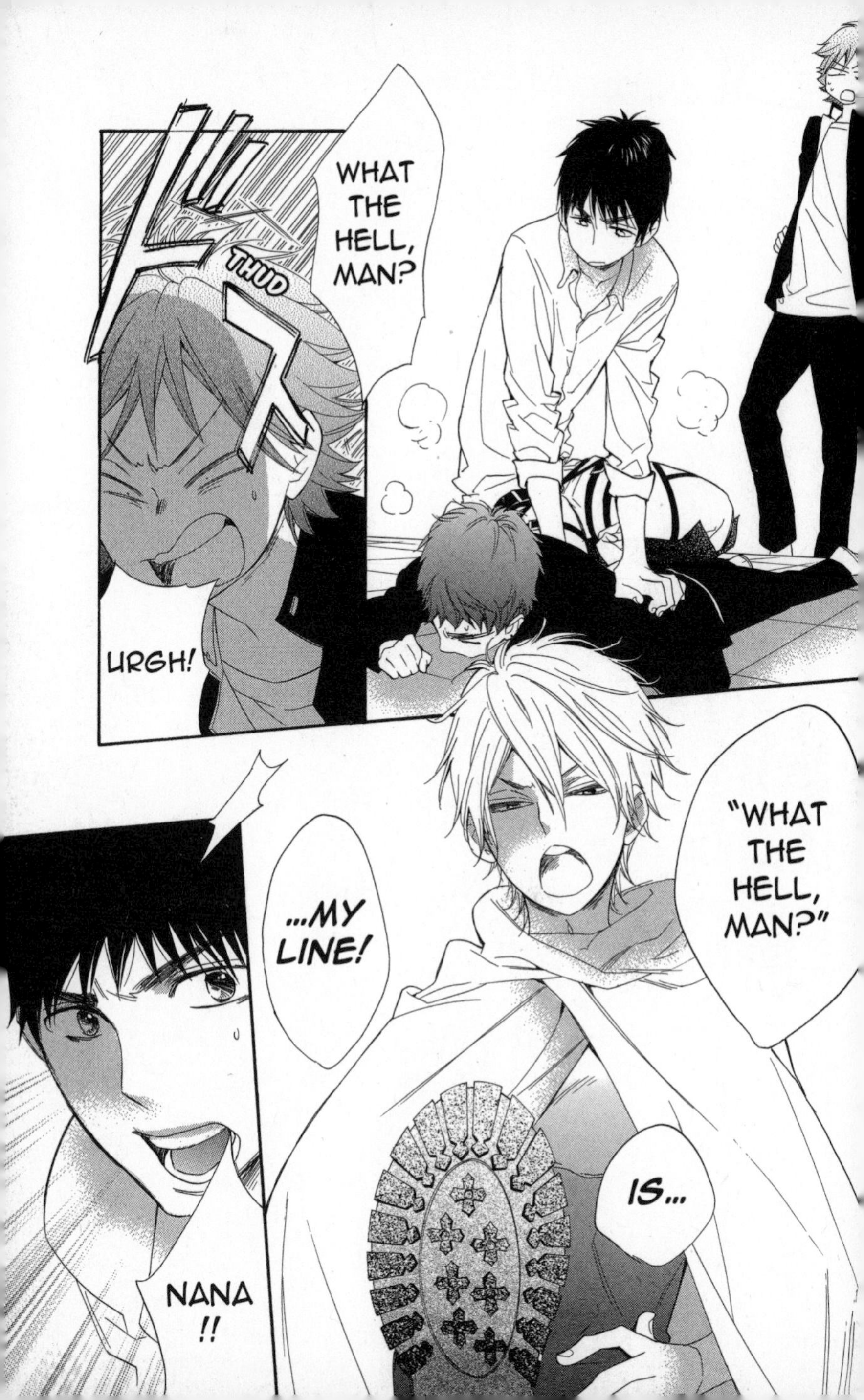
WHAT THE HELL, MAN?
THUD
URGH!
"WHAT THE HELL, MAN?"
IS...
...MY LINE!
NANA !!

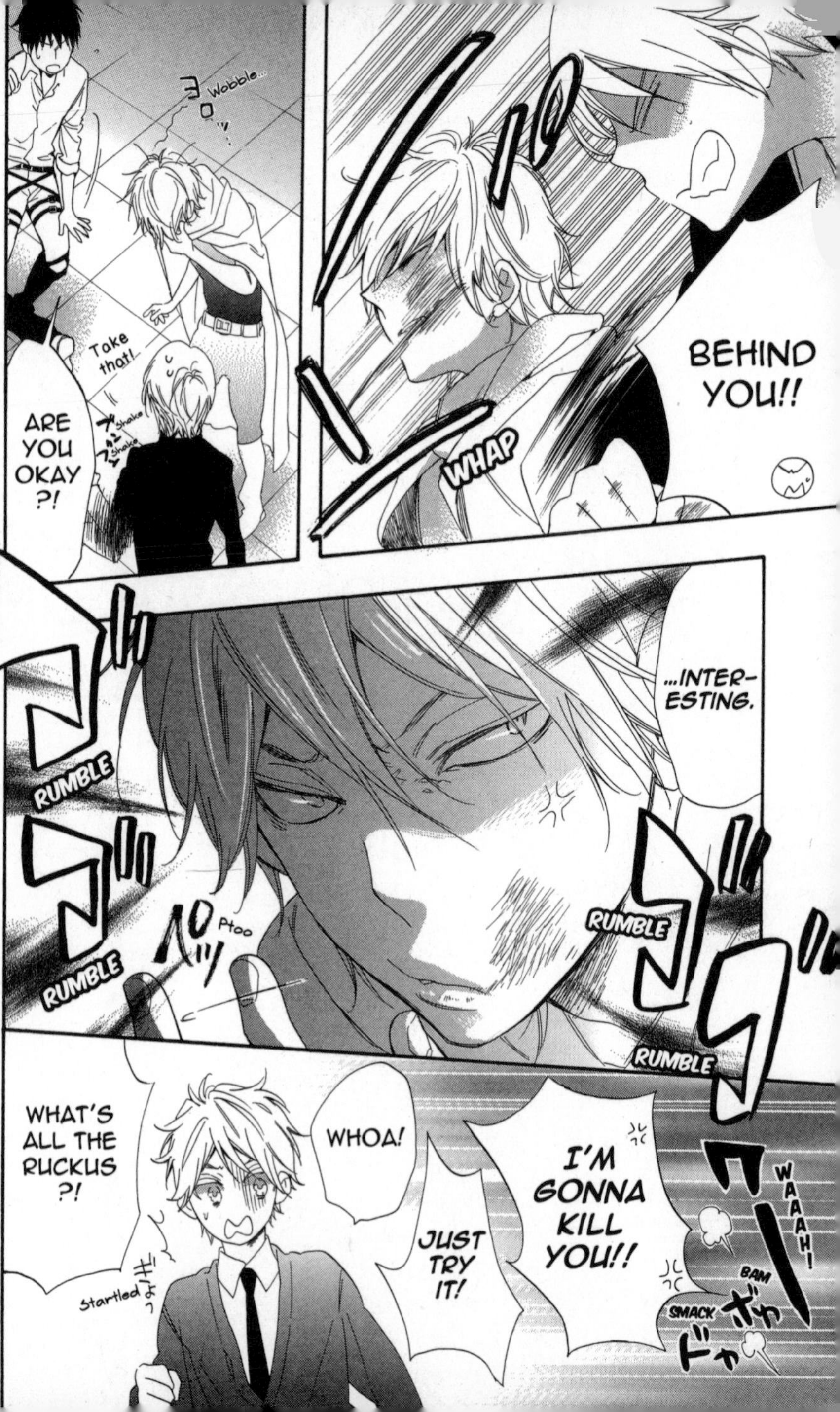
BEHIND YOU!!
WHAP
Wobble...
Take that!
Shake
Shake
ARE YOU OKAY ?!
...INTER-ESTING.
RUMBLE
RUMBLE
RUMBLE
RUMBLE
Ptoo
WAAAH!
BAM
SMACK
I'M GONNA KILL YOU!!
JUST TRY IT!
WHOA!
WHAT'S ALL THE RUCKUS ?!
Startled

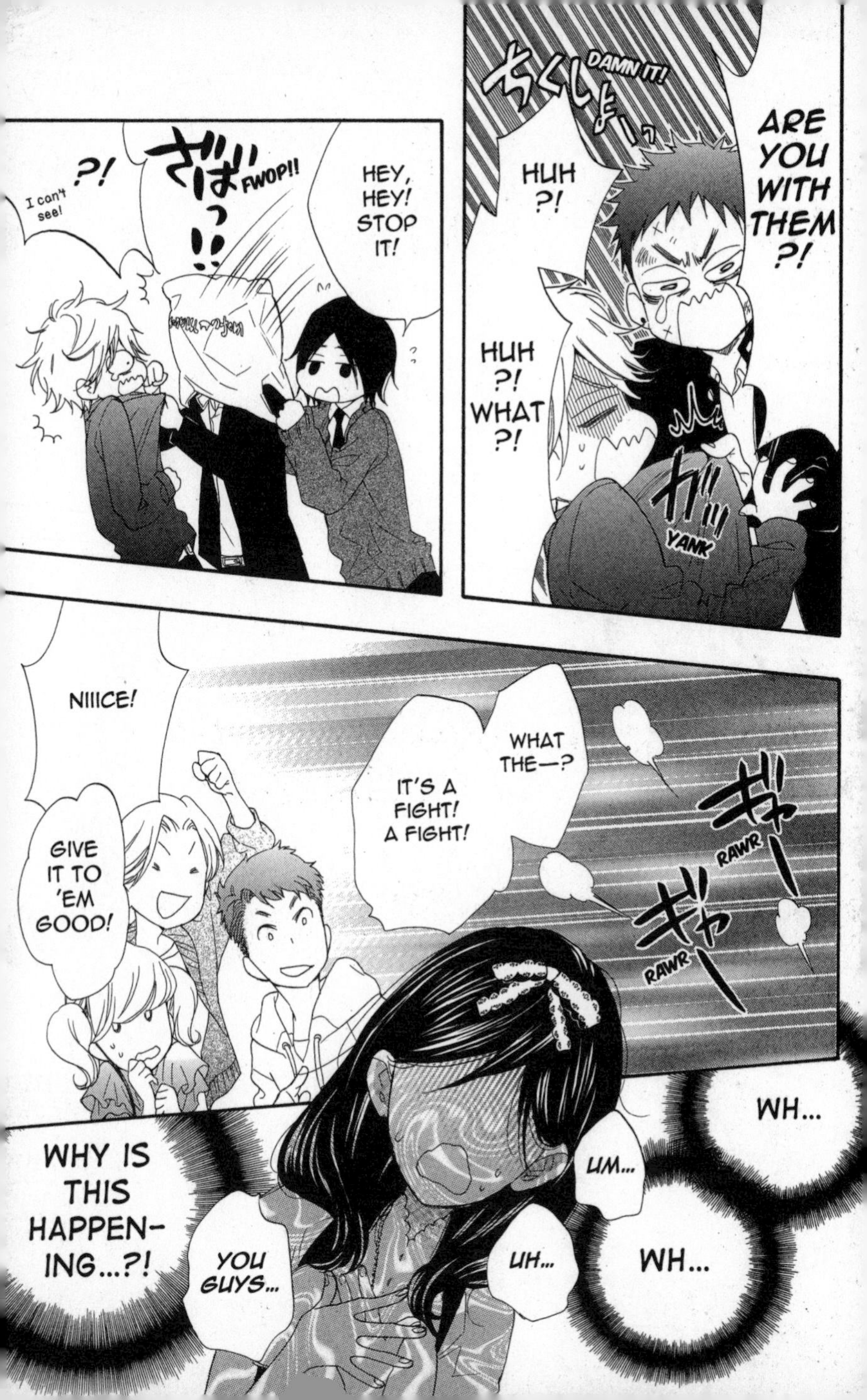

DAMN IT!
ARE YOU WITH THEM?!
HUH?!
HUH?! WHAT?!
YANK
HEY, HEY! STOP IT!
FWOP!!
?!
I can't see!
WHAT THE—?
IT'S A FIGHT! A FIGHT!
RAWR
RAWR
NIIICE!
GIVE IT TO 'EM GOOD!
WH...
UM...
WH...
UH...
YOU GUYS...
WHY IS THIS HAPPEN-ING...?!

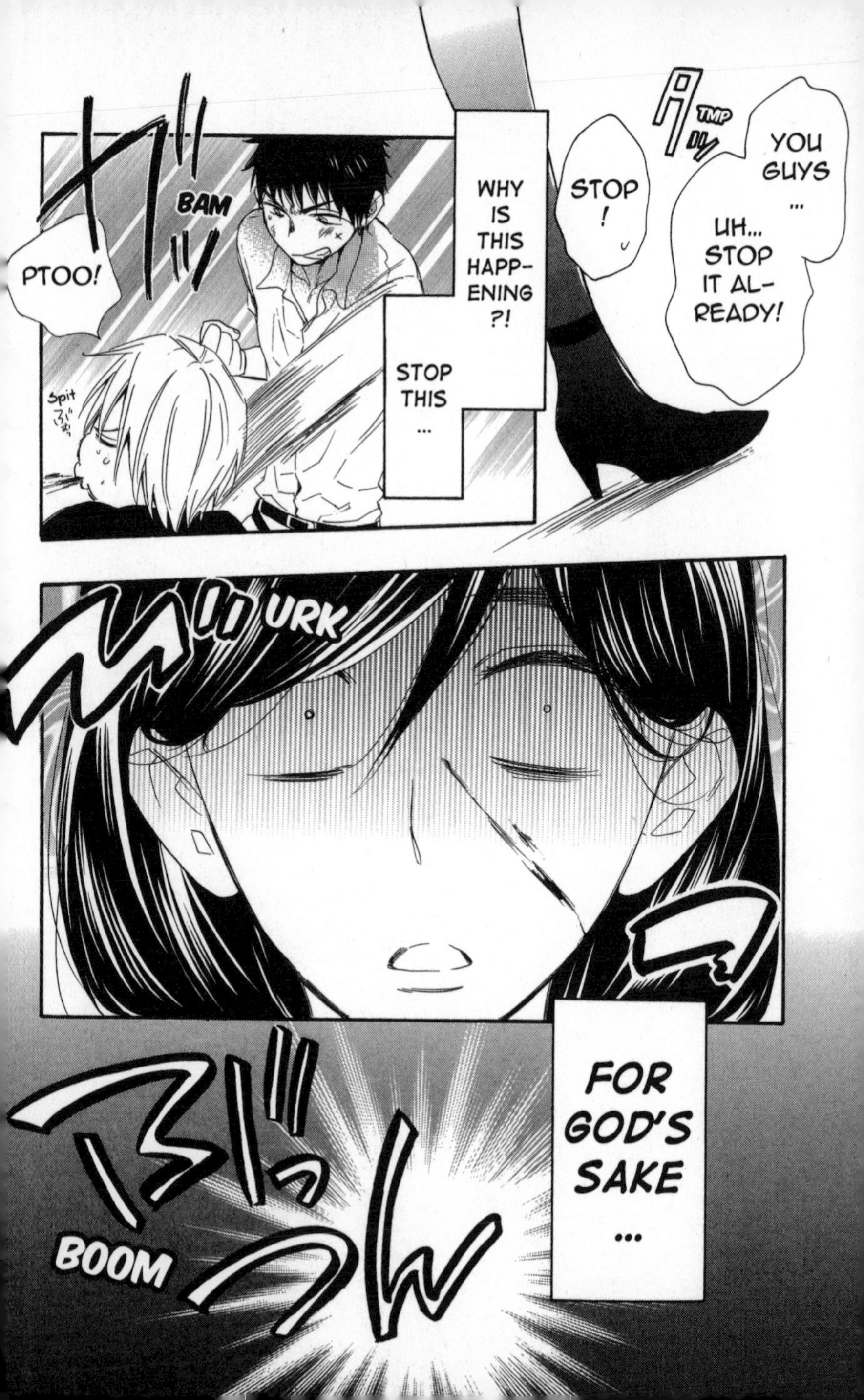
TMP
YOU GUYS ... UH... STOP IT AL-READY!
STOP!
WHY IS THIS HAPP-ENING?!
STOP THIS ...
BAM
PTOO!
Spit
URK
FOR GOD'S SAKE ...
BOOM

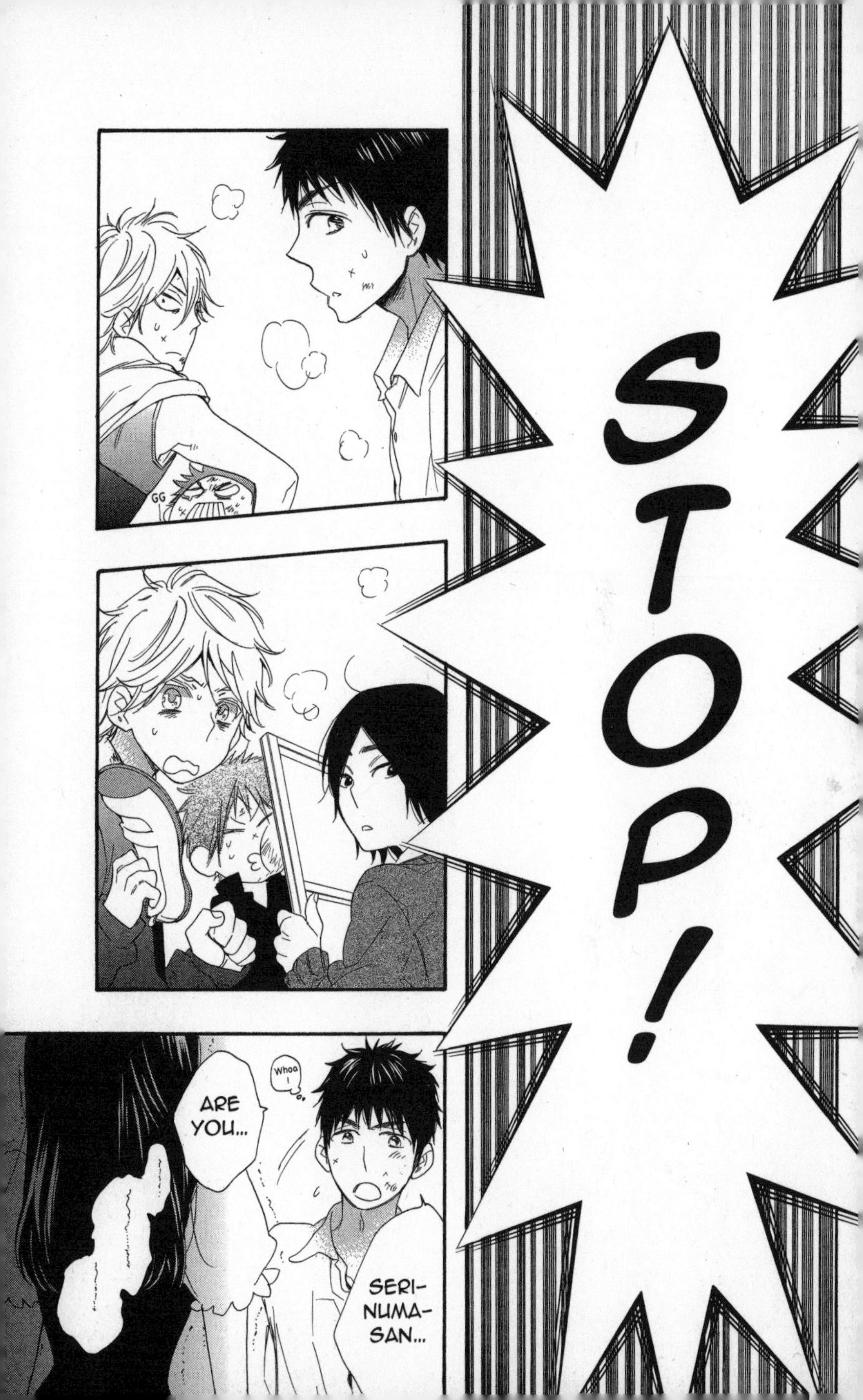
STOP!
GG
Whoa!
ARE YOU...
SERI-NUMA-SAN...

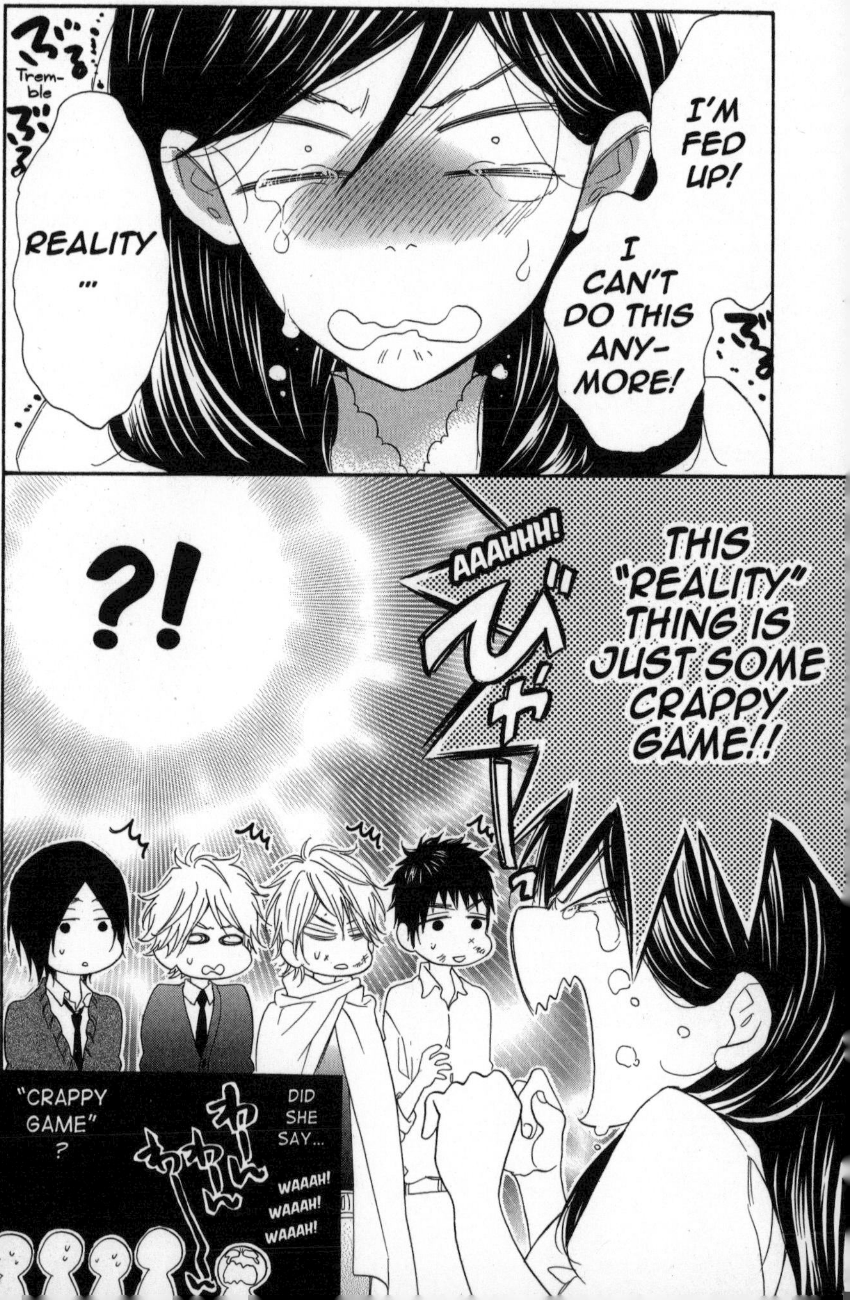
I'M FED UP!
I CAN'T DO THIS ANYMORE!
ぶる
ぶるぶる
Trem-ble
REALITY ...
THIS "REALITY" THING IS JUST SOME CRAPPY GAME!!
AAAHHH!
?!
DID SHE SAY...
"CRAPPY GAME"?
WAAAH! WAAAH! WAAAH!

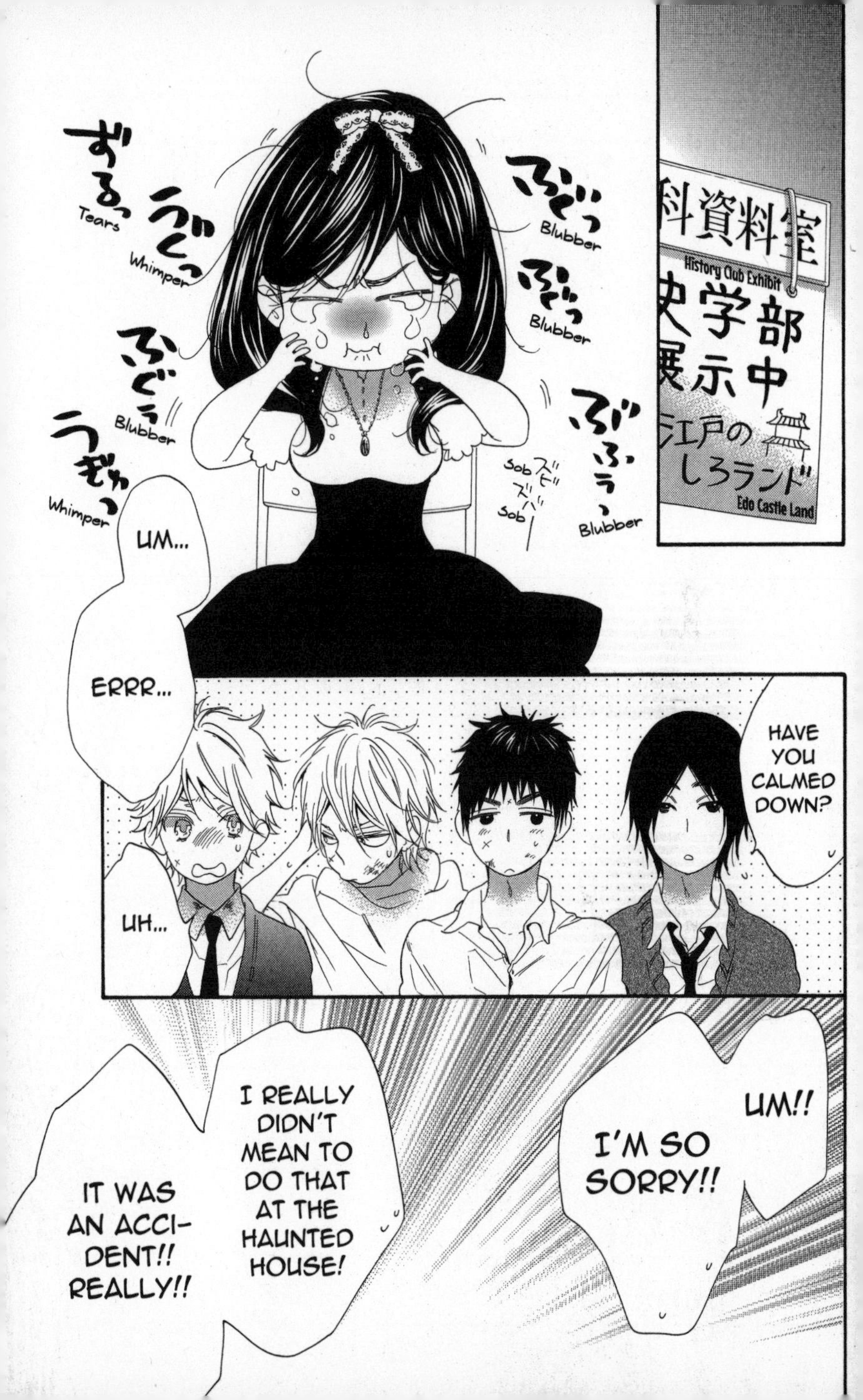

科資料室
History Club Exhibit
史学部
展示中
江戸のしろランド
Edo Castle Land
Blubber
Blubber
Blubber
Sob Sob
Tears
Whimper
Blubber
Whimper
UM...
ERRR...
HAVE YOU CALMED DOWN?
UH...
UM!!
I'M SO SORRY!!
I REALLY DIDN'T MEAN TO DO THAT AT THE HAUNTED HOUSE!
IT WAS AN ACCI-DENT!! REALLY!!

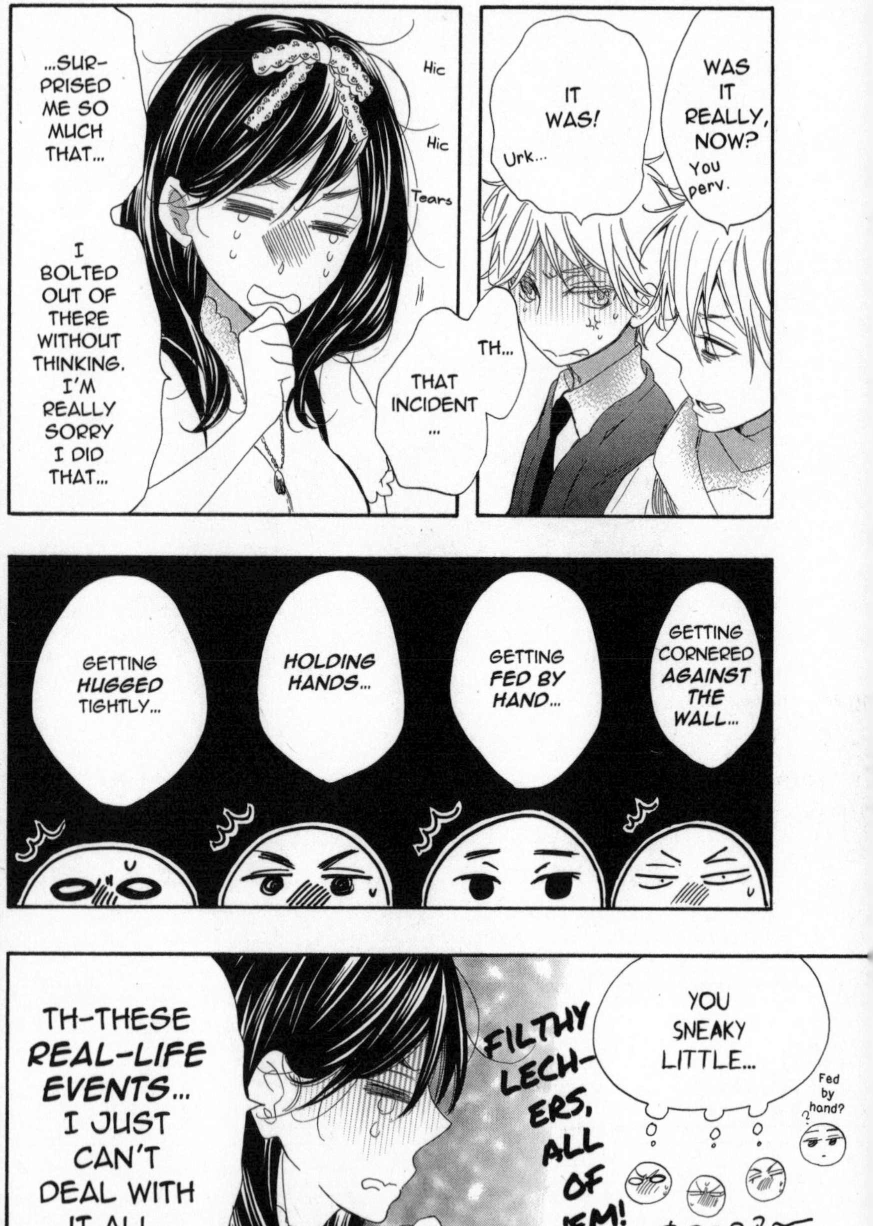

WAS IT REALLY, NOW?
You perv.
IT WAS!
Urk...
TH...
THAT INCIDENT ...
...SUR-PRISED ME SO MUCH THAT...
Hic
Hic
Tears
I BOLTED OUT OF THERE WITHOUT THINKING. I'M REALLY SORRY I DID THAT...
GETTING CORNERED AGAINST THE WALL...
GETTING FED BY HAND...
HOLDING HANDS...
GETTING HUGGED TIGHTLY...
YOU SNEAKY LITTLE...
Fed by hand?
FILTHY LECH-ERS, ALL OF 'EM!
Blushhh
TH-THESE REAL-LIFE EVENTS... I JUST CAN'T DEAL WITH IT ALL.

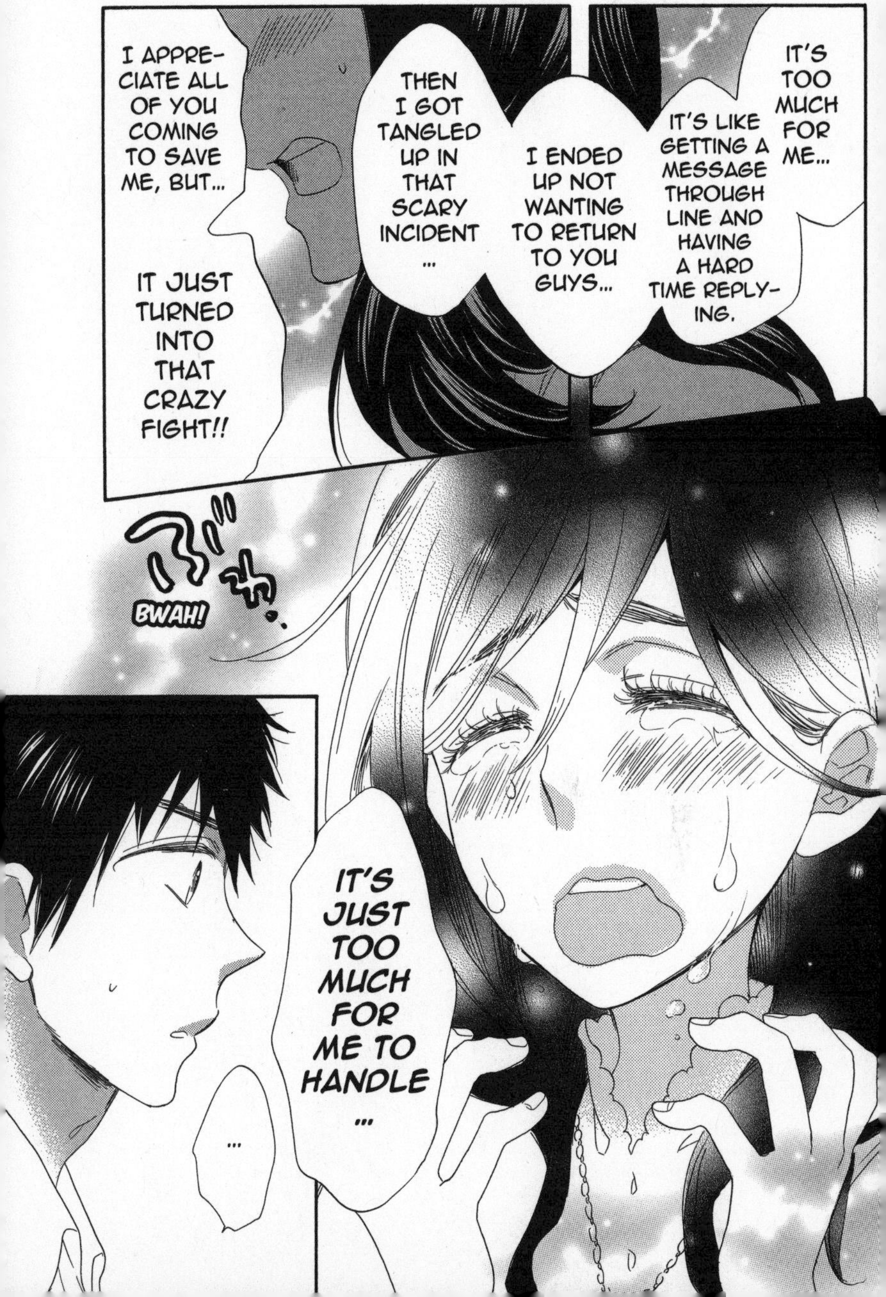
I APPRECIATE ALL OF YOU COMING TO SAVE ME, BUT...
IT JUST TURNED INTO THAT CRAZY FIGHT!!
THEN I GOT TANGLED UP IN THAT SCARY INCIDENT...
I ENDED UP NOT WANTING TO RETURN TO YOU GUYS...
IT'S LIKE GETTING A MESSAGE THROUGH LINE AND HAVING A HARD TIME REPLYING.
IT'S TOO MUCH FOR ME...
BWAH!
IT'S JUST TOO MUCH FOR ME TO HANDLE...
...

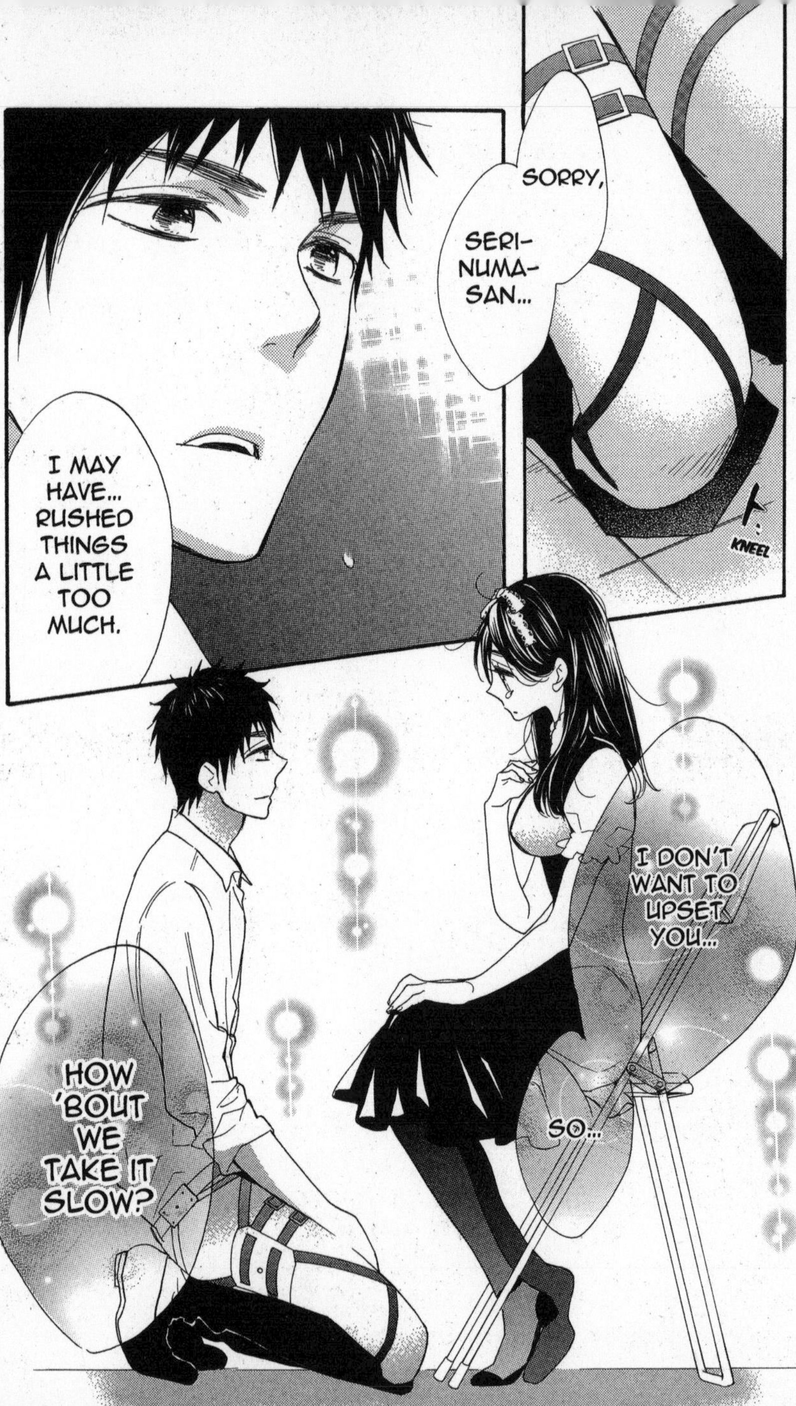
SORRY,
SERI-NUMA-SAN...
KNEEL
I MAY HAVE... RUSHED THINGS A LITTLE TOO MUCH.
I DON'T WANT TO UPSET YOU...
SO...
HOW 'BOUT WE TAKE IT SLOW?

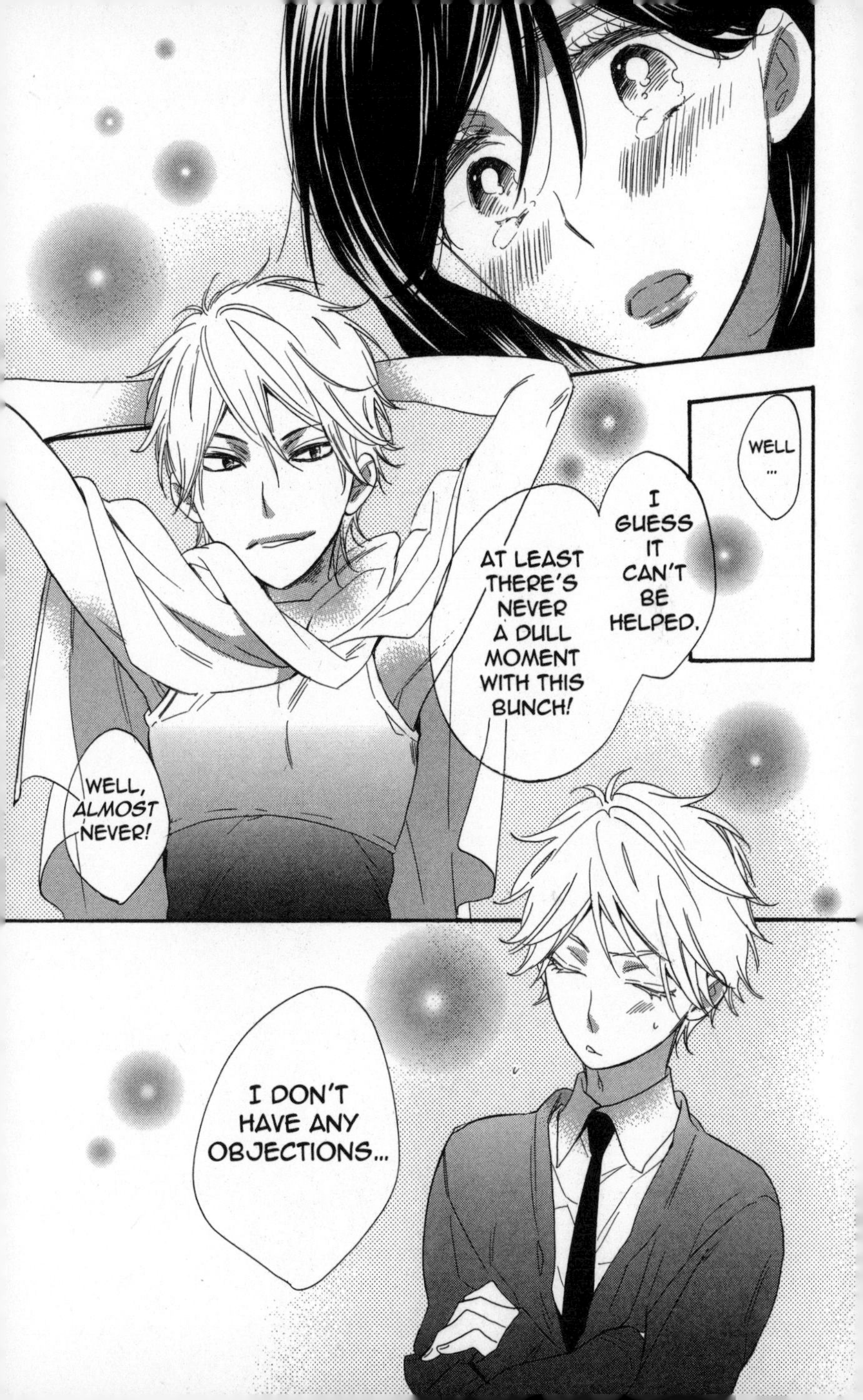
WELL ...
I GUESS IT CAN'T BE HELPED.
AT LEAST THERE'S NEVER A DULL MOMENT WITH THIS BUNCH!
WELL, ALMOST NEVER!
I DON'T HAVE ANY OBJECTIONS...

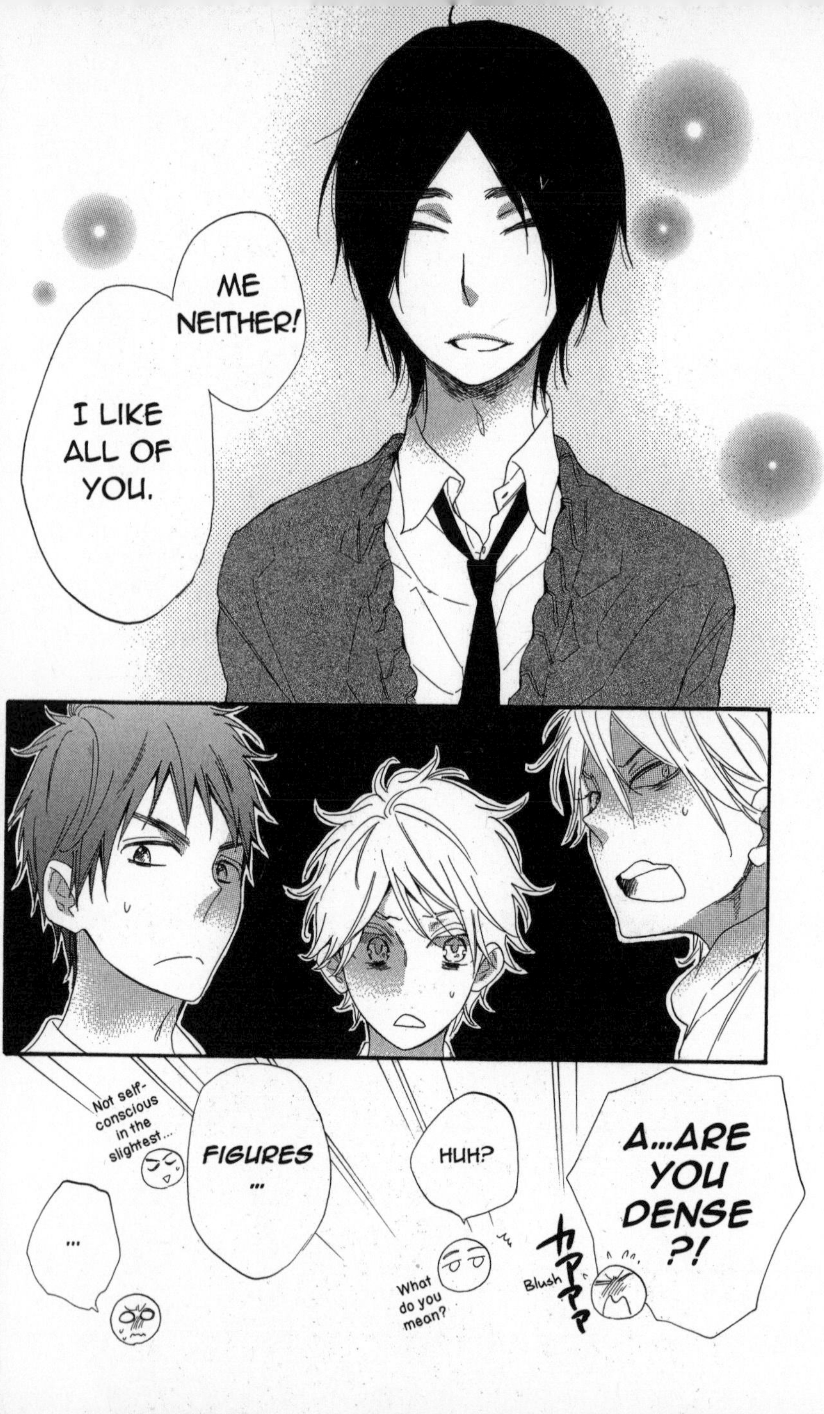
ME NEITHER!
I LIKE ALL OF YOU.
A...ARE YOU DENSE?!
カアァァ
Blush
HUH?
What do you mean?
FIGURES...
Not self-conscious in the slightest...
...

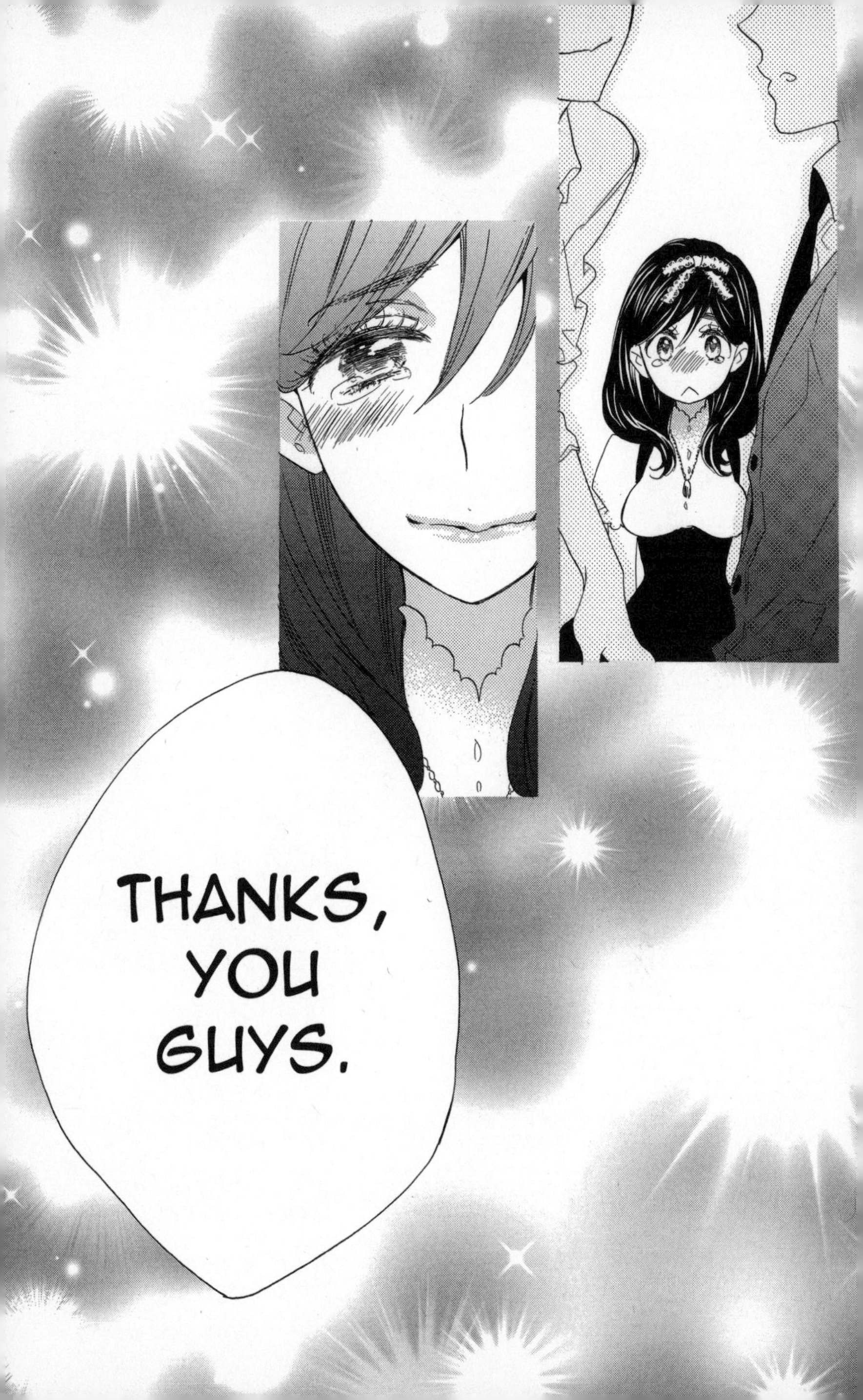
THANKS, YOU GUYS.

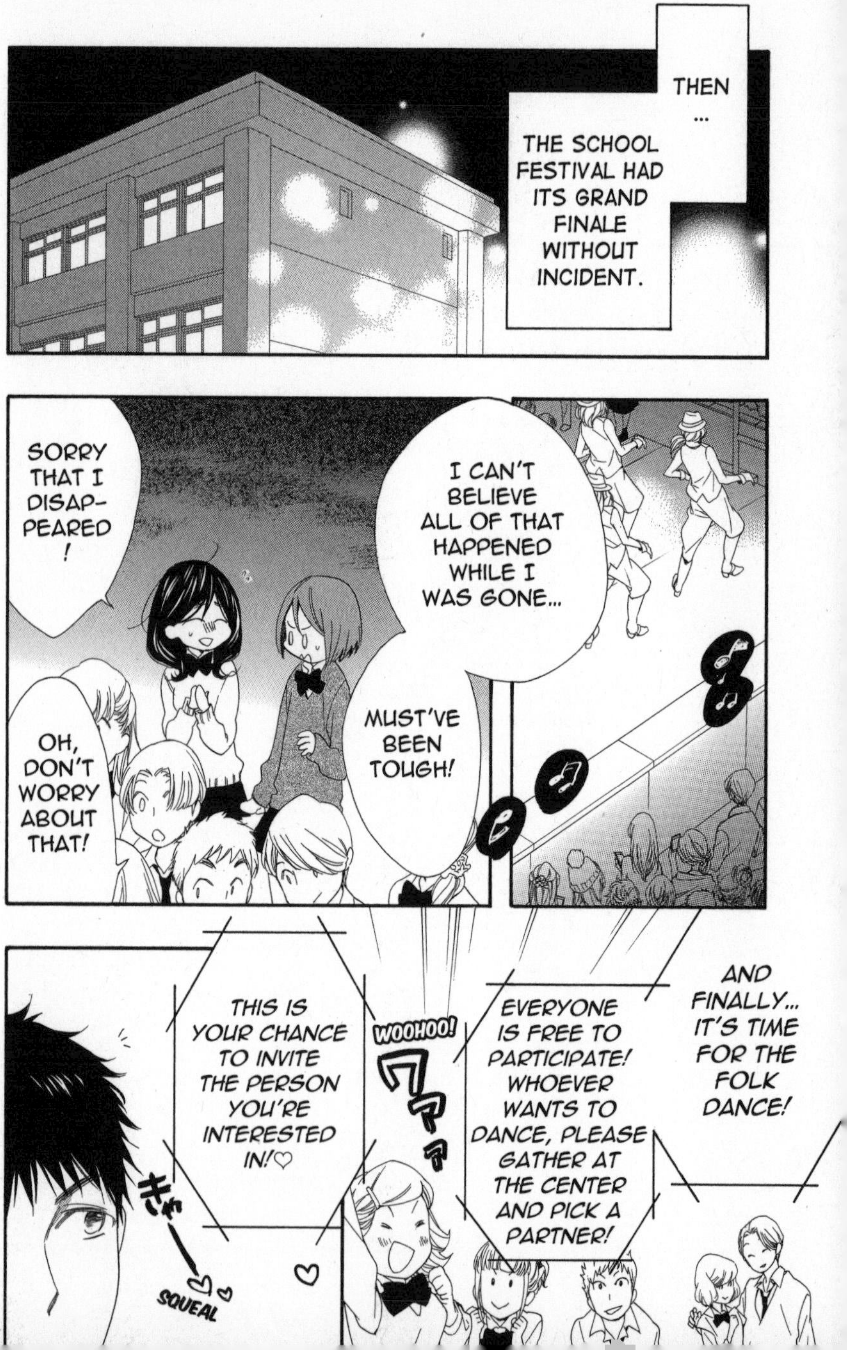
THEN ...
THE SCHOOL FESTIVAL HAD ITS GRAND FINALE WITHOUT INCIDENT.
I CAN'T BELIEVE ALL OF THAT HAPPENED WHILE I WAS GONE...
SORRY THAT I DISAP-PEARED!
MUST'VE BEEN TOUGH!
OH, DON'T WORRY ABOUT THAT!
AND FINALLY... IT'S TIME FOR THE FOLK DANCE!
EVERYONE IS FREE TO PARTICIPATE! WHOEVER WANTS TO DANCE, PLEASE GATHER AT THE CENTER AND PICK A PARTNER!
WOOHOO!
THIS IS YOUR CHANCE TO INVITE THE PERSON YOU'RE INTERESTED IN!♡
SQUEAL

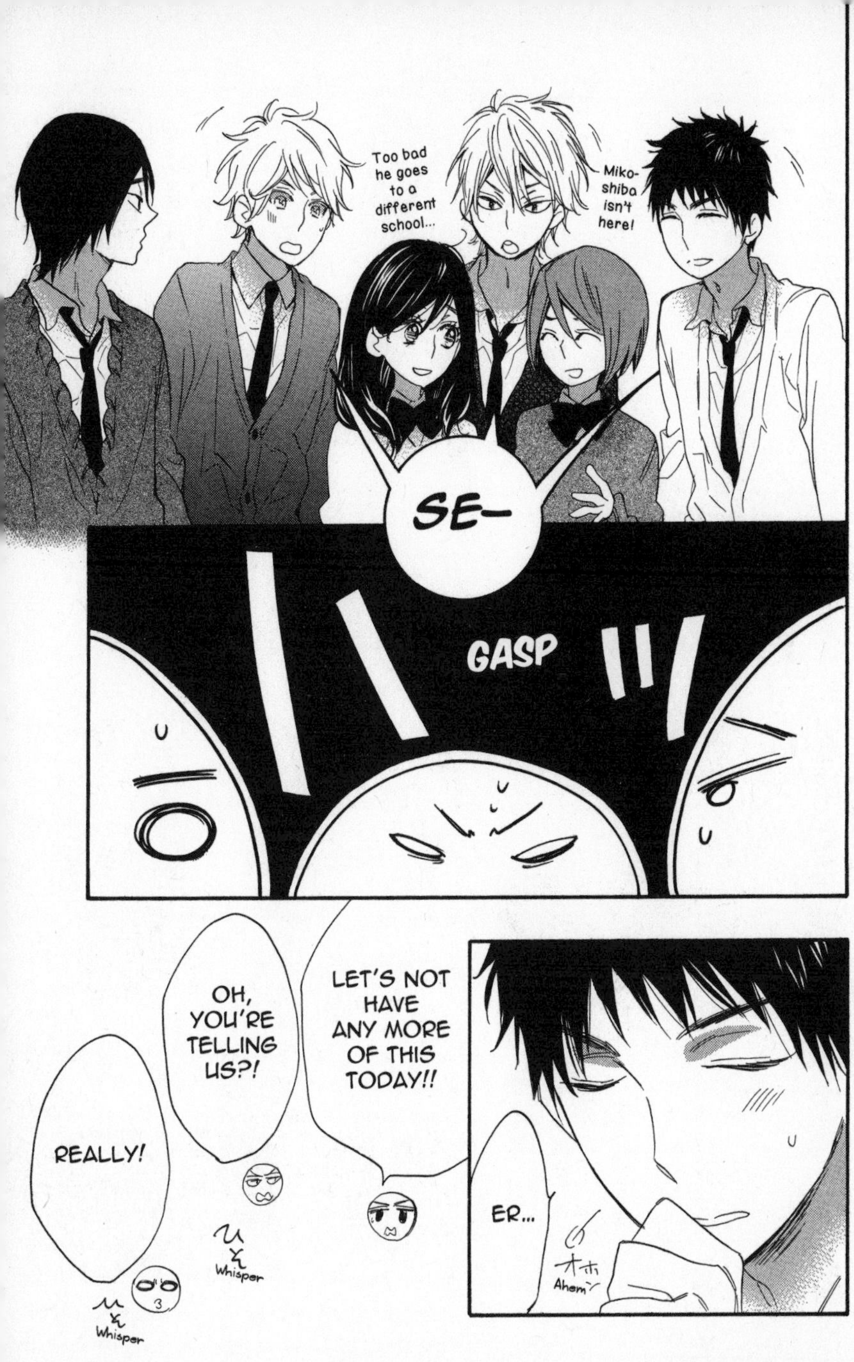
Miko-shiba isn't here!
Too bad he goes to a different school...
SE—
GASP
ER...
オホ
Ahem
LET'S NOT HAVE ANY MORE OF THIS TODAY!!
OH, YOU'RE TELLING US?!
ひそ
Whisper
REALLY!
ひそ
Whisper

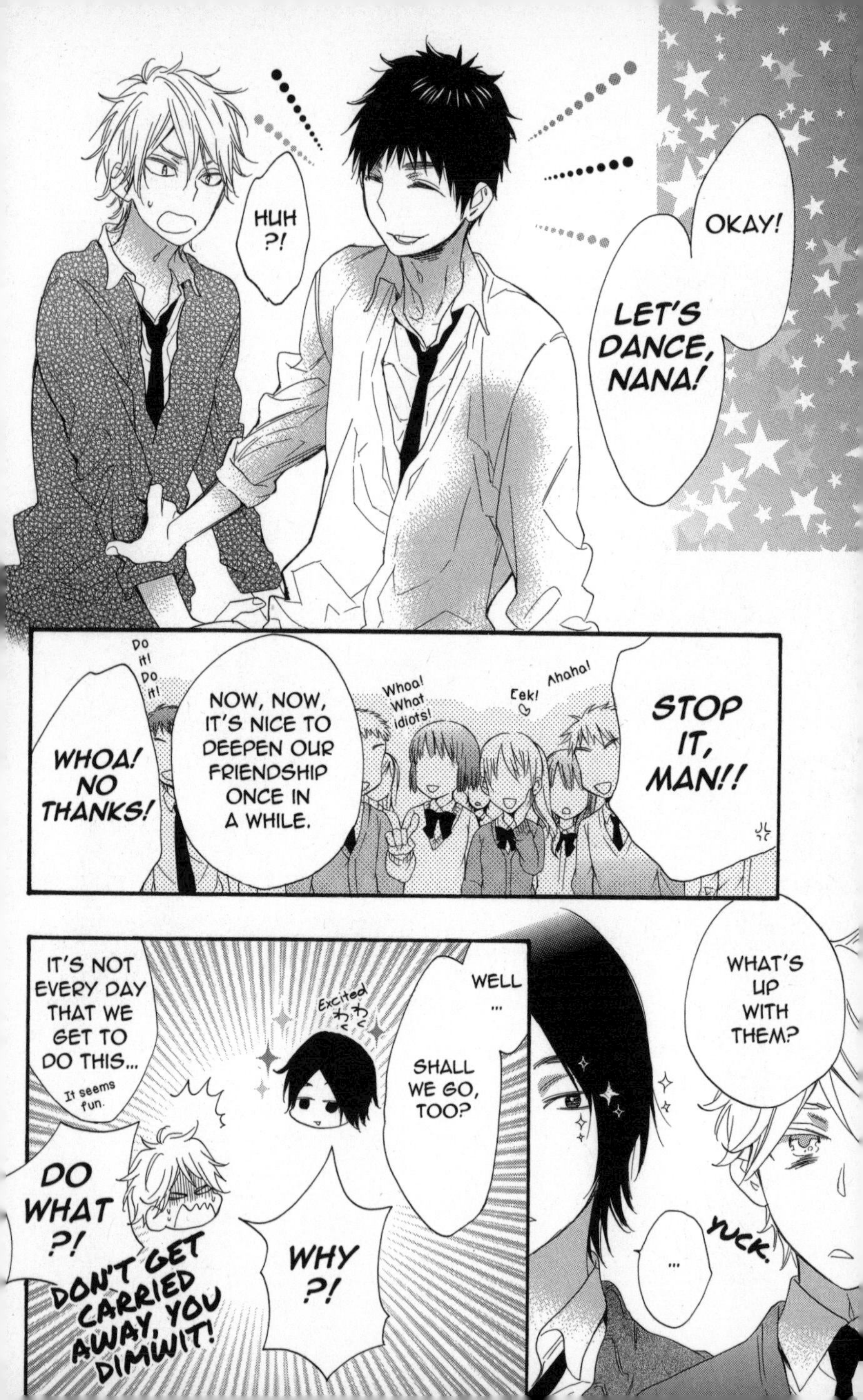
OKAY!
LET'S DANCE, NANA!
HUH ?!
STOP IT, MAN!!
Ahaha!
Eek!
Whoa! What idiots!
NOW, NOW, IT'S NICE TO DEEPEN OUR FRIENDSHIP ONCE IN A WHILE.
Do it! Do it!
WHOA! NO THANKS!
WHAT'S UP WITH THEM?
YUCK.
...
WELL ... SHALL WE GO, TOO?
Excited
WHY ?!
IT'S NOT EVERY DAY THAT WE GET TO DO THIS...
It seems fun.
DO WHAT ?!
DON'T GET CARRIED AWAY, YOU DIMWIT!

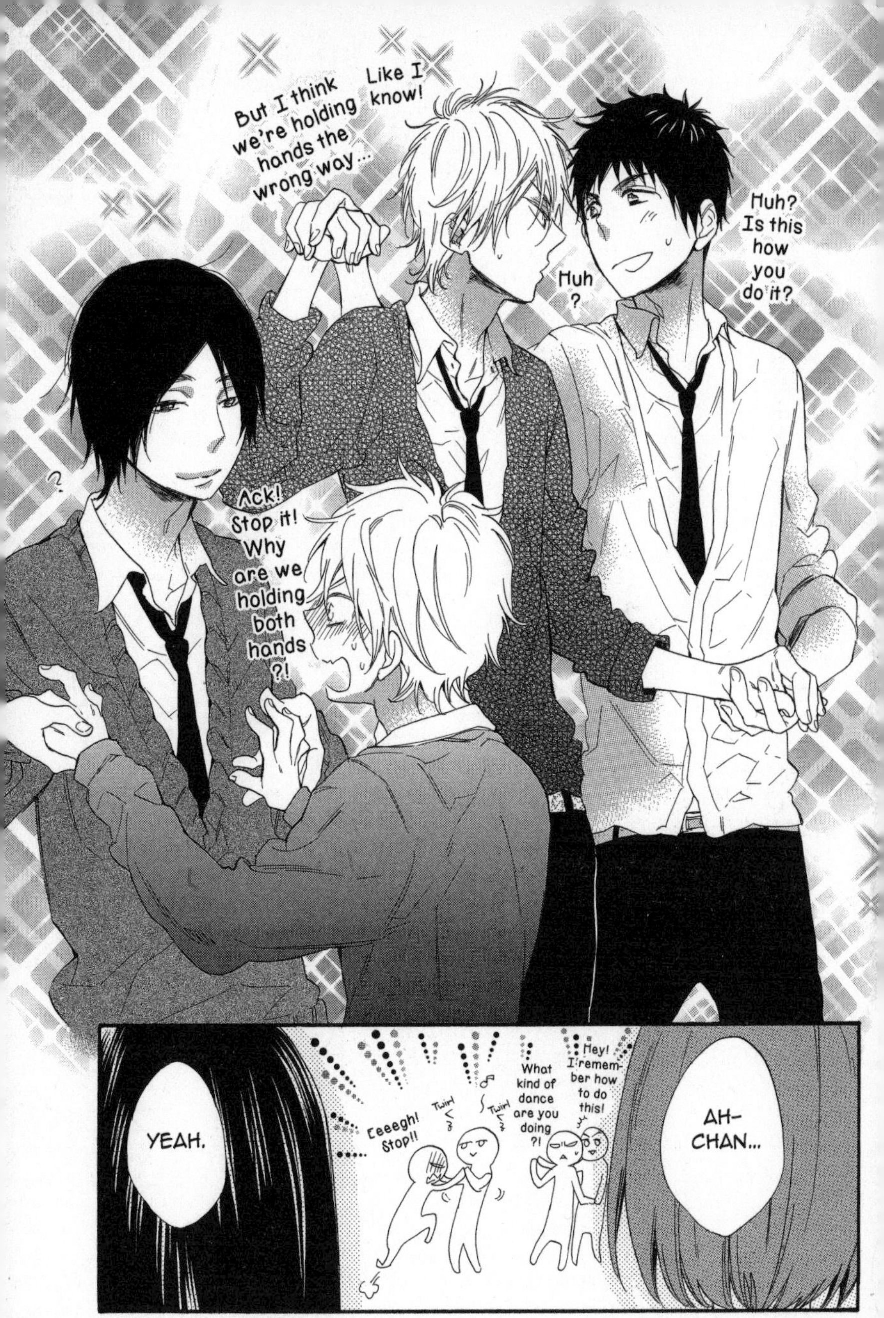
Huh? Is this how you do it?
Huh?
Like I know!
But I think we're holding hands the wrong way...
?
Ack! Stop it! Why are we holding both hands?!
AH-CHAN...
Hey! I remember how to do this!
What kind of dance are you doing?!
Twirl
Twirl
Eeeegh! Stop!!
YEAH.

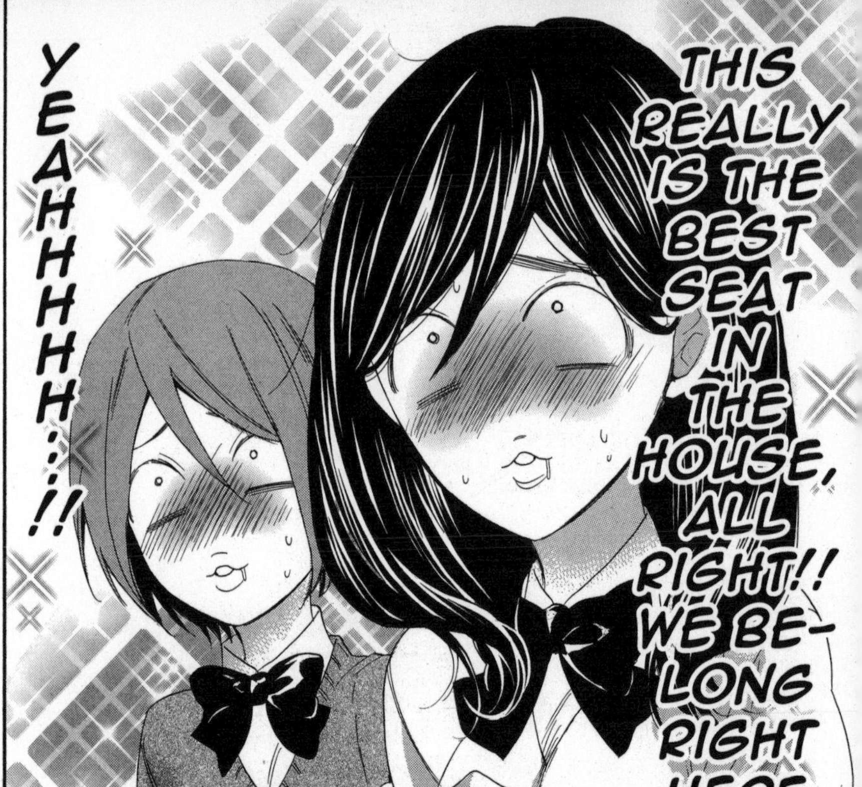
THIS REALLY IS THE BEST SEAT IN THE HOUSE, ALL RIGHT!! WE BE-LONG RIGHT HERE!!
YEAHHHHHH...!!

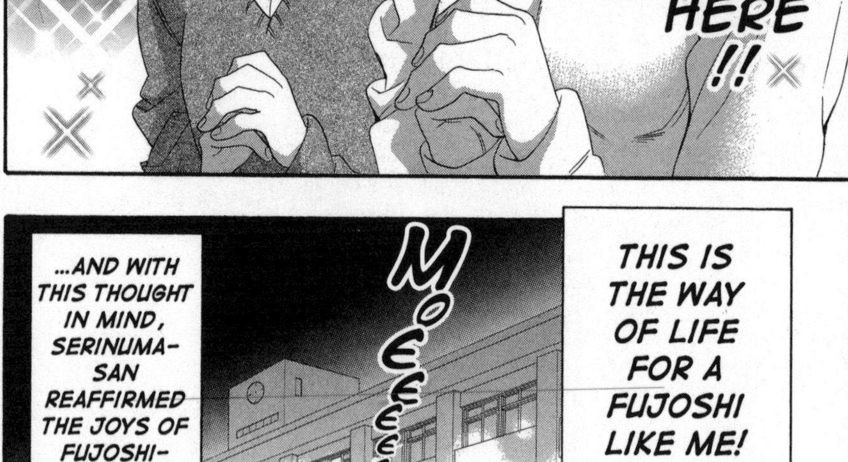
THIS IS THE WAY OF LIFE FOR A FUJOSHI LIKE ME!
MOEEEEEEE!!
...AND WITH THIS THOUGHT IN MIND, SERINUMA-SAN REAFFIRMED THE JOYS OF FUJOSHI-HOOD.

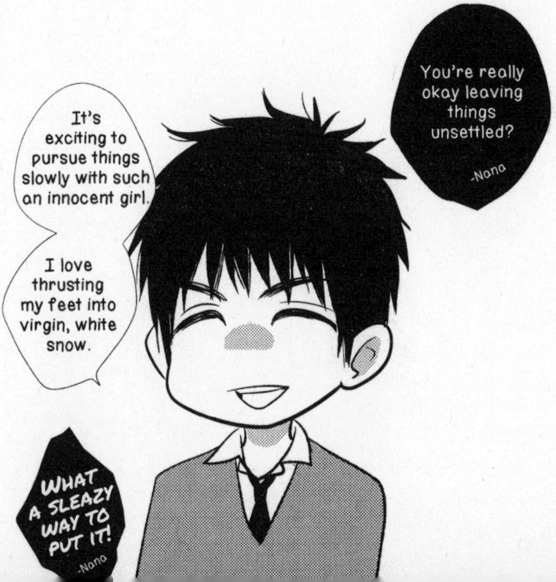
You're really okay leaving things unsettled?
-Nana
It's exciting to pursue things slowly with such an innocent girl.
I love thrusting my feet into virgin, white snow.
WHAT A SLEAZY WAY TO PUT IT!
-Nana

KiSS HiM, NOT ME!

#8 CHRISTMAS IN THE HOLY LAND

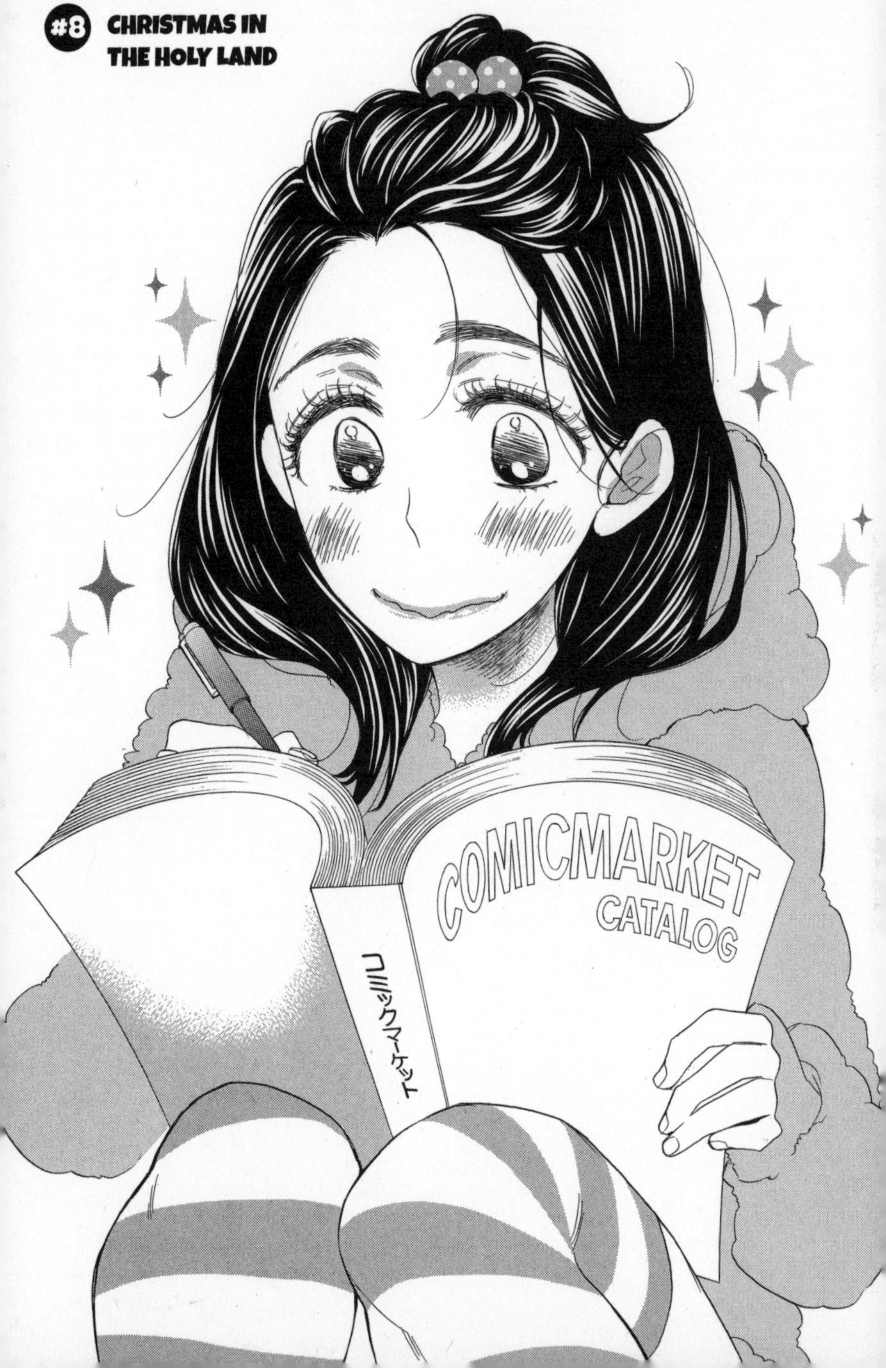
COMICMARKET
CATALOG
コミックマーケット

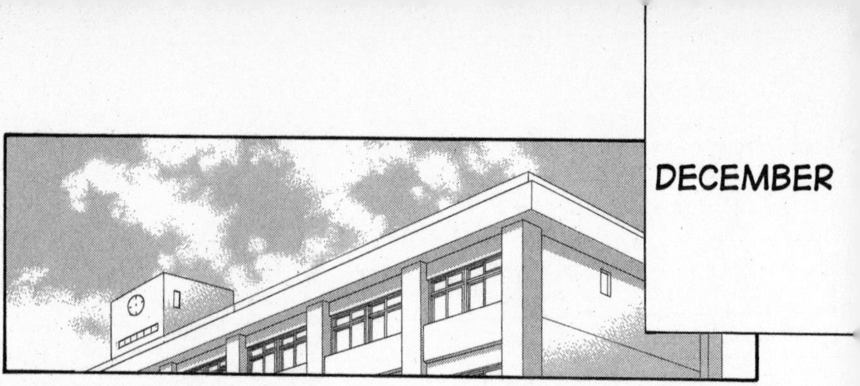
DECEMBER

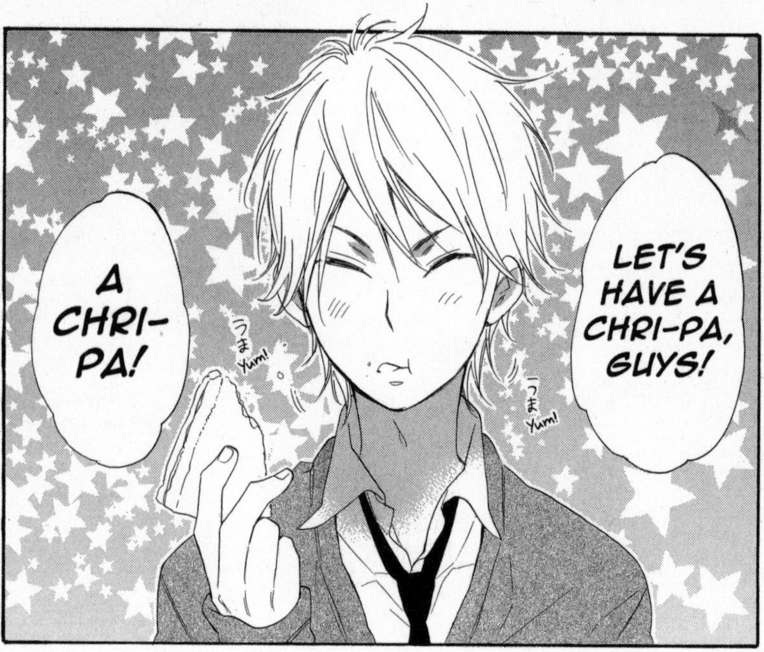
LET'S HAVE A CHRI-PA, GUYS!
うま Yum!
うま Yum!
A CHRI-PA!

KiSS HiM, NOT ME!

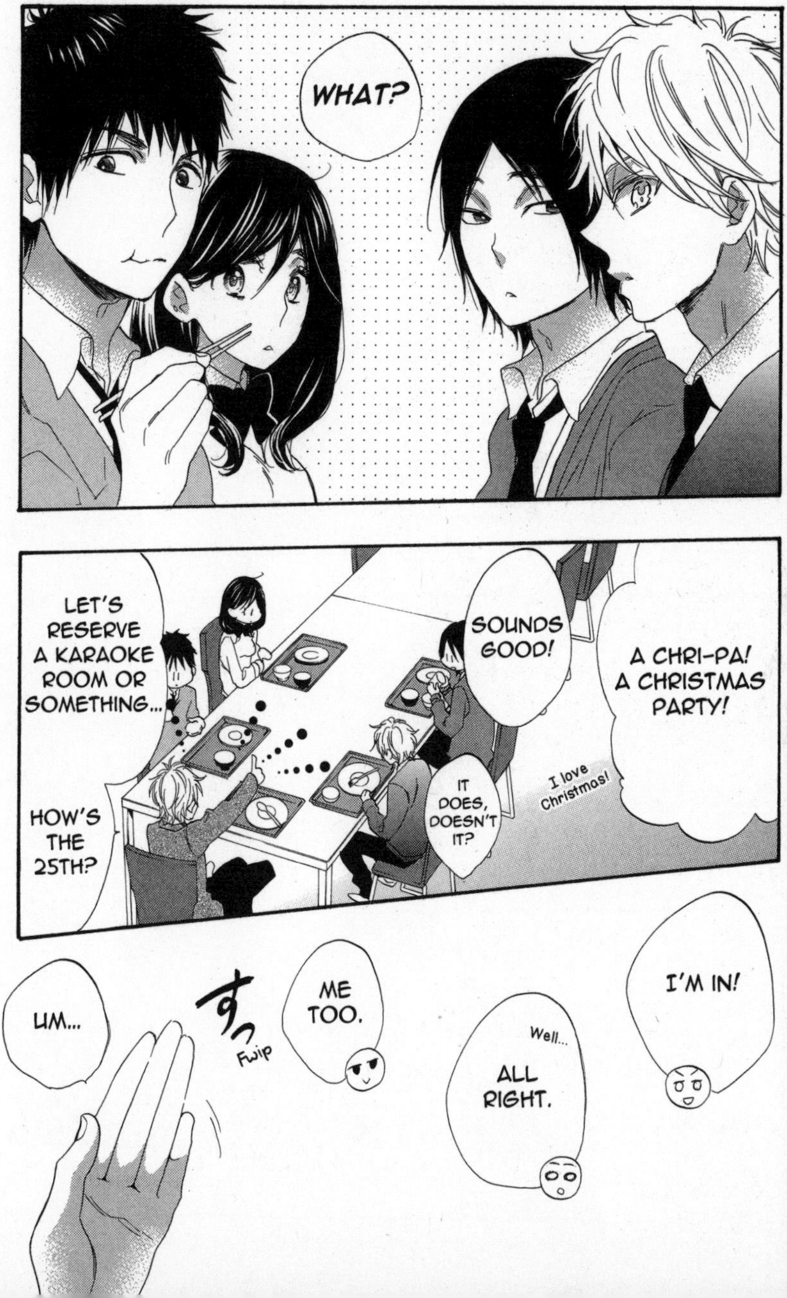
WHAT?
A CHRI-PA! A CHRISTMAS PARTY!
I love Christmas!
SOUNDS GOOD!
IT DOES, DOESN'T IT?
LET'S RESERVE A KARAOKE ROOM OR SOMETHING...
HOW'S THE 25TH?
I'M IN!
Well...
ALL RIGHT.
ME TOO.
すっ
Fwip
UM...

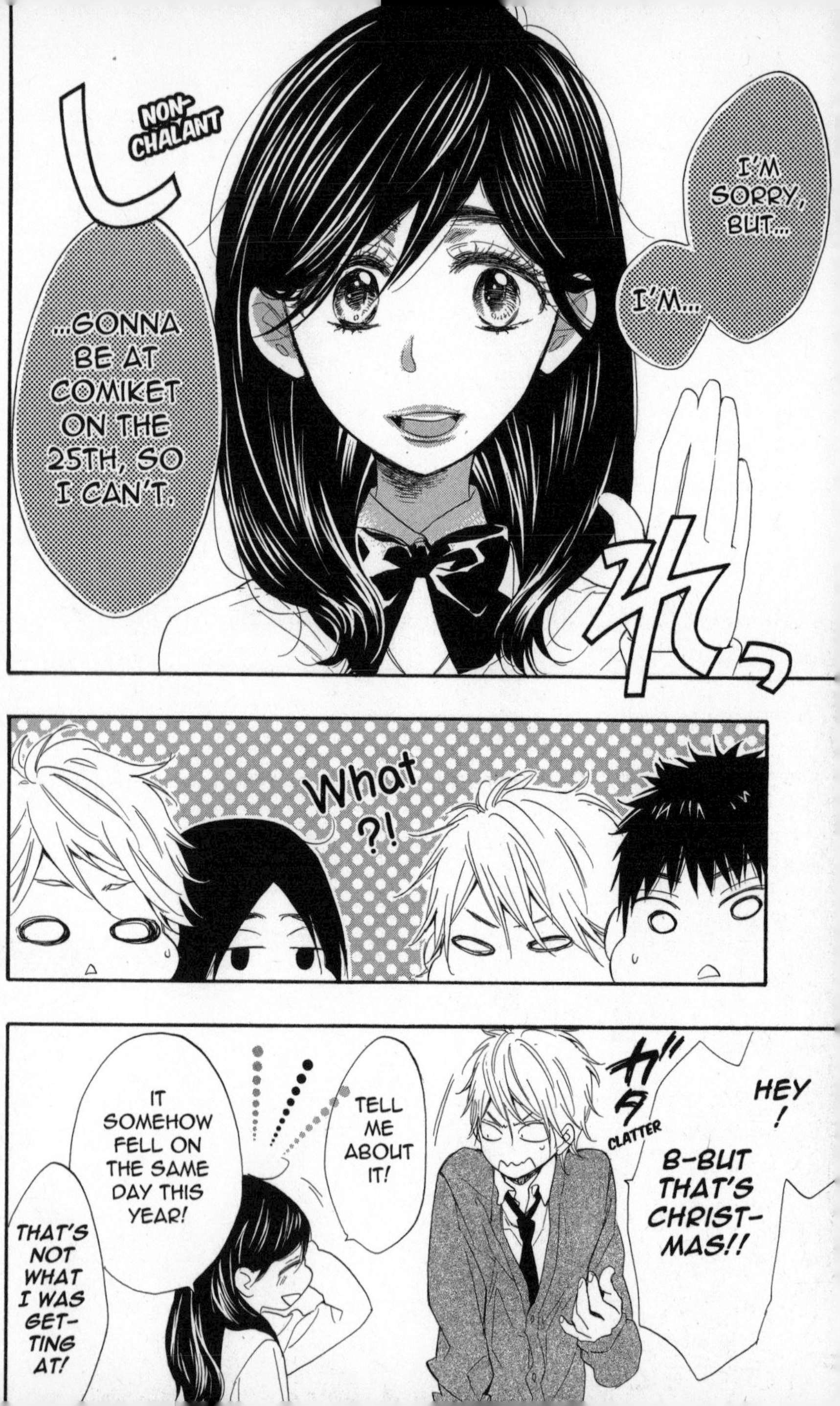
I'M SORRY, BUT...
I'M...
NON-CHALANT
...GONNA BE AT COMIKET ON THE 25TH, SO I CAN'T.
What ?!
CLATTER
HEY!
B-BUT THAT'S CHRIST-MAS!!
TELL ME ABOUT IT!
IT SOMEHOW FELL ON THE SAME DAY THIS YEAR!
THAT'S NOT WHAT I WAS GET-TING AT!

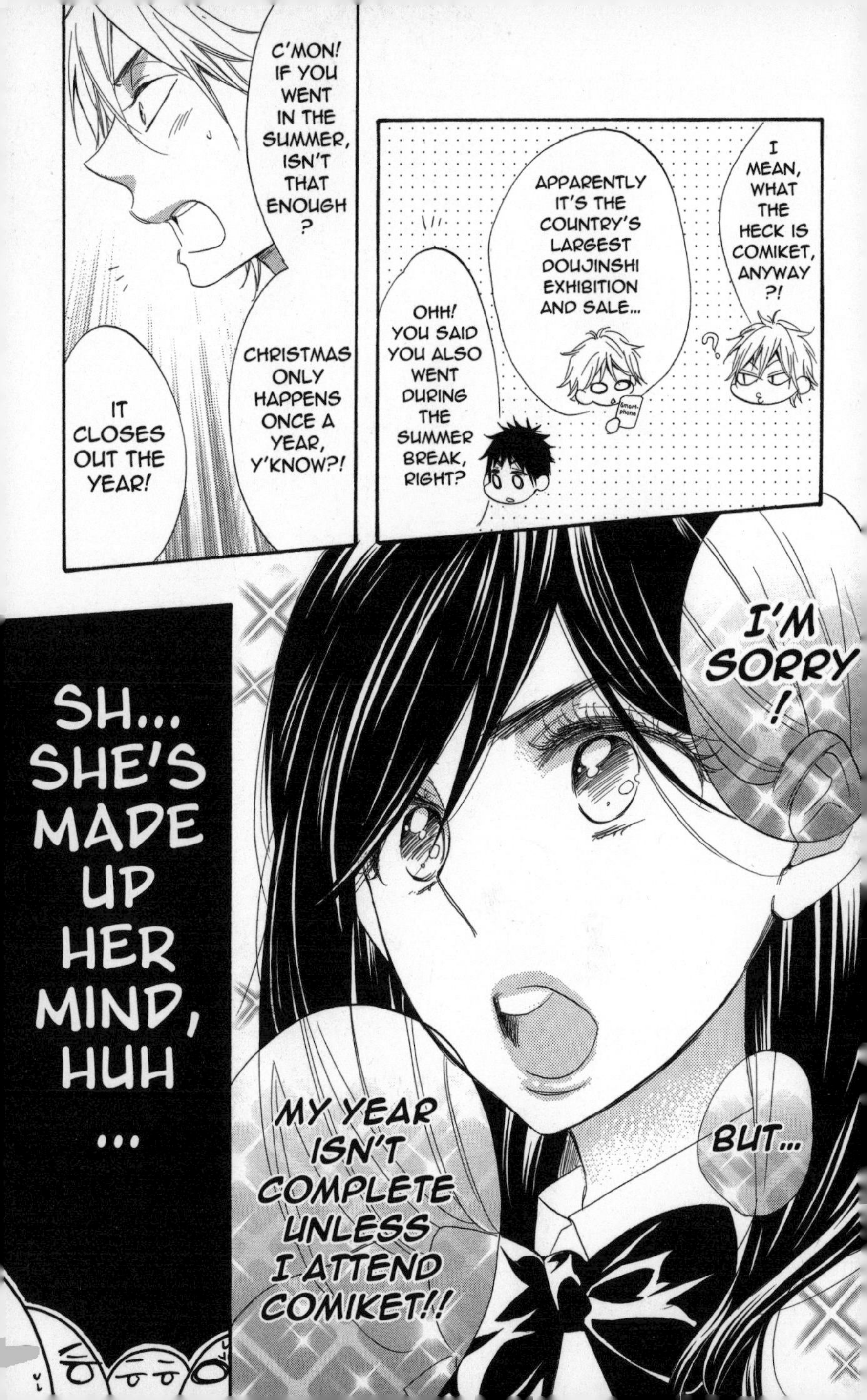
I MEAN, WHAT THE HECK IS COMIKET, ANYWAY?!
APPARENTLY IT'S THE COUNTRY'S LARGEST DOUJINSHI EXHIBITION AND SALE...
Smart-phone
OHH! YOU SAID YOU ALSO WENT DURING THE SUMMER BREAK, RIGHT?
C'MON! IF YOU WENT IN THE SUMMER, ISN'T THAT ENOUGH?
CHRISTMAS ONLY HAPPENS ONCE A YEAR, Y'KNOW?!
IT CLOSES OUT THE YEAR!
I'M SORRY!
BUT...
MY YEAR ISN'T COMPLETE UNLESS I ATTEND COMIKET!!
SH... SHE'S MADE UP HER MIND, HUH...

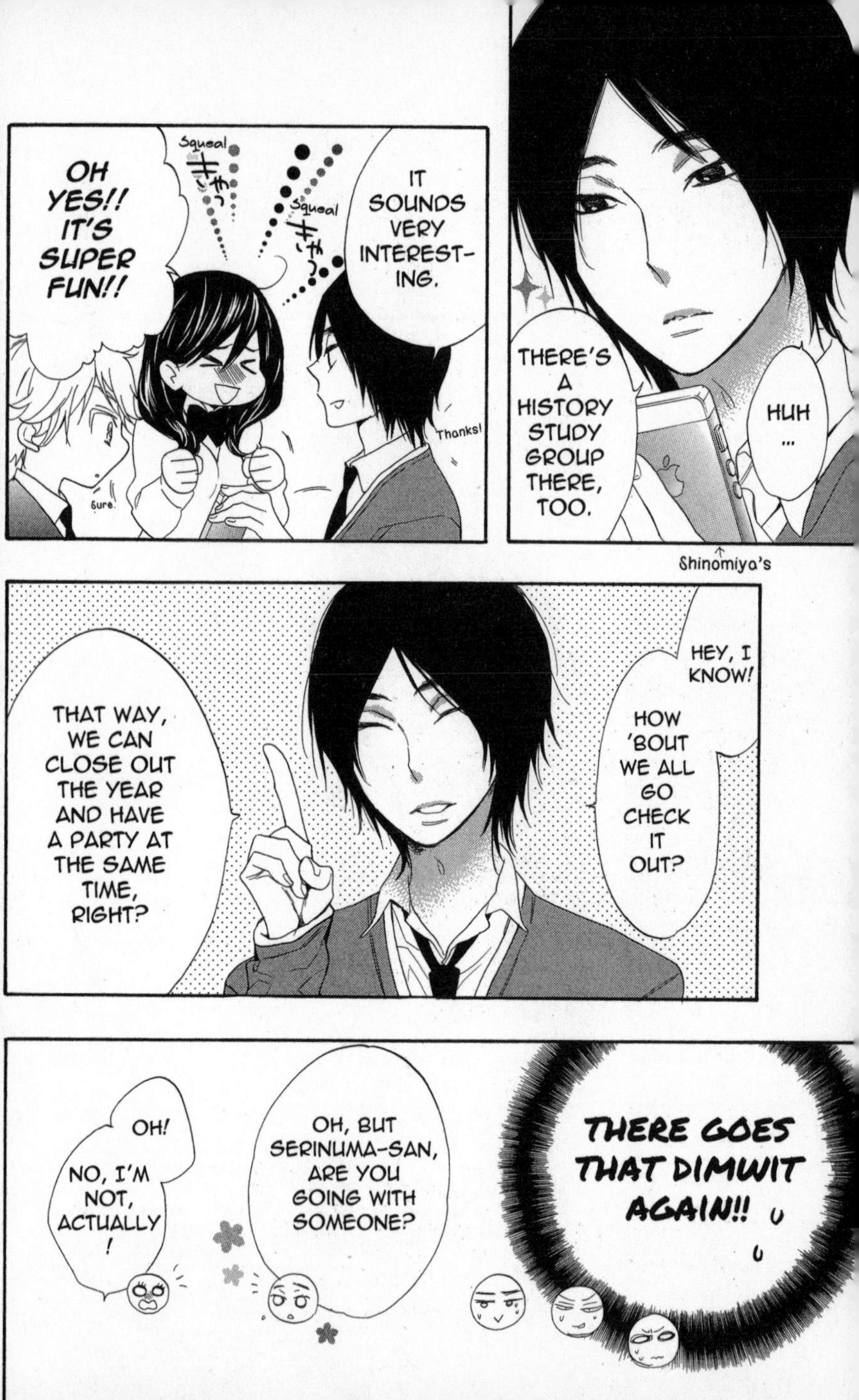
HUH ...
THERE'S A HISTORY STUDY GROUP THERE, TOO.
Shinomiya's
IT SOUNDS VERY INTEREST-ING.
Squeal
きゃっ
Squeal
きゃっ
OH YES!! IT'S SUPER FUN!!
Thanks!
Sure.
HEY, I KNOW!
HOW 'BOUT WE ALL GO CHECK IT OUT?
THAT WAY, WE CAN CLOSE OUT THE YEAR AND HAVE A PARTY AT THE SAME TIME, RIGHT?
THERE GOES THAT DIMWIT AGAIN!!
OH, BUT SERINUMA-SAN, ARE YOU GOING WITH SOMEONE?
OH!
NO, I'M NOT, ACTUALLY!

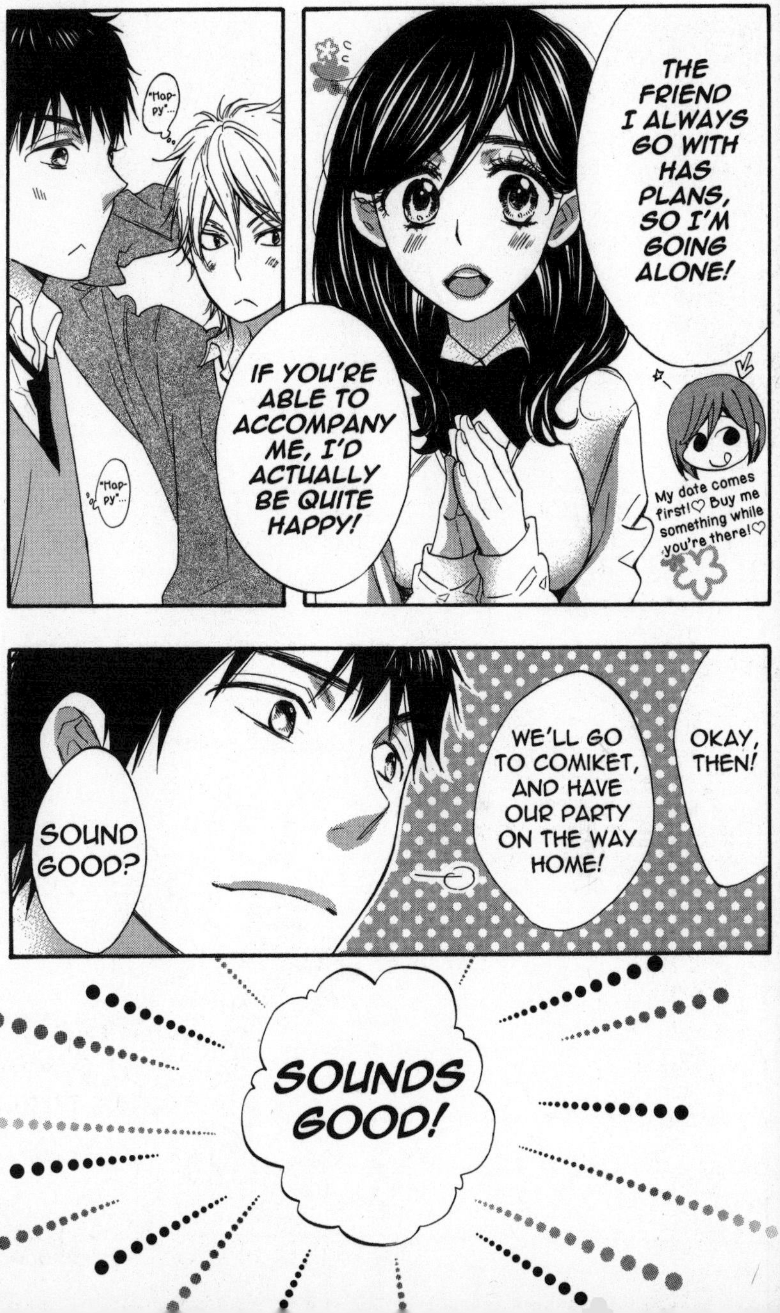
THE FRIEND I ALWAYS GO WITH HAS PLANS, SO I'M GOING ALONE!
IF YOU'RE ABLE TO ACCOMPANY ME, I'D ACTUALLY BE QUITE HAPPY!
My date comes first!♡ Buy me something while you're there!♡
"Hap-py"...
"Hap-py"...
OKAY, THEN!
WE'LL GO TO COMIKET, AND HAVE OUR PARTY ON THE WAY HOME!
SOUND GOOD?
SOUNDS GOOD!

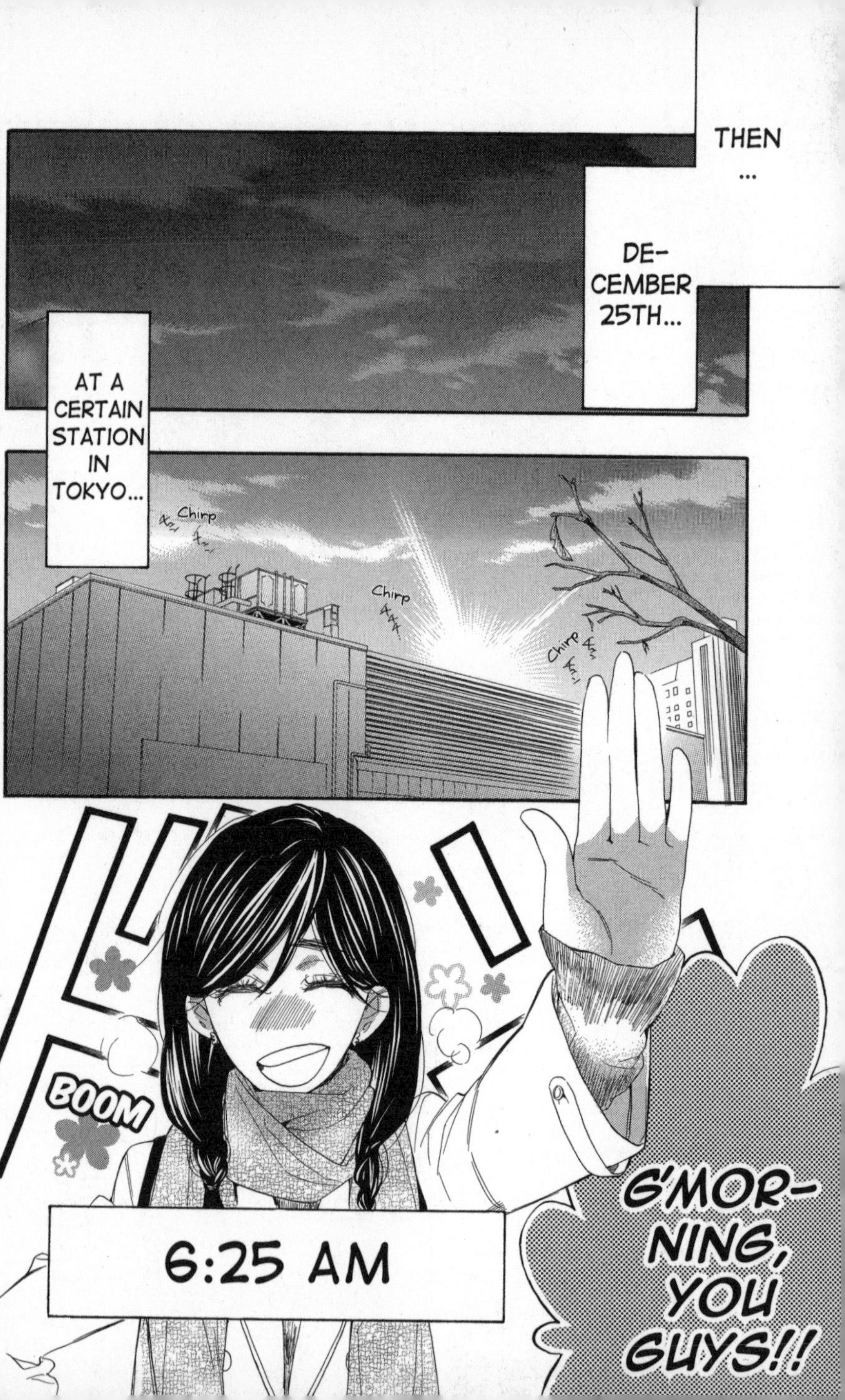
THEN ...
DE-CEMBER 25TH...
AT A CERTAIN STATION IN TOKYO...
Chirp
Chirp
Chirp
G'MOR-NING, YOU GUYS!!
BOOM
6:25 AM

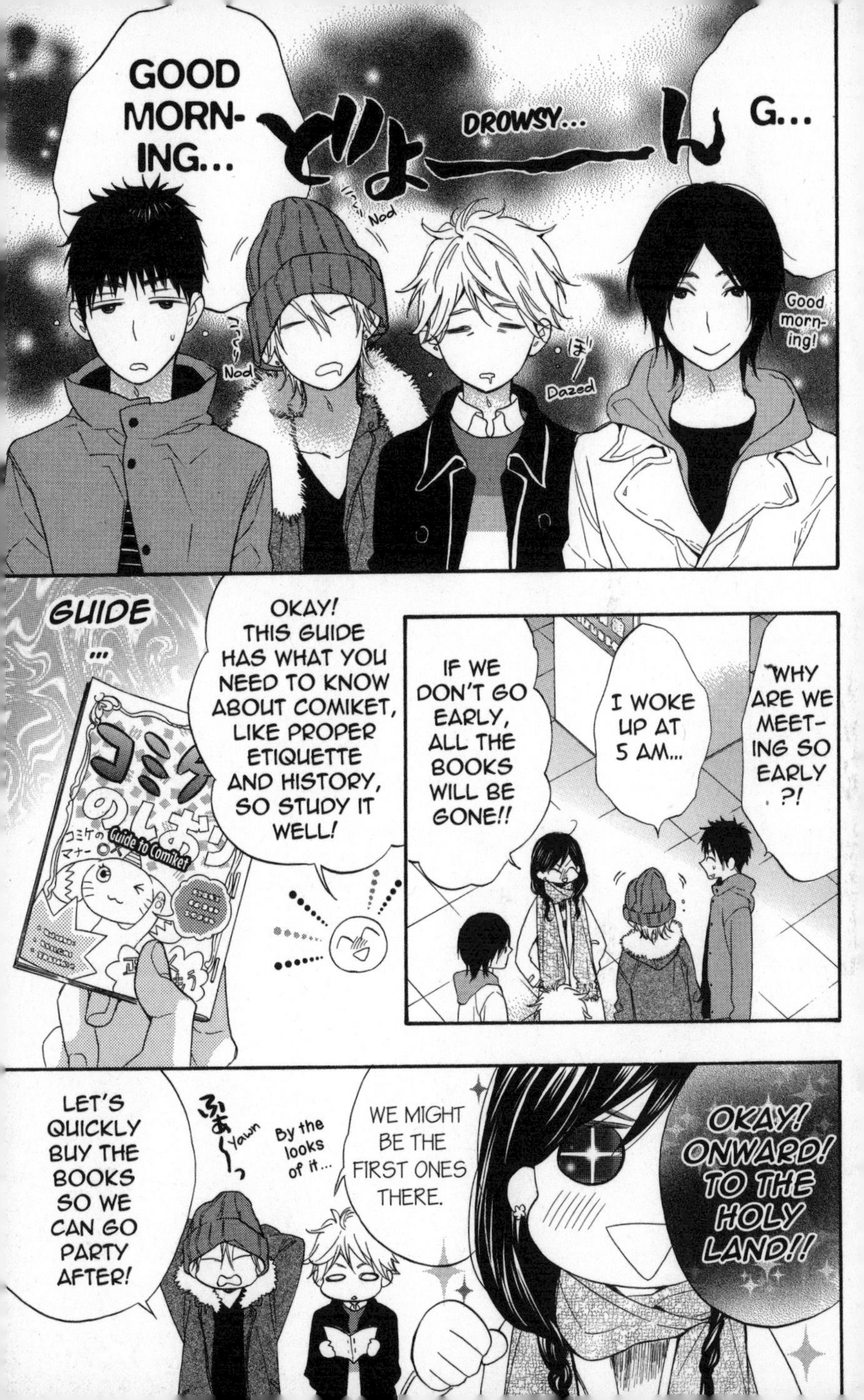
G...
Good morning!
DROWSY...
Dazed
Nod
GOOD MORNING...
Nod
WHY ARE WE MEETING SO EARLY?!
I WOKE UP AT 5 AM...
IF WE DON'T GO EARLY, ALL THE BOOKS WILL BE GONE!!
OKAY! THIS GUIDE HAS WHAT YOU NEED TO KNOW ABOUT COMIKET, LIKE PROPER ETIQUETTE AND HISTORY, SO STUDY IT WELL!
GUIDE...
Guide to Comiket
OKAY! ONWARD! TO THE HOLY LAND!!
WE MIGHT BE THE FIRST ONES THERE.
By the looks of it...
Yawn
LET'S QUICKLY BUY THE BOOKS SO WE CAN GO PARTY AFTER!

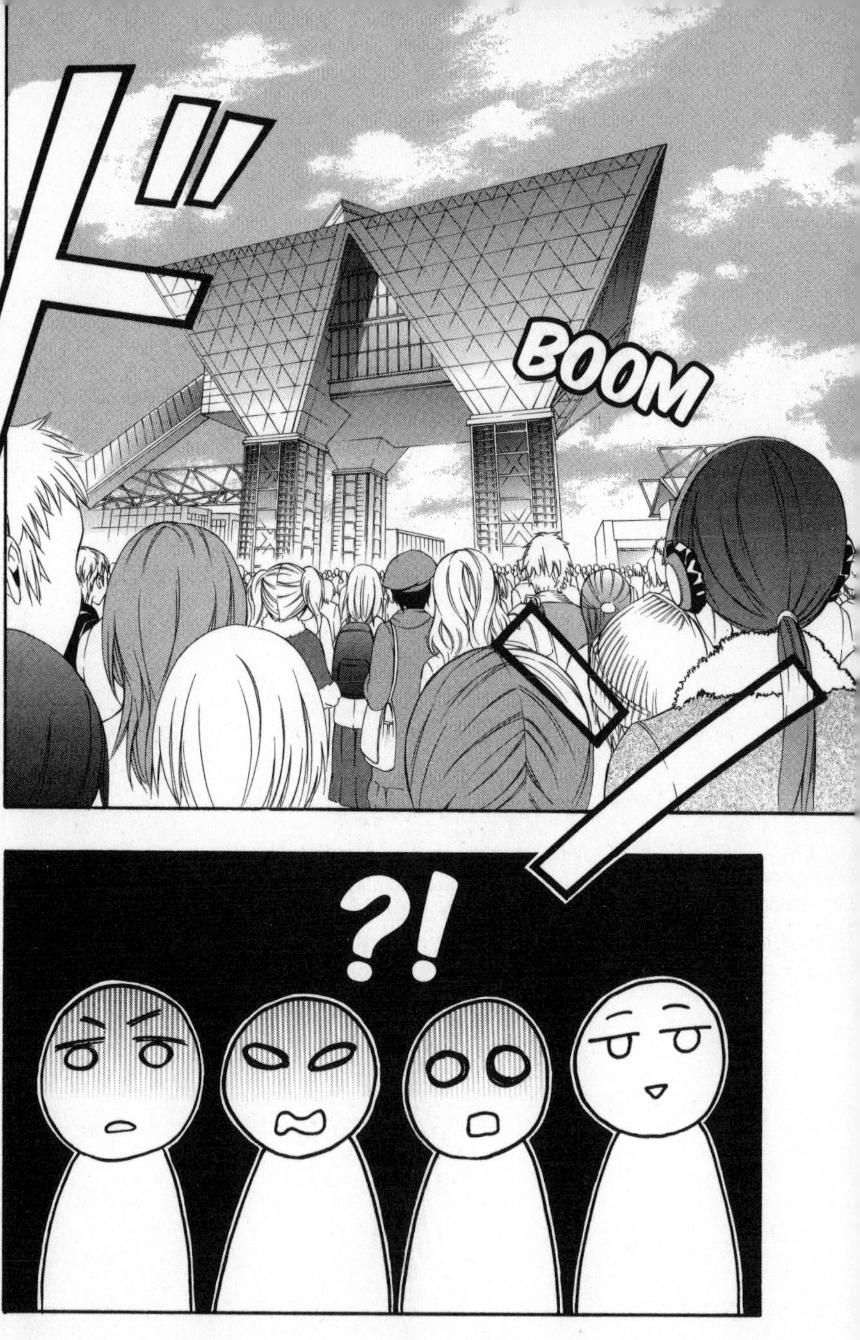
ドン
BOOM
?!

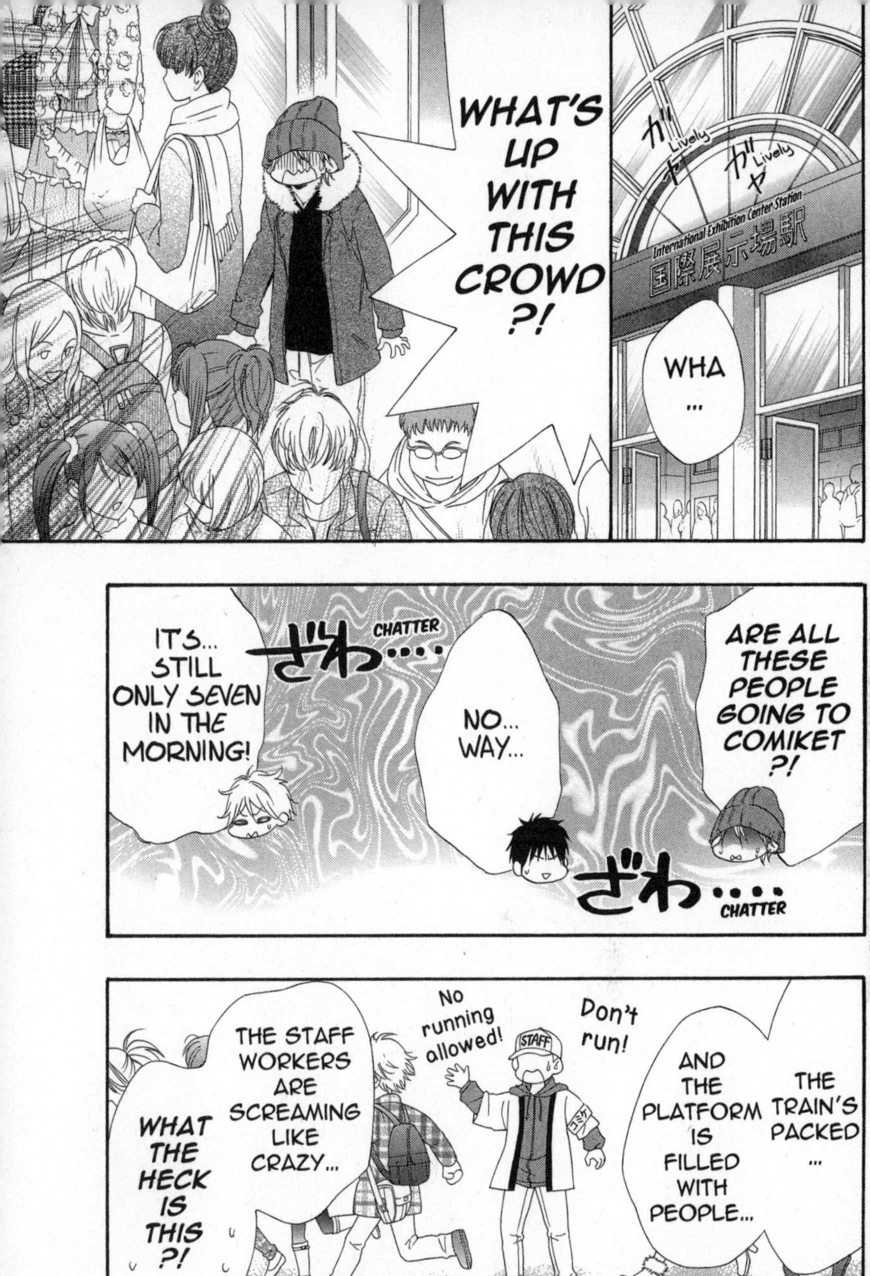
ガヤ Lively
ガヤ Lively
International Exhibition Center Station
国際展示場駅
WHA ...
WHAT'S UP WITH THIS CROWD ?!
ARE ALL THESE PEOPLE GOING TO COMIKET ?!
ざわ.... CHATTER
NO... WAY...
ざわ.... CHATTER
IT'S... STILL ONLY SEVEN IN THE MORNING!
THE TRAIN'S PACKED ...
AND THE PLATFORM IS FILLED WITH PEOPLE...
Don't run!
STAFF
No running allowed!
THE STAFF WORKERS ARE SCREAMING LIKE CRAZY...
WHAT THE HECK IS THIS ?!

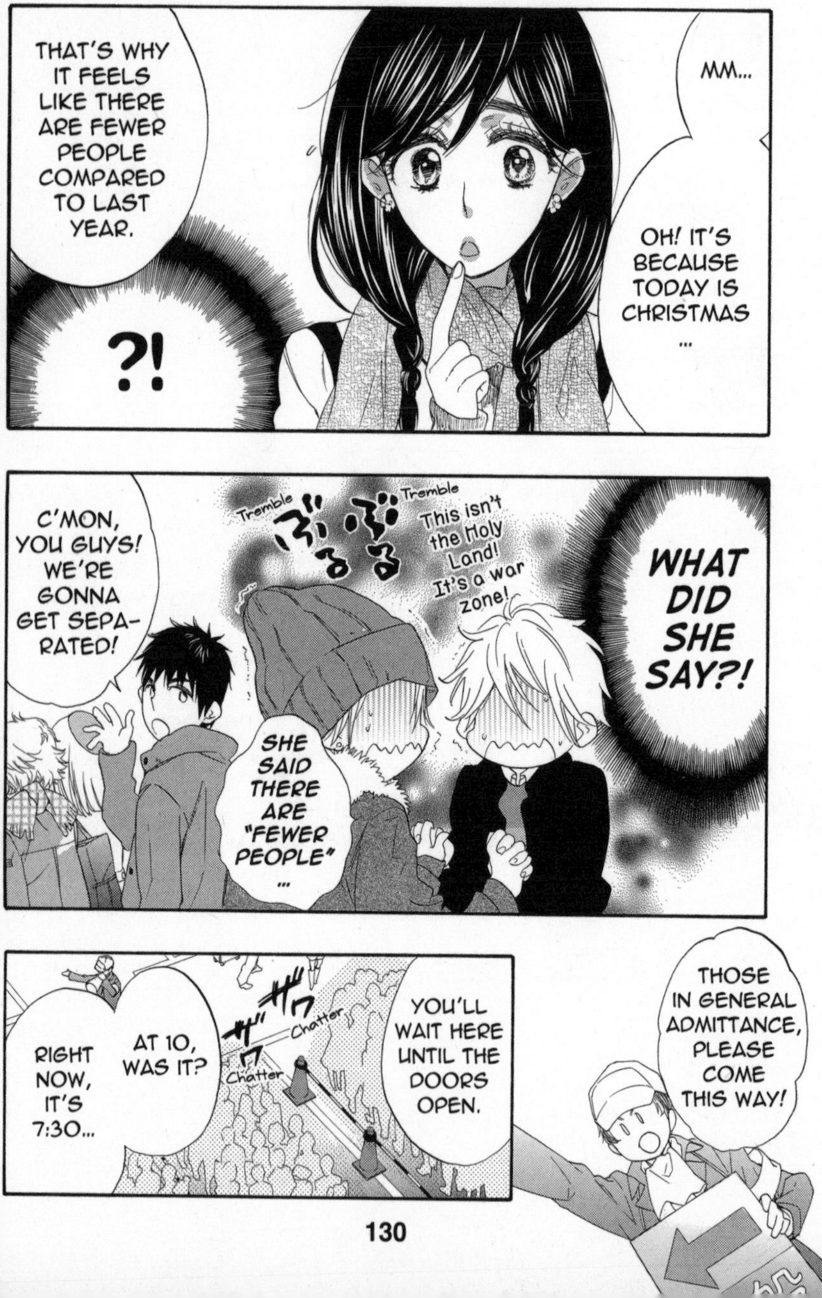
MM...
OH! IT'S BECAUSE TODAY IS CHRISTMAS ...
THAT'S WHY IT FEELS LIKE THERE ARE FEWER PEOPLE COMPARED TO LAST YEAR.
?!
WHAT DID SHE SAY?!
Tremble Tremble
This isn't the Holy Land! It's a war zone!
SHE SAID THERE ARE "FEWER PEOPLE" ...
C'MON, YOU GUYS! WE'RE GONNA GET SEPA-RATED!
THOSE IN GENERAL ADMITTANCE, PLEASE COME THIS WAY!
YOU'LL WAIT HERE UNTIL THE DOORS OPEN.
Chatter Chatter
AT 10, WAS IT?
RIGHT NOW, IT'S 7:30...

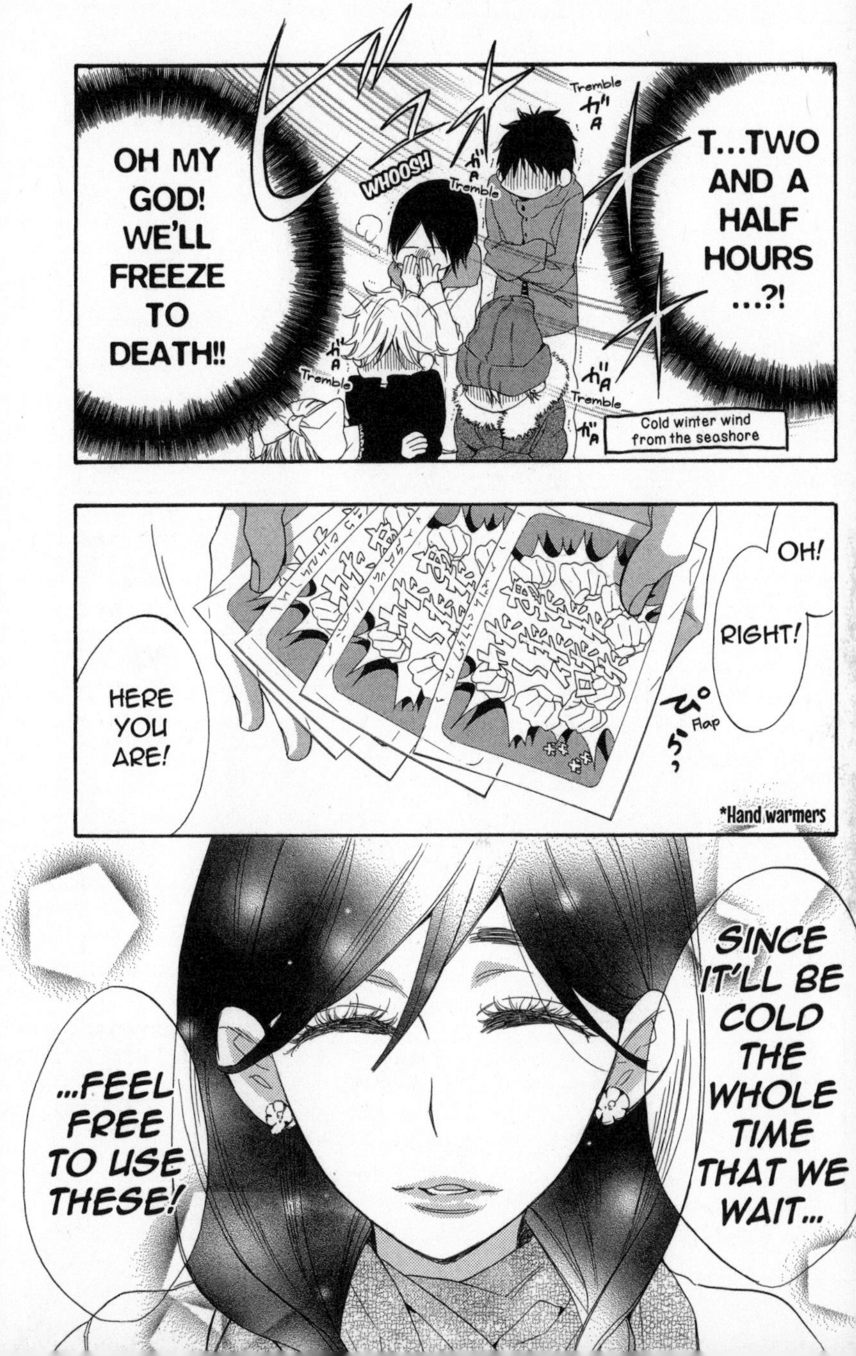

Tremble
T...TWO AND A HALF HOURS ...?!
WHOOSH
Tremble
OH MY GOD! WE'LL FREEZE TO DEATH!!
Tremble
Tremble
Cold winter wind from the seashore
OH!
RIGHT!
Flap
HERE YOU ARE!
*Hand warmers
SINCE IT'LL BE COLD THE WHOLE TIME THAT WE WAIT...
...FEEL FREE TO USE THESE!

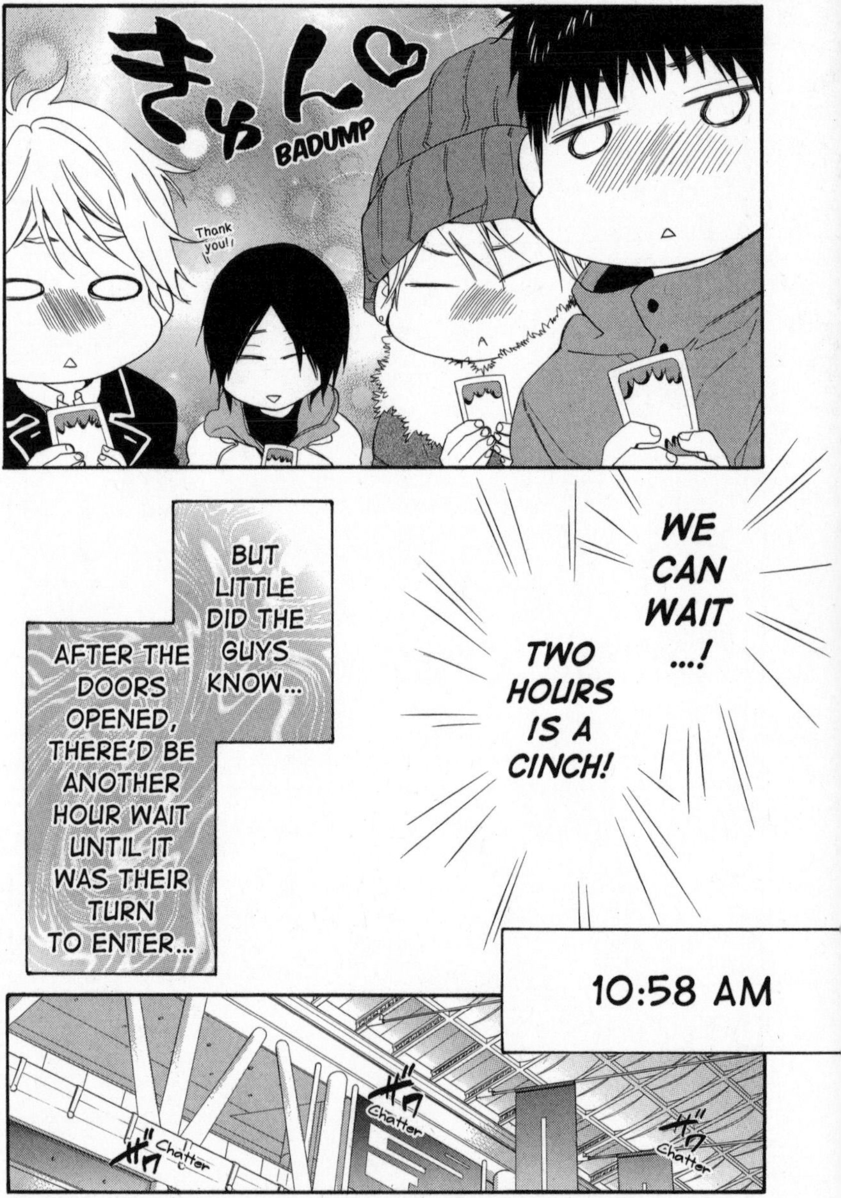
きゅん♡
BADUMP
Thank you!!
WE CAN WAIT ...!
TWO HOURS IS A CINCH!
BUT LITTLE DID THE GUYS KNOW...
AFTER THE DOORS OPENED, THERE'D BE ANOTHER HOUR WAIT UNTIL IT WAS THEIR TURN TO ENTER...
10:58 AM
ザワ Chatter
ザワ Chatter
ザワ Chatter

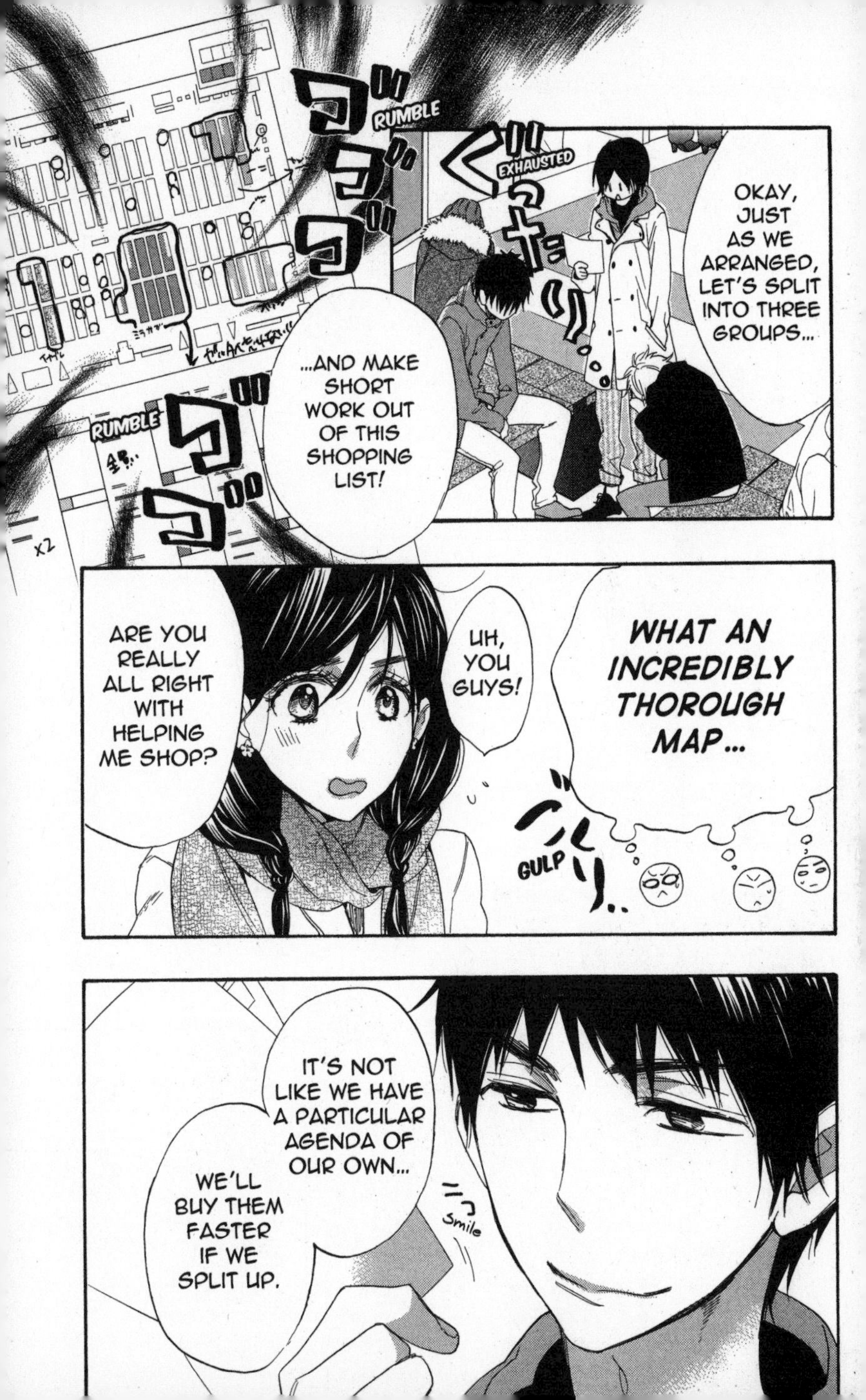
OKAY, JUST AS WE ARRANGED, LET'S SPLIT INTO THREE GROUPS...
EXHAUSTED
...AND MAKE SHORT WORK OUT OF THIS SHOPPING LIST!
RUMBLE
RUMBLE
X2
WHAT AN INCREDIBLY THOROUGH MAP...
GULP
UH, YOU GUYS!
ARE YOU REALLY ALL RIGHT WITH HELPING ME SHOP?
IT'S NOT LIKE WE HAVE A PARTICULAR AGENDA OF OUR OWN...
Smile
WE'LL BUY THEM FASTER IF WE SPLIT UP.

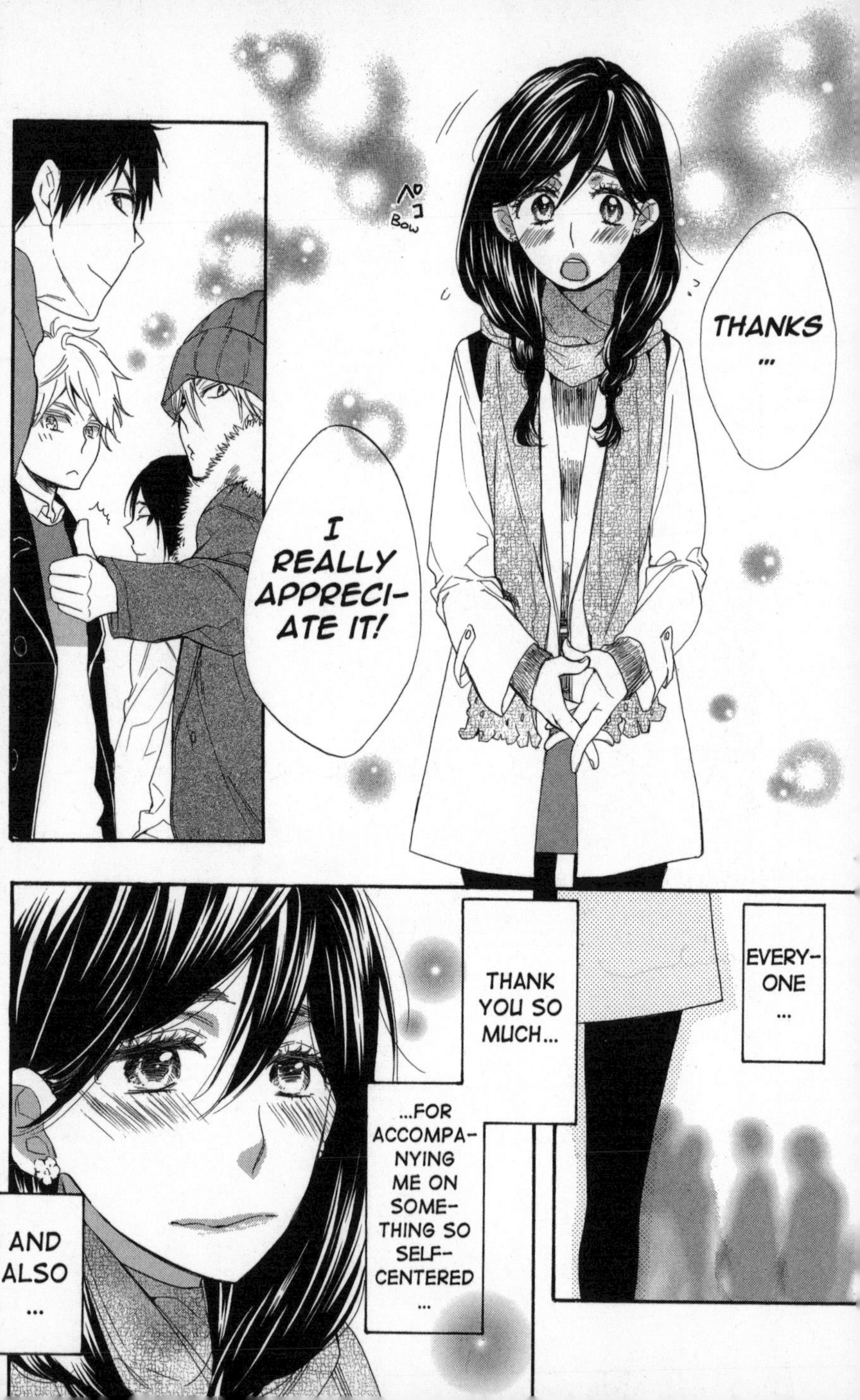
THANKS...
Bow
I REALLY APPRECIATE IT!
EVERY-ONE...
THANK YOU SO MUCH...
...FOR ACCOMPANYING ME ON SOMETHING SO SELF-CENTERED...
AND ALSO...

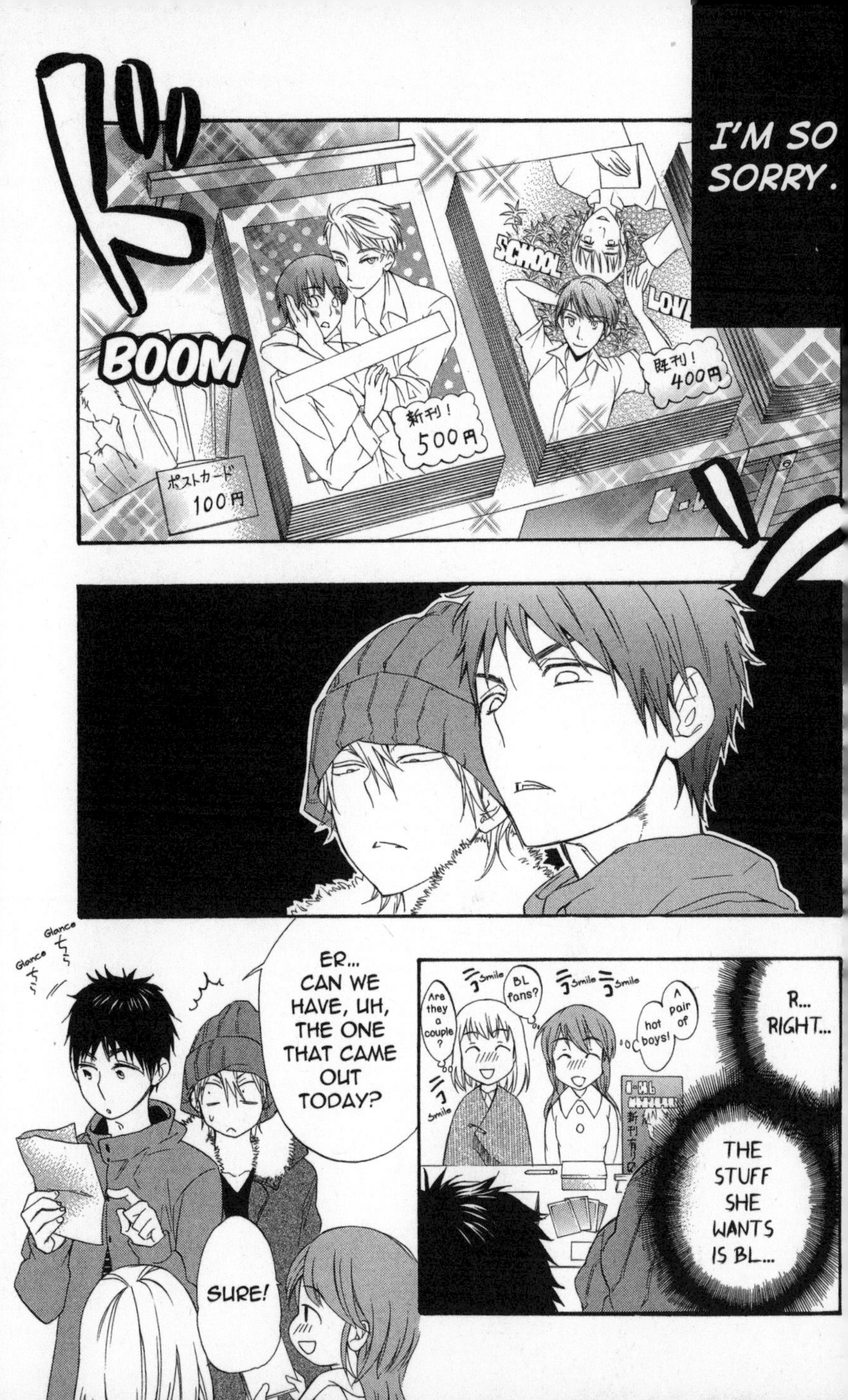
I'M SO SORRY.
BOOM
SCHOOL
既刊！400円
新刊！500円
ポストカード 100円
R... RIGHT...
A pair of hot boys!
Smile
BL fans?
Smile
Are they a couple?
Smile
THE STUFF SHE WANTS IS BL...
Glance
Glance
ER... CAN WE HAVE, UH, THE ONE THAT CAME OUT TODAY?
SURE!

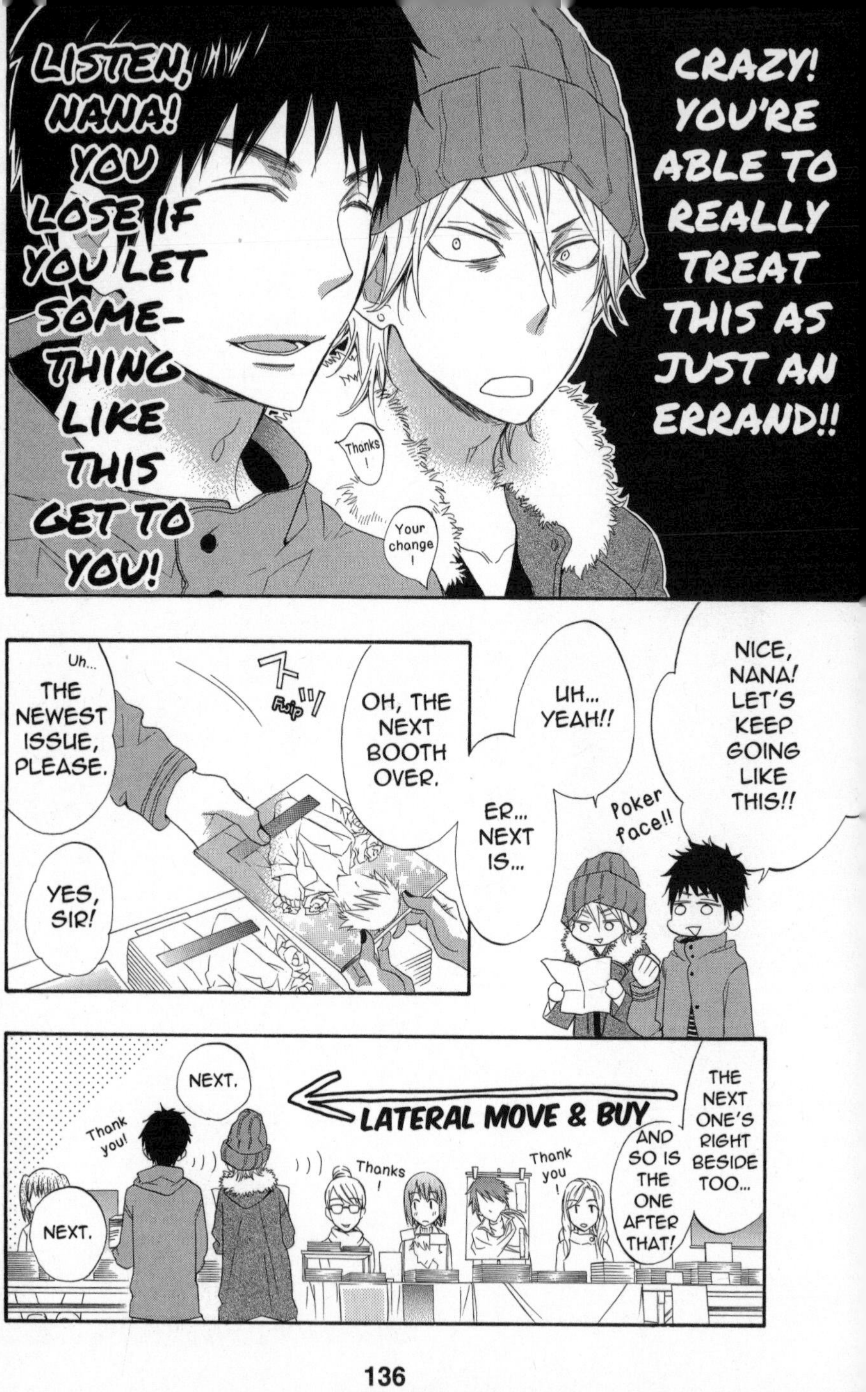
CRAZY! YOU'RE ABLE TO REALLY TREAT THIS AS JUST AN ERRAND!!
LISTEN, NANA! YOU LOSE IF YOU LET SOME-THING LIKE THIS GET TO YOU!
Thanks!
Your change!
NICE, NANA! LET'S KEEP GOING LIKE THIS!!
Poker face!!
UH... YEAH!!
ER... NEXT IS...
OH, THE NEXT BOOTH OVER.
Fwip
Uh... THE NEWEST ISSUE, PLEASE.
YES, SIR!
THE NEXT ONE'S RIGHT BESIDE TOO...
AND SO IS THE ONE AFTER THAT!
LATERAL MOVE & BUY
Thank you!
Thanks!
NEXT.
Thank you!
NEXT.

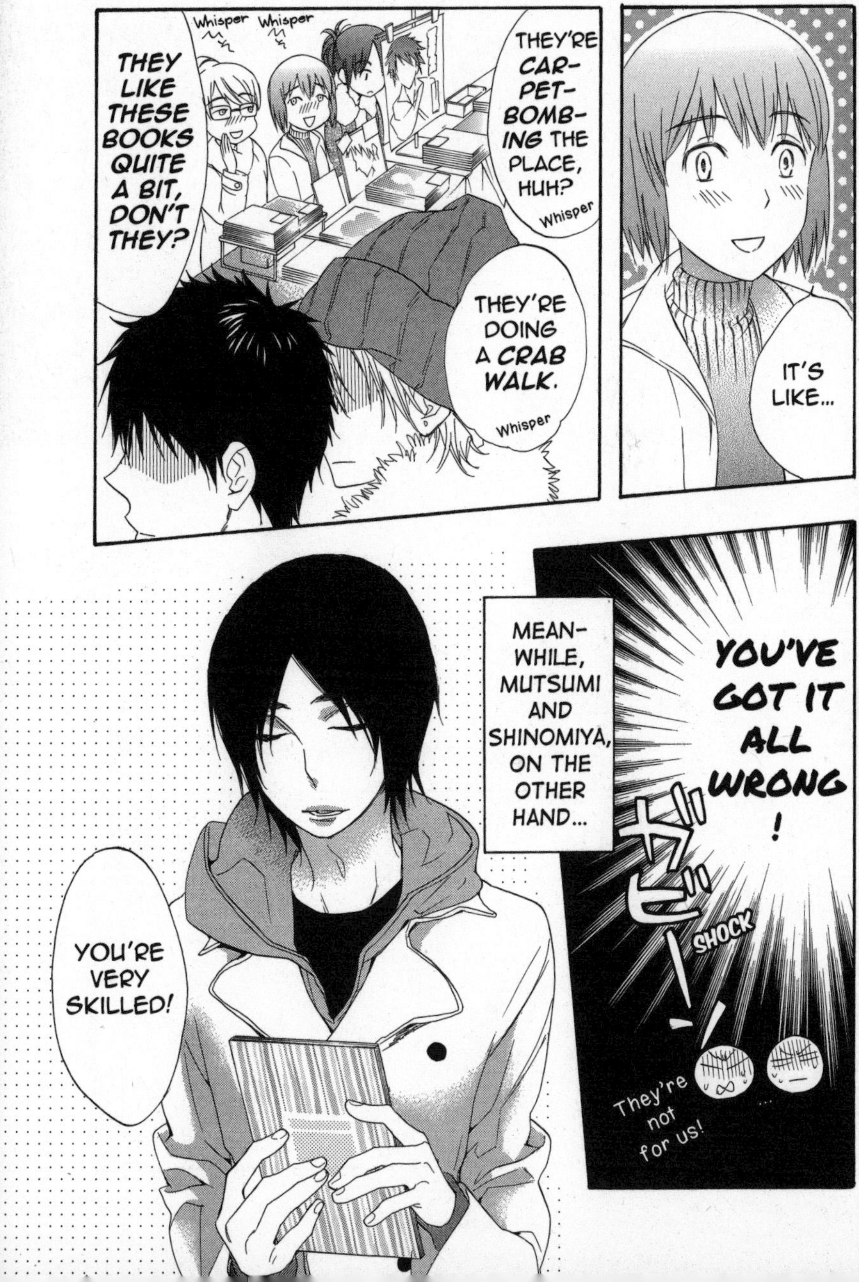
IT'S LIKE...
THEY'RE CARPET-BOMBING THE PLACE, HUH?
Whisper
Whisper Whisper
THEY LIKE THESE BOOKS QUITE A BIT, DON'T THEY?
THEY'RE DOING A CRAB WALK.
Whisper
YOU'VE GOT IT ALL WRONG!
SHOCK
They're not for us!
...
MEANWHILE, MUTSUMI AND SHINOMIYA, ON THE OTHER HAND...
YOU'RE VERY SKILLED!

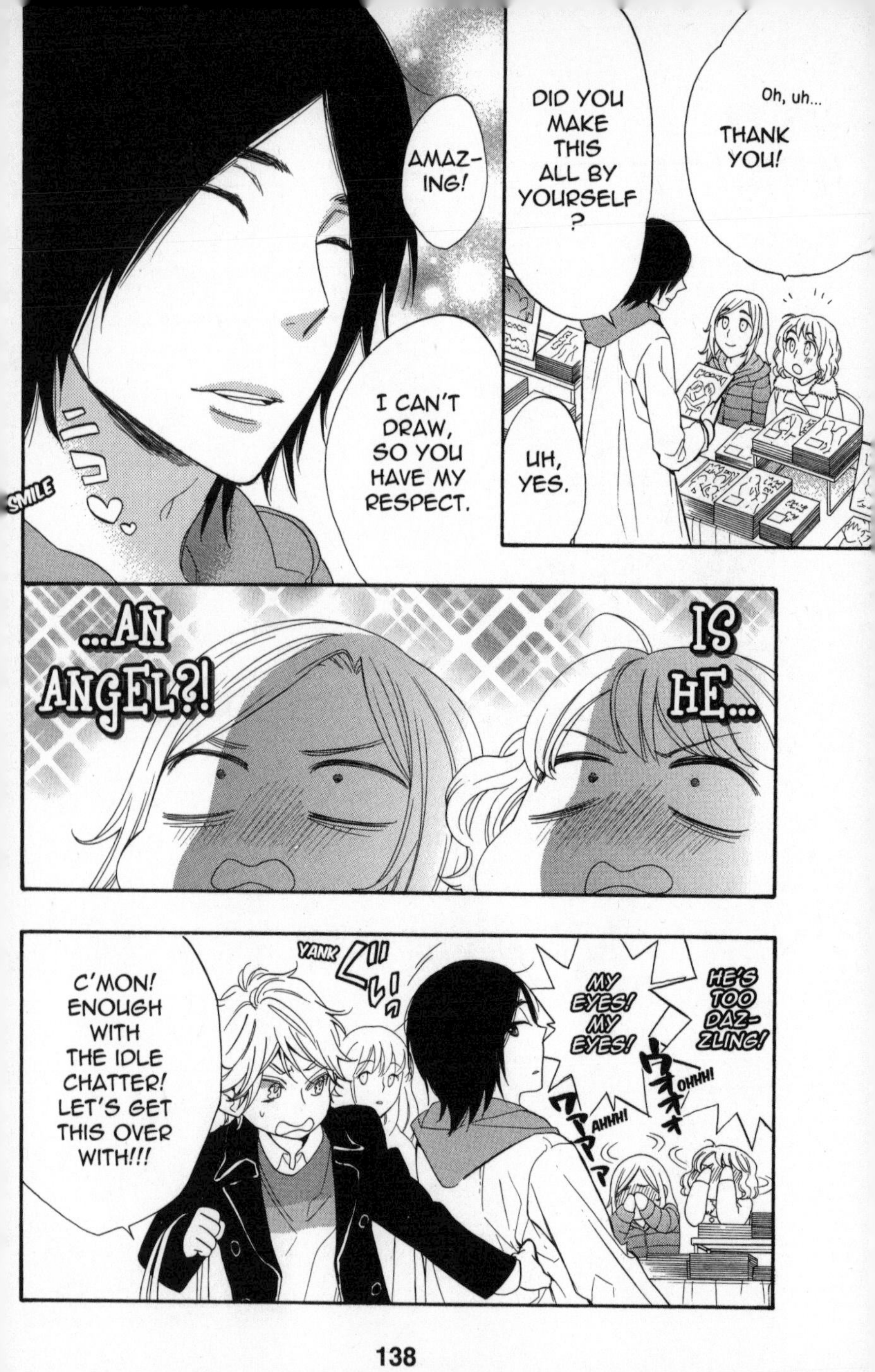
Oh, uh...
THANK YOU!
DID YOU MAKE THIS ALL BY YOURSELF?
UH, YES.
AMAZ-ING!
I CAN'T DRAW, SO YOU HAVE MY RESPECT.
SMILE
IS HE...
...AN ANGEL?!
HE'S TOO DAZ-ZLING!
MY EYES! MY EYES!
OHHH!
AHHH!
YANK
C'MON! ENOUGH WITH THE IDLE CHATTER! LET'S GET THIS OVER WITH!!!

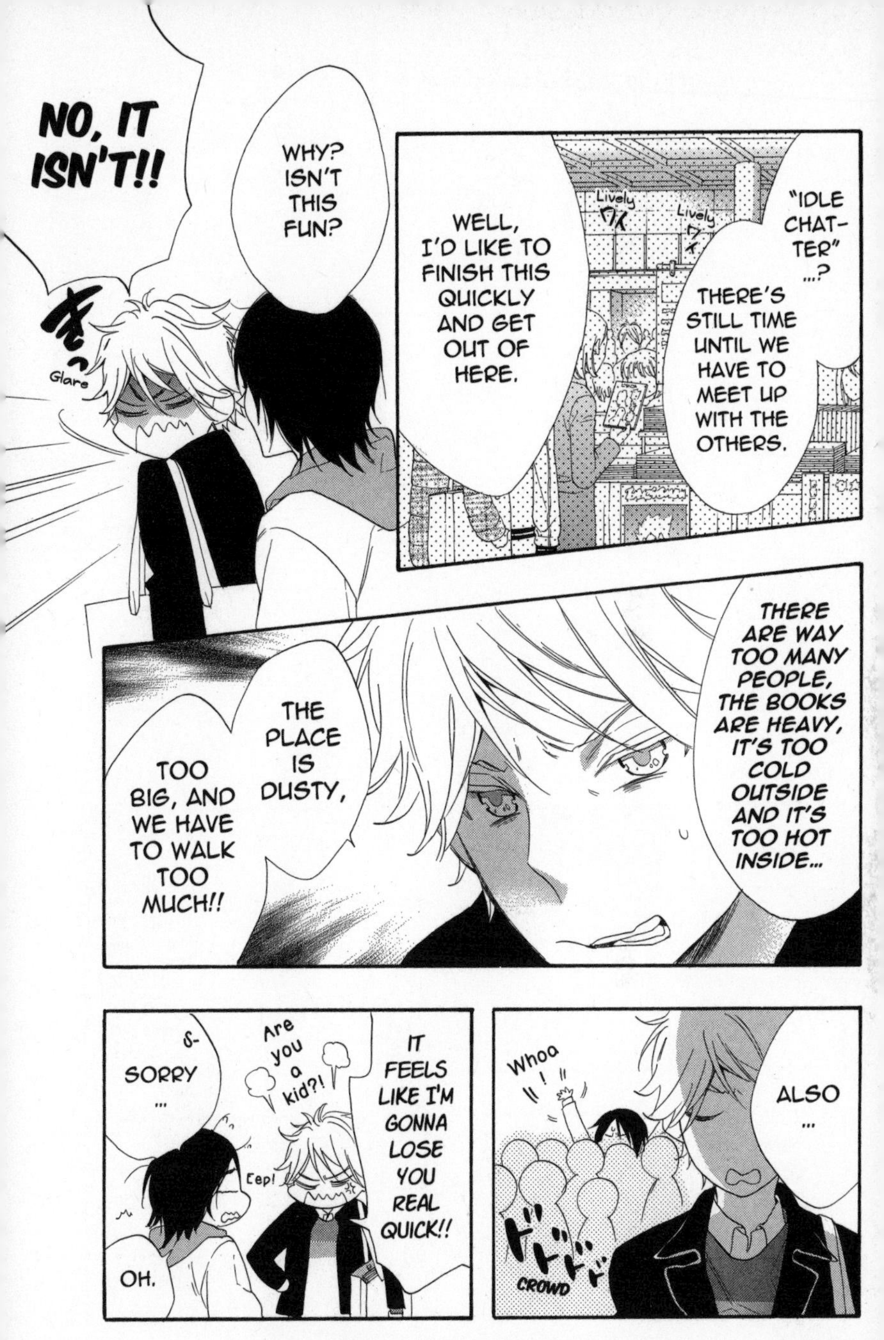
"IDLE CHAT-TER" ...?
THERE'S STILL TIME UNTIL WE HAVE TO MEET UP WITH THE OTHERS.
Lively
Lively
WELL, I'D LIKE TO FINISH THIS QUICKLY AND GET OUT OF HERE.
WHY? ISN'T THIS FUN?
NO, IT ISN'T!!
Glare
THERE ARE WAY TOO MANY PEOPLE, THE BOOKS ARE HEAVY, IT'S TOO COLD OUTSIDE AND IT'S TOO HOT INSIDE...
THE PLACE IS DUSTY,
TOO BIG, AND WE HAVE TO WALK TOO MUCH!!
ALSO ...
Whoa !
CROWD
IT FEELS LIKE I'M GONNA LOSE YOU REAL QUICK!!
Are you a kid?!
S-SORRY ...
Eep!
OH.

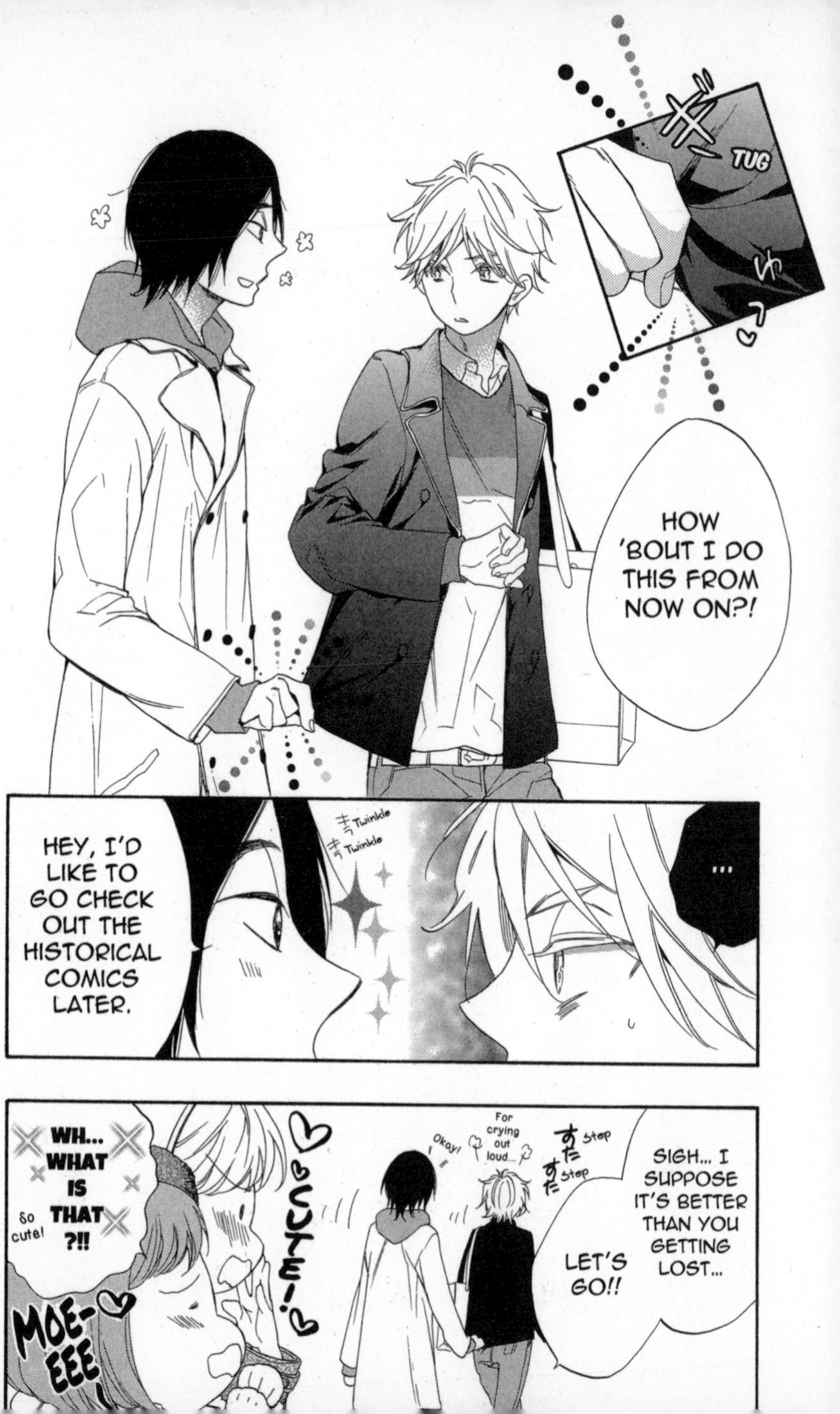

TUG
HOW 'BOUT I DO THIS FROM NOW ON?!
...
Twinkle
Twinkle
HEY, I'D LIKE TO GO CHECK OUT THE HISTORICAL COMICS LATER.
SIGH... I SUPPOSE IT'S BETTER THAN YOU GETTING LOST...
LET'S GO!!
Step
Step
For crying out loud...
Okay!
CUTE!
WH... WHAT IS THAT?!!
So cute!
MOE-EEE

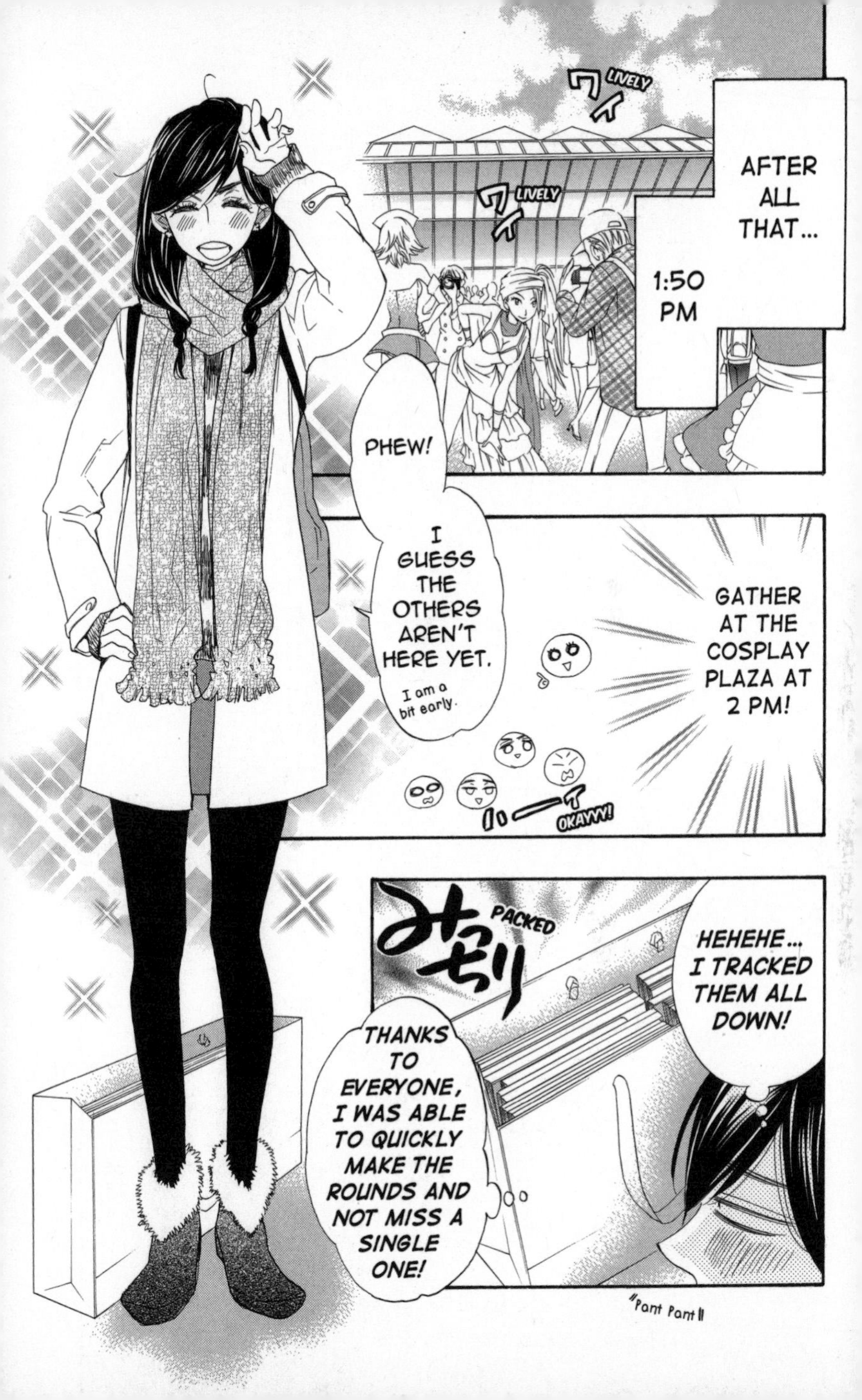

LIVELY
LIVELY
AFTER ALL THAT...
1:50 PM
GATHER AT THE COSPLAY PLAZA AT 2 PM!
OKAYYY!
PACKED
HEHEHE... I TRACKED THEM ALL DOWN!
THANKS TO EVERYONE, I WAS ABLE TO QUICKLY MAKE THE ROUNDS AND NOT MISS A SINGLE ONE!
"Pant Pant"
PHEW!
I GUESS THE OTHERS AREN'T HERE YET.
I am a bit early.

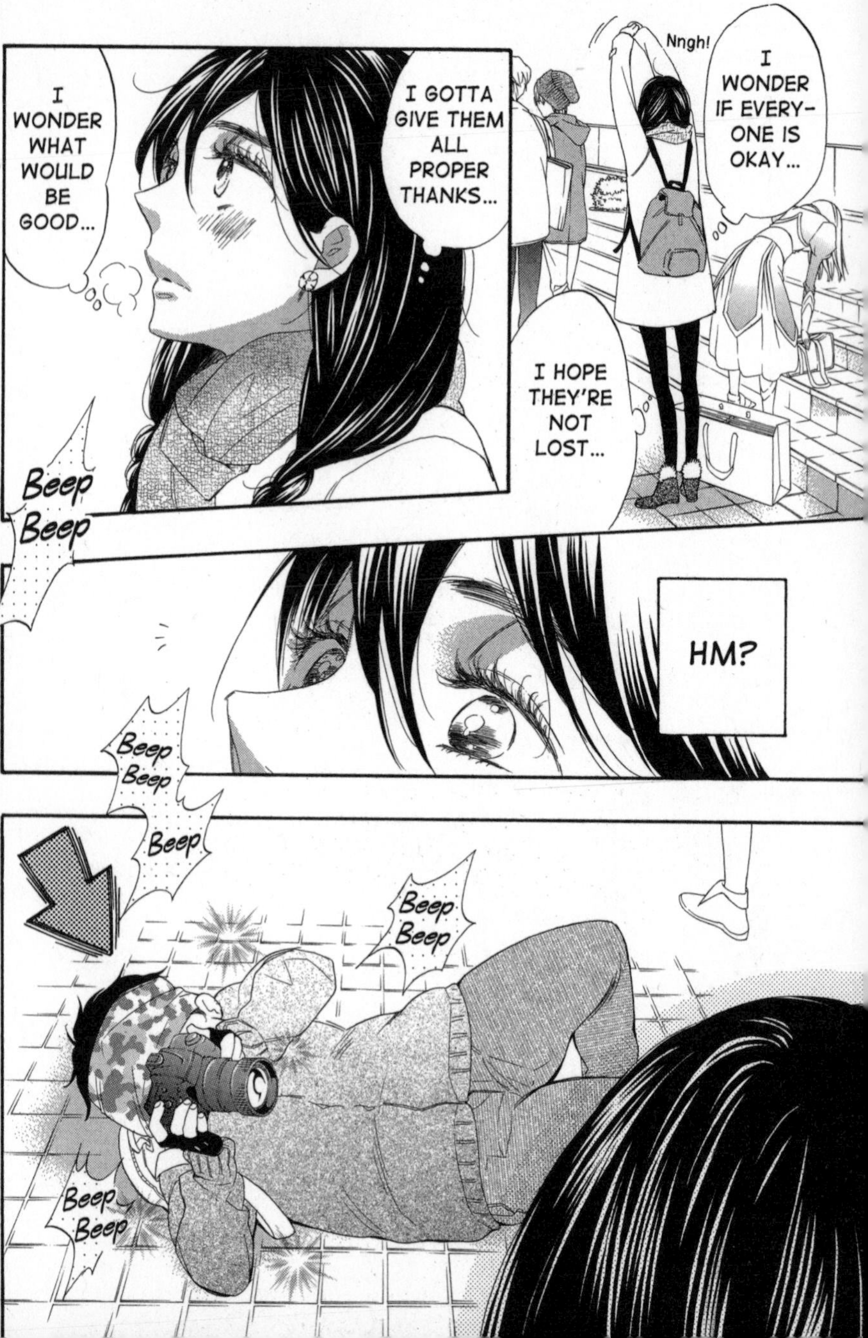

Nngh!
I WONDER IF EVERY-ONE IS OKAY...
I HOPE THEY'RE NOT LOST...
I GOTTA GIVE THEM ALL PROPER THANKS...
I WONDER WHAT WOULD BE GOOD...
Beep Beep
HM?
Beep Beep
Beep
Beep Beep
Beep Beep

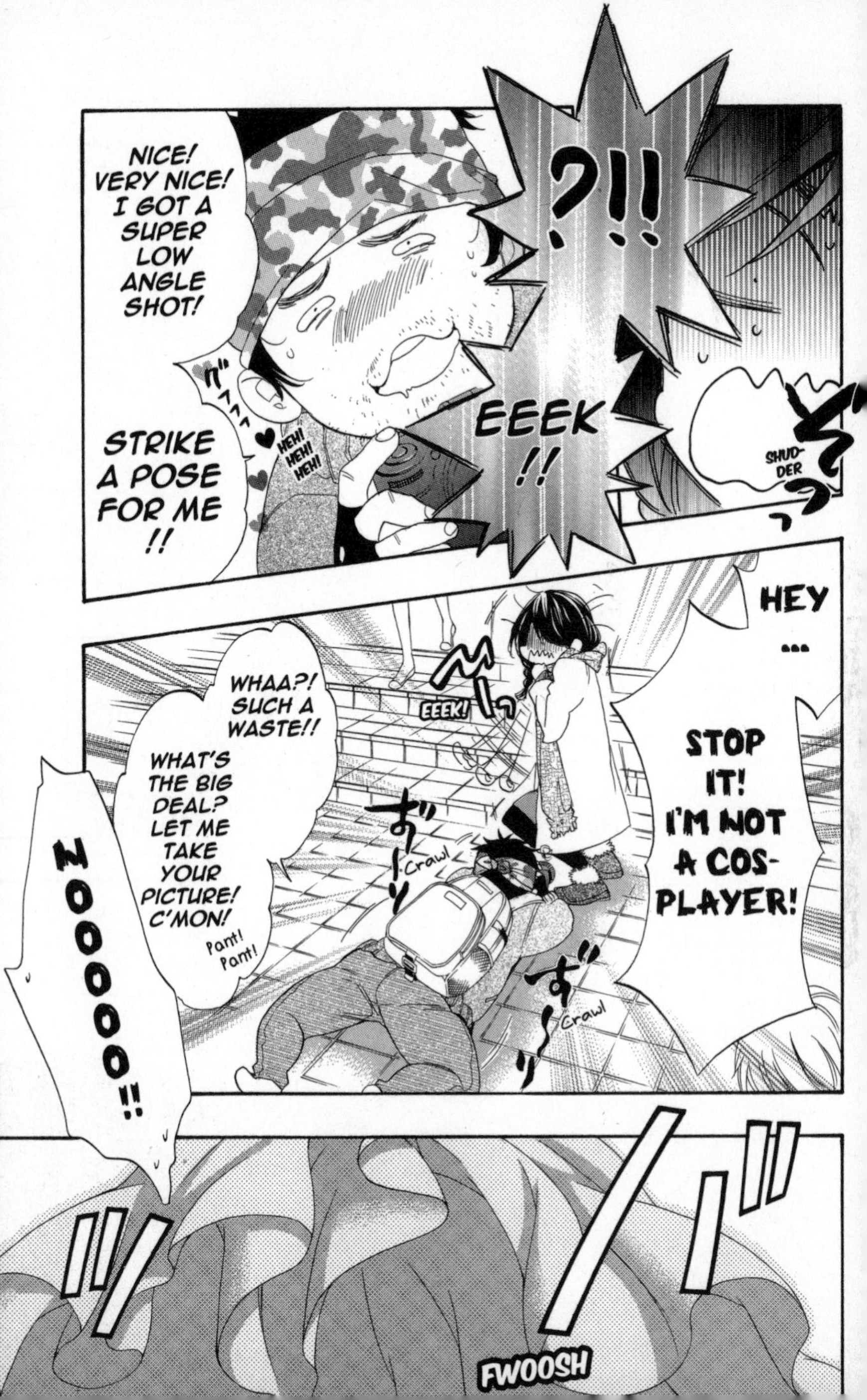
?!!
SHUD-DER
EEEK!!
NICE! VERY NICE! I GOT A SUPER LOW ANGLE SHOT!
HEH! HEH! HEH!
STRIKE A POSE FOR ME!!
HEY...
STOP IT! I'M NOT A COS-PLAYER!
EEEK!
WHAA?! SUCH A WASTE!!
WHAT'S THE BIG DEAL? LET ME TAKE YOUR PICTURE! C'MON!
Crawl
Pant! Pant!
Crawl
NOOOOO!!
FWOOSH

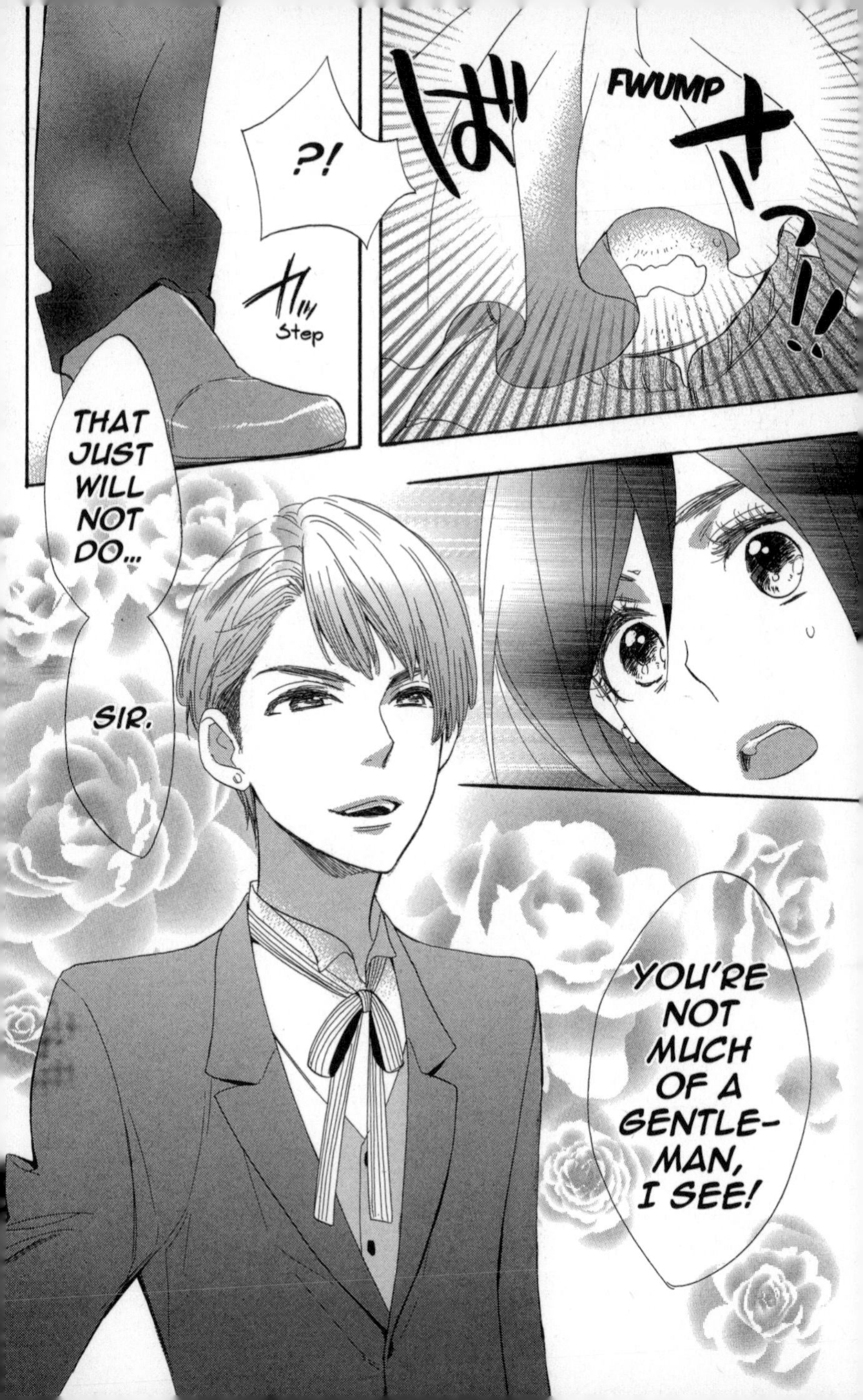
FWUMP
ばっ
さーっ!!
?!
Step
THAT JUST WILL NOT DO...
SIR.
YOU'RE NOT MUCH OF A GENTLE-MAN, I SEE!

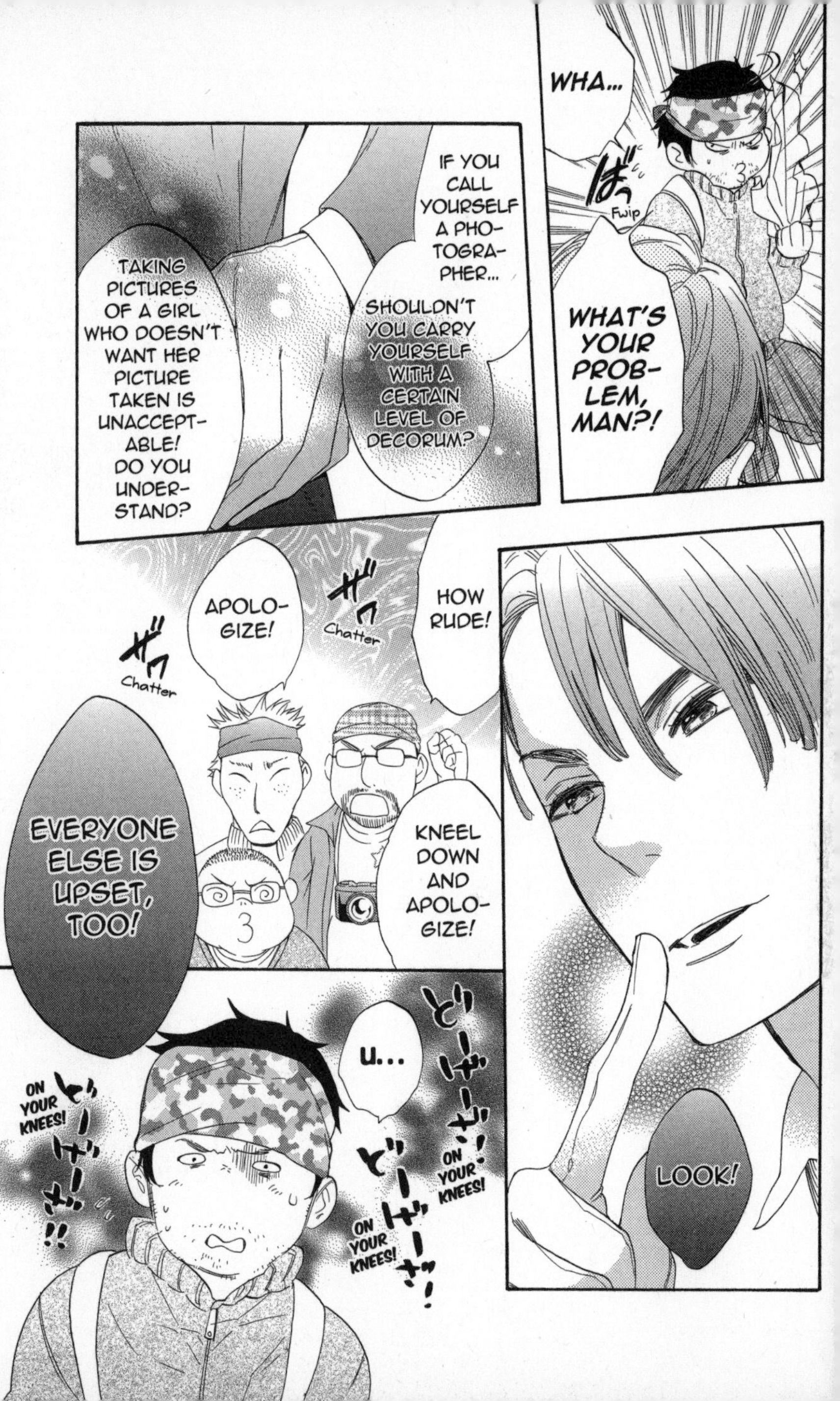

WHA...
Fwip
WHAT'S YOUR PROBLEM, MAN?!
IF YOU CALL YOURSELF A PHOTOGRAPHER...
SHOULDN'T YOU CARRY YOURSELF WITH A CERTAIN LEVEL OF DECORUM?
TAKING PICTURES OF A GIRL WHO DOESN'T WANT HER PICTURE TAKEN IS UNACCEPTABLE! DO YOU UNDERSTAND?
LOOK!
HOW RUDE!
Chatter
APOLOGIZE!
Chatter
KNEEL DOWN AND APOLOGIZE!
EVERYONE ELSE IS UPSET, TOO!
U...
ON YOUR KNEES!
ON YOUR KNEES!
ON YOUR KNEES!

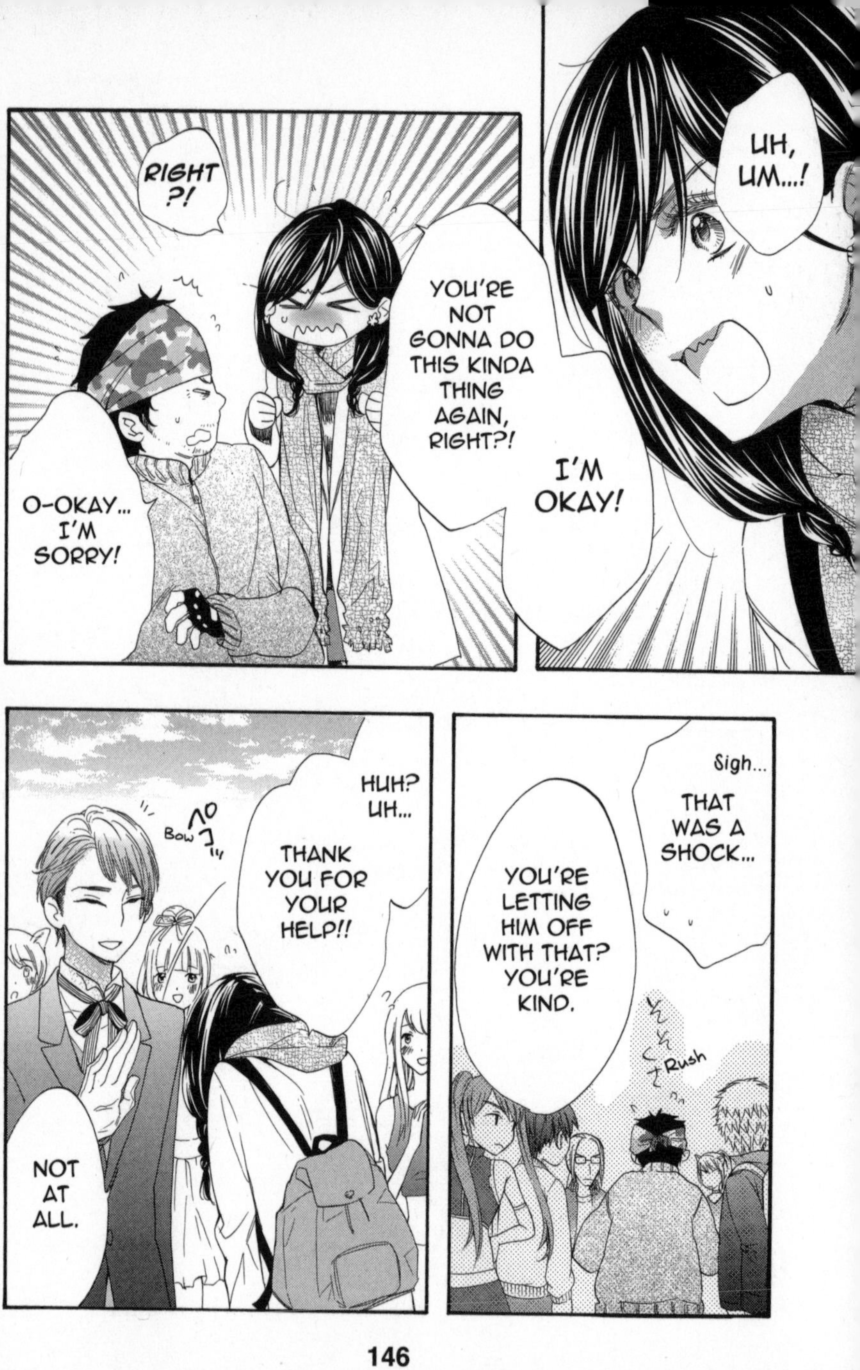
UH, UM...!
I'M OKAY!
YOU'RE NOT GONNA DO THIS KINDA THING AGAIN, RIGHT?!
RIGHT ?!
O-OKAY... I'M SORRY!
Sigh...
THAT WAS A SHOCK...
YOU'RE LETTING HIM OFF WITH THAT? YOU'RE KIND.
Rush
HUH? UH...
THANK YOU FOR YOUR HELP!!
Bow
NOT AT ALL.

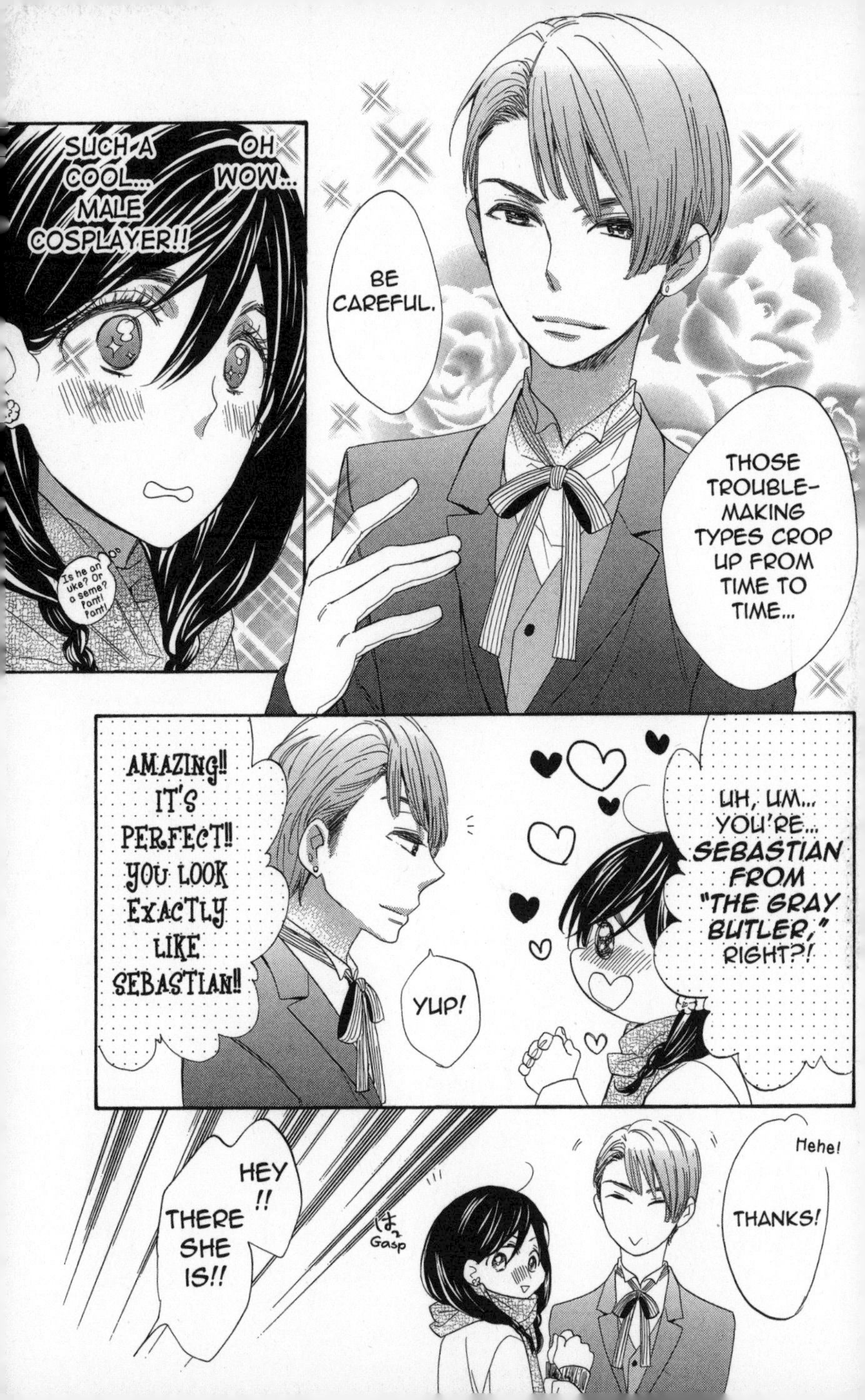
BE CAREFUL.
THOSE TROUBLE-MAKING TYPES CROP UP FROM TIME TO TIME...
OH WOW...
SUCH A COOL... MALE COSPLAYER!!
Is he an uke? Or a seme? Pant! Pant!
UH, UM... YOU'RE... SEBASTIAN FROM "THE GRAY BUTLER," RIGHT?!
YUP!
AMAZING!! IT'S PERFECT!! YOU LOOK EXACTLY LIKE SEBASTIAN!!
Hehe!
THANKS!
は
Gasp
HEY!!
THERE SHE IS!!

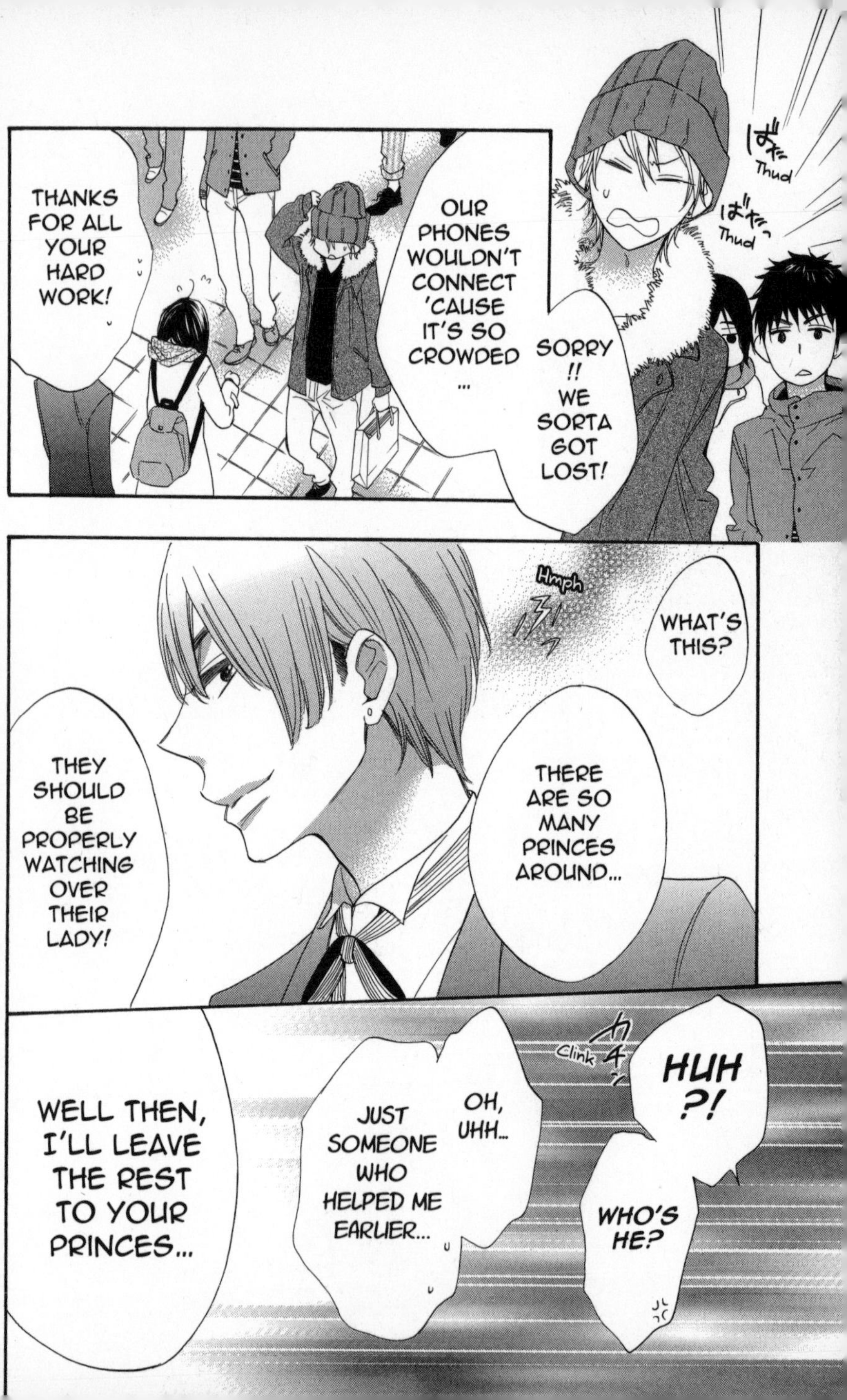
Thud
Thud
SORRY!! WE SORTA GOT LOST!
OUR PHONES WOULDN'T CONNECT 'CAUSE IT'S SO CROWDED...
THANKS FOR ALL YOUR HARD WORK!
Hmph
WHAT'S THIS?
THERE ARE SO MANY PRINCES AROUND...
THEY SHOULD BE PROPERLY WATCHING OVER THEIR LADY!
HUH?!
Clink
WHO'S HE?
OH, UHH...
JUST SOMEONE WHO HELPED ME EARLIER...
WELL THEN, I'LL LEAVE THE REST TO YOUR PRINCES...

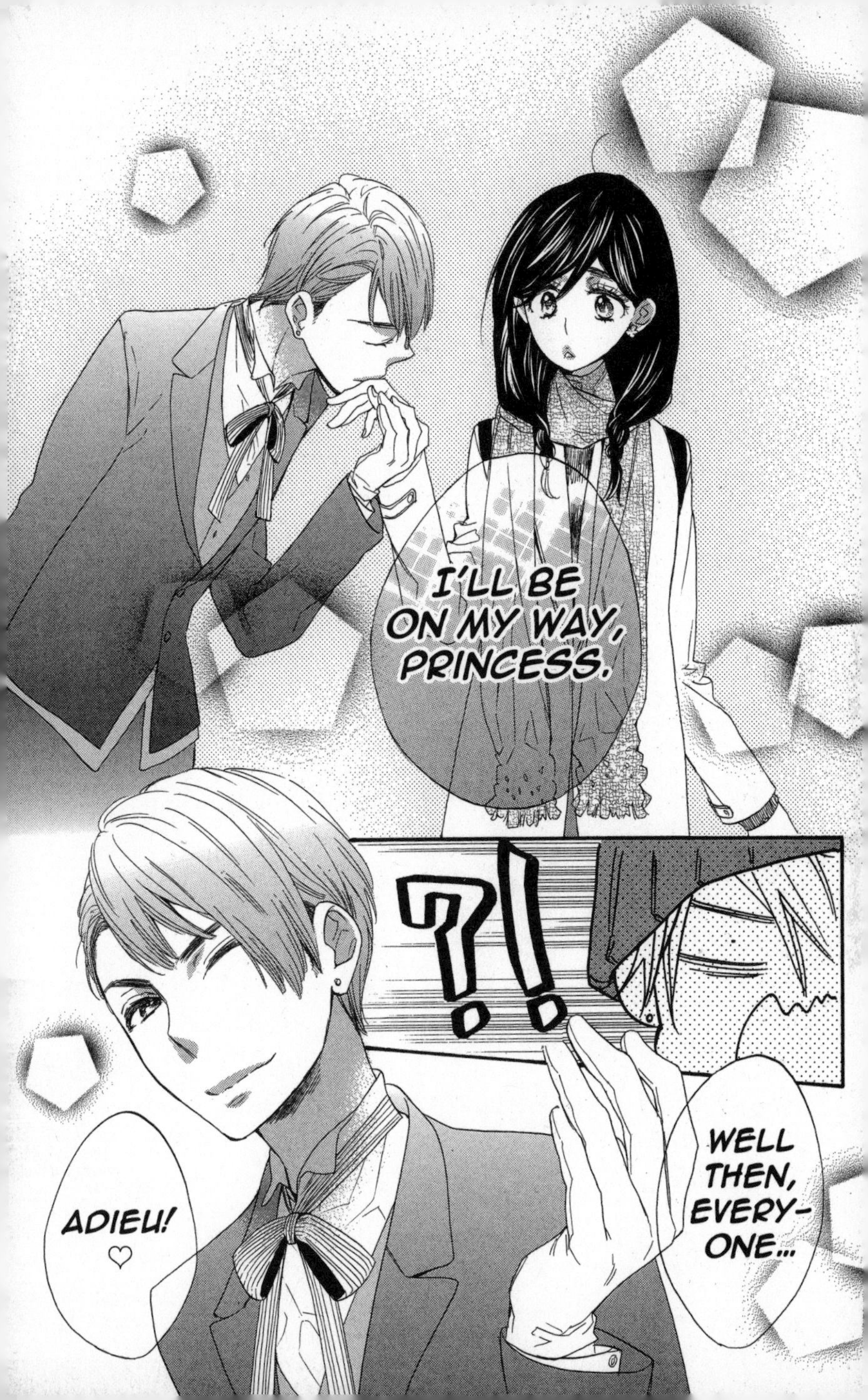
I'LL BE ON MY WAY, PRINCESS.
?!
WELL THEN, EVERY-ONE...
ADIEU! ♡

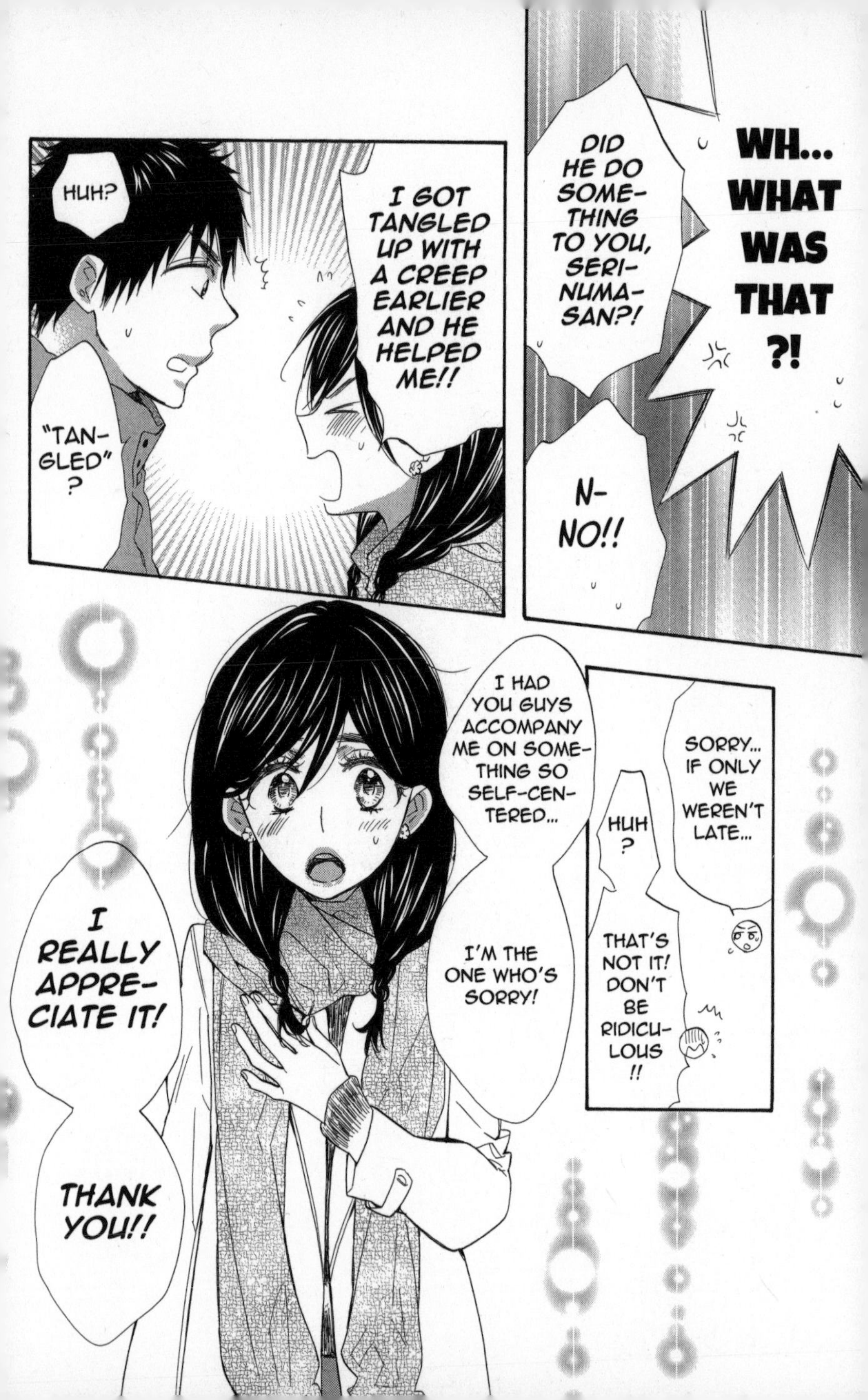
WH... WHAT WAS THAT ?!
DID HE DO SOME-THING TO YOU, SERI-NUMA-SAN?!
N-NO!!
I GOT TANGLED UP WITH A CREEP EARLIER AND HE HELPED ME!!
HUH?
"TAN-GLED" ?
SORRY... IF ONLY WE WEREN'T LATE...
HUH ?
THAT'S NOT IT! DON'T BE RIDICU-LOUS !!
I HAD YOU GUYS ACCOMPANY ME ON SOME-THING SO SELF-CEN-TERED...
I'M THE ONE WHO'S SORRY!
I REALLY APPRE-CIATE IT!
THANK YOU!!

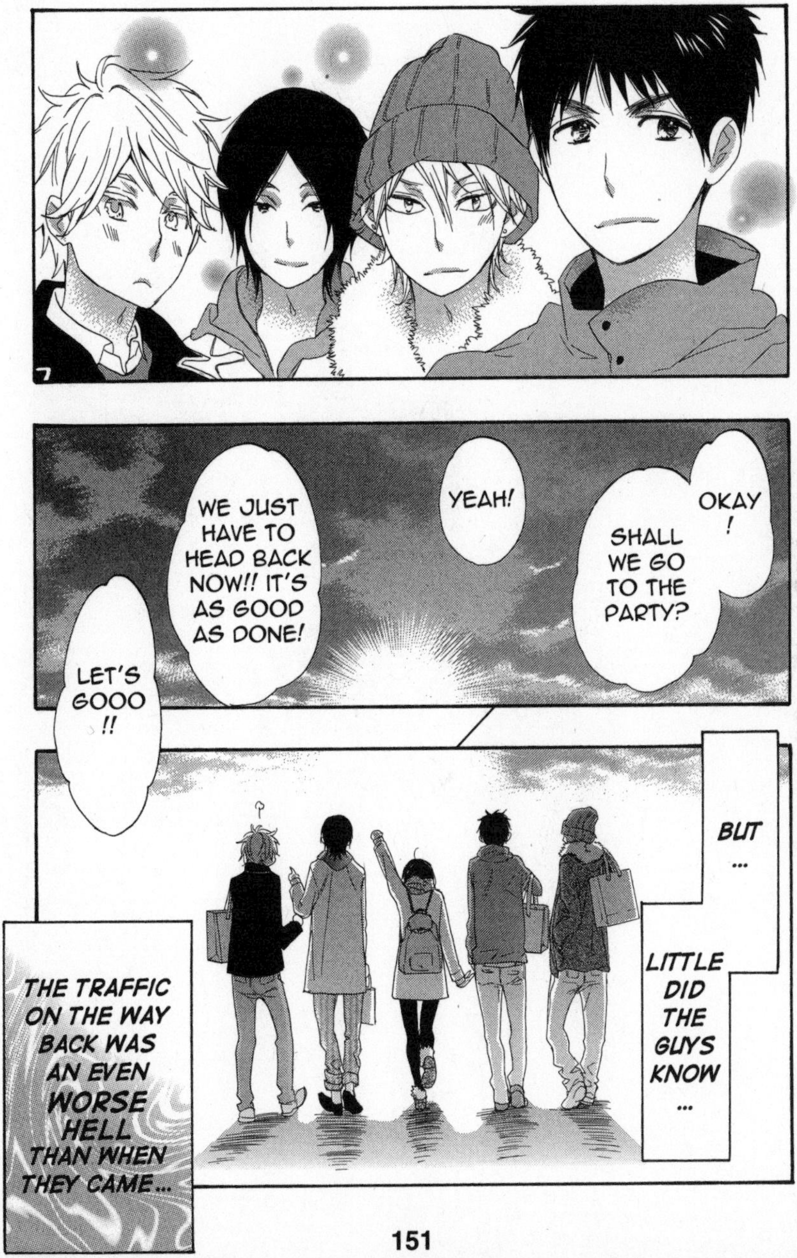
OKAY!
SHALL WE GO TO THE PARTY?
YEAH!
WE JUST HAVE TO HEAD BACK NOW!! IT'S AS GOOD AS DONE!
LET'S GOOO!!
BUT...
LITTLE DID THE GUYS KNOW...
THE TRAFFIC ON THE WAY BACK WAS AN EVEN WORSE HELL THAN WHEN THEY CAME...

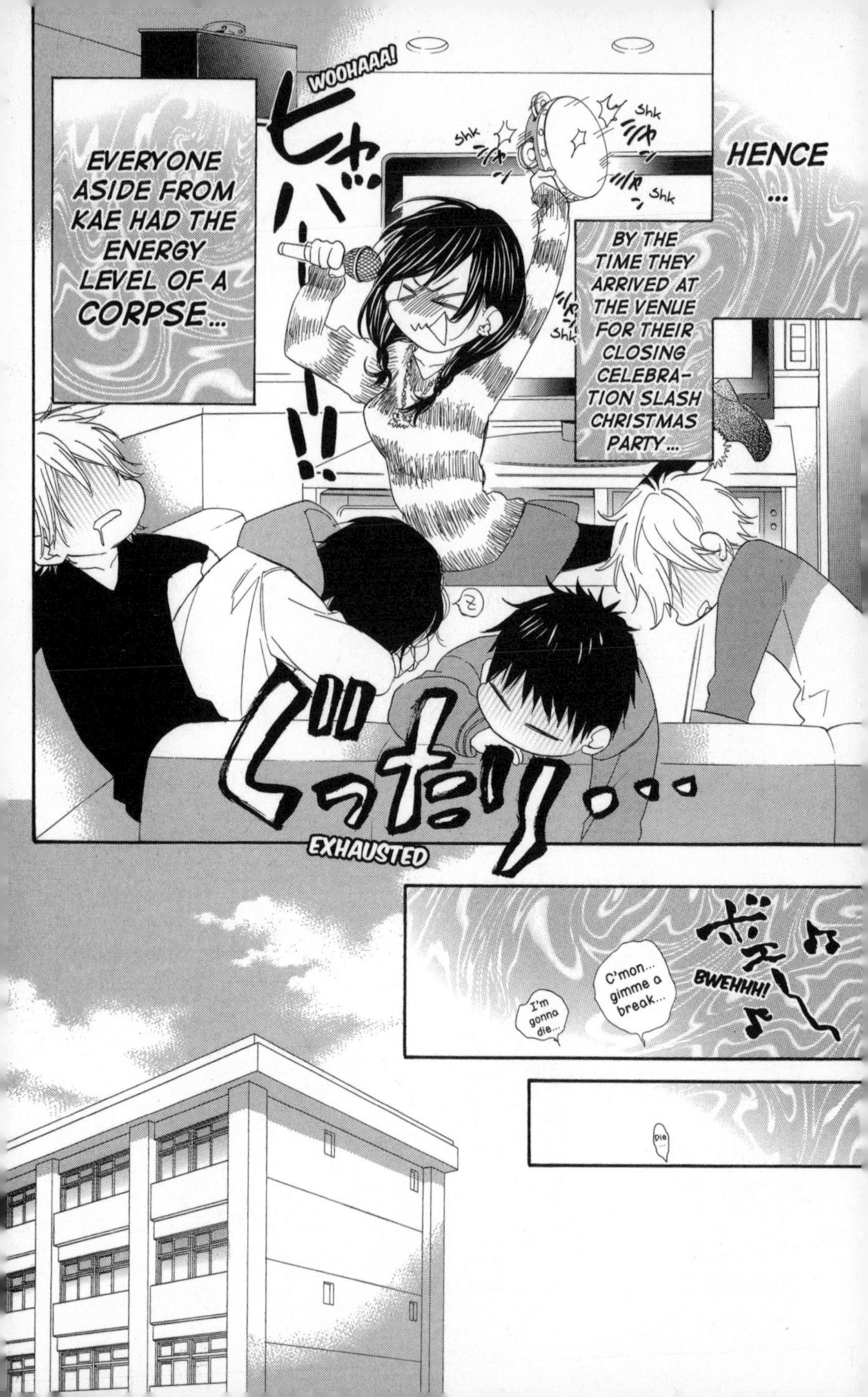
HENCE ...
BY THE TIME THEY ARRIVED AT THE VENUE FOR THEIR CLOSING CELEBRA-TION SLASH CHRISTMAS PARTY...
Shk
Shk
WOOHAAA!
EVERYONE ASIDE FROM KAE HAD THE ENERGY LEVEL OF A CORPSE...
Shk
Shk
ぐったり・・・
EXHAUSTED
BWEHHH!
C'mon... gimme a break...
I'm gonna die...
Die...

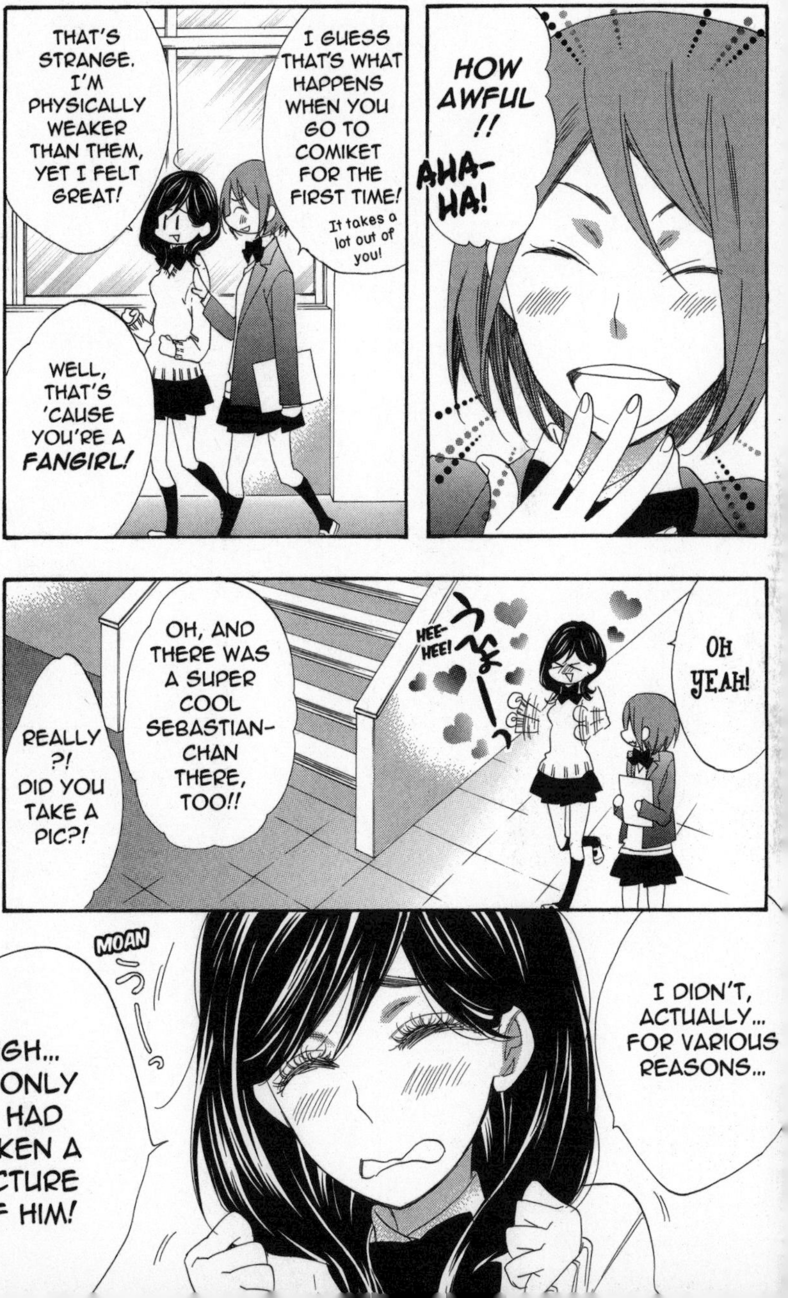
HOW AWFUL!!
AHA-HA!
I GUESS THAT'S WHAT HAPPENS WHEN YOU GO TO COMIKET FOR THE FIRST TIME!
It takes a lot out of you!
THAT'S STRANGE. I'M PHYSICALLY WEAKER THAN THEM, YET I FELT GREAT!
WELL, THAT'S 'CAUSE YOU'RE A FANGIRL!
OH YEAH!
HEE-HEE!
OH, AND THERE WAS A SUPER COOL SEBASTIAN-CHAN THERE, TOO!!
REALLY?! DID YOU TAKE A PIC?!
I DIDN'T, ACTUALLY... FOR VARIOUS REASONS...
MOAN
UGH... IF ONLY I HAD TAKEN A PICTURE OF HIM!

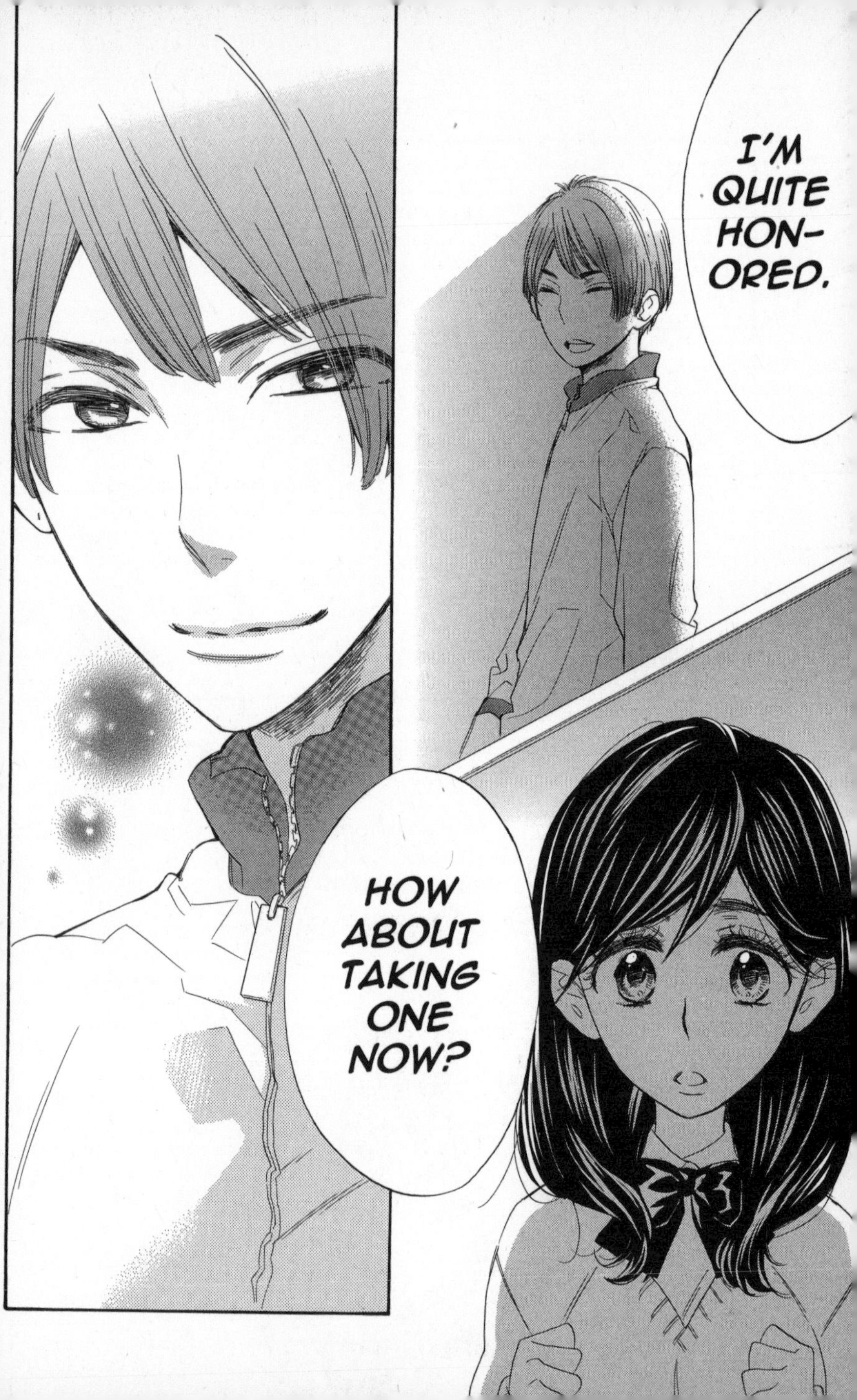
I'M QUITE HON-ORED.
HOW ABOUT TAKING ONE NOW?

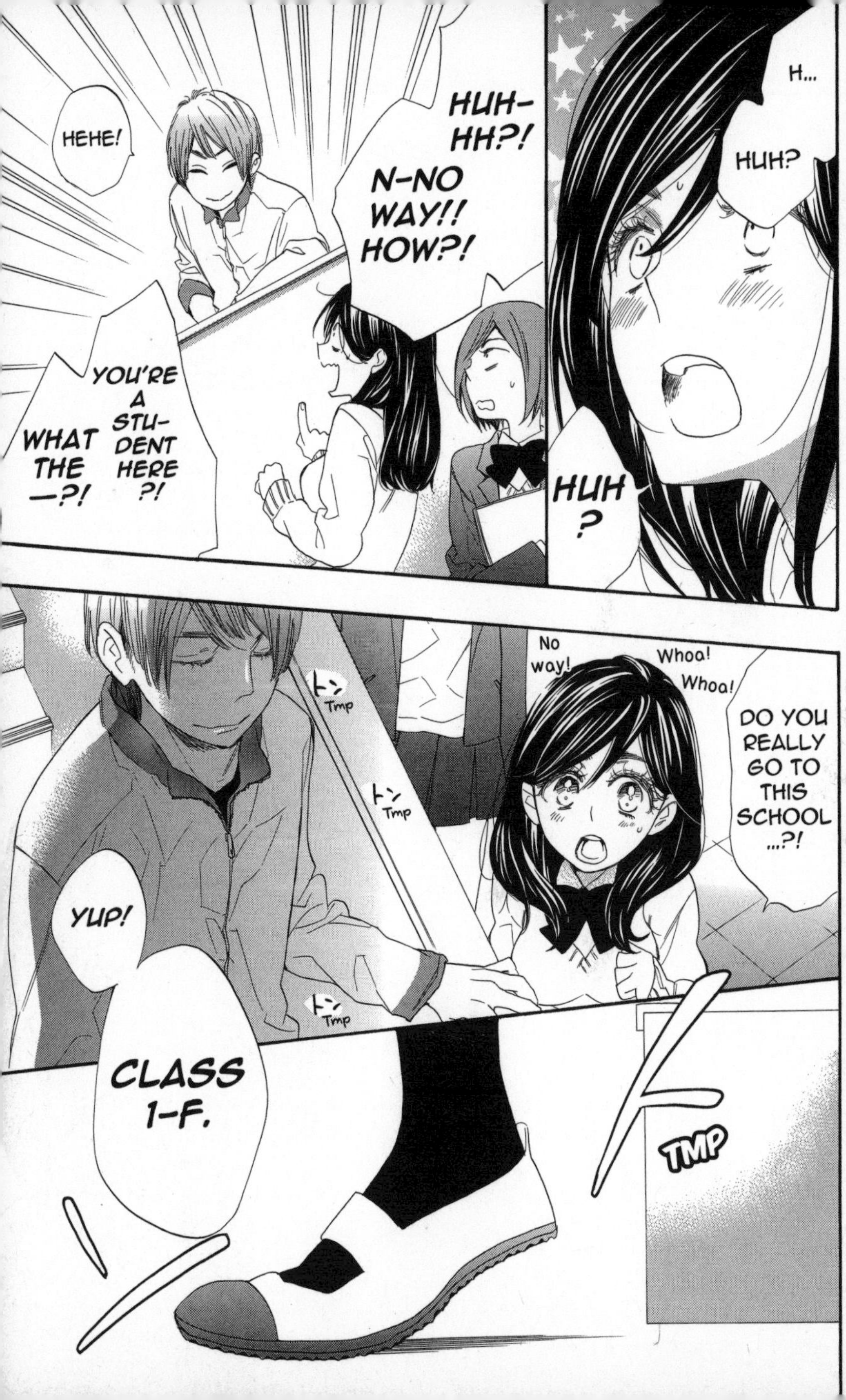
H...
HUH?
HUH?
HUH-HH?! N-NO WAY!! HOW?!
HEHE!
YOU'RE A STUDENT HERE?!
WHAT THE—?!
No way!
Whoa! Whoa!
DO YOU REALLY GO TO THIS SCHOOL...?!
Tmp
Tmp
Tmp
YUP!
TMP
CLASS 1-F.

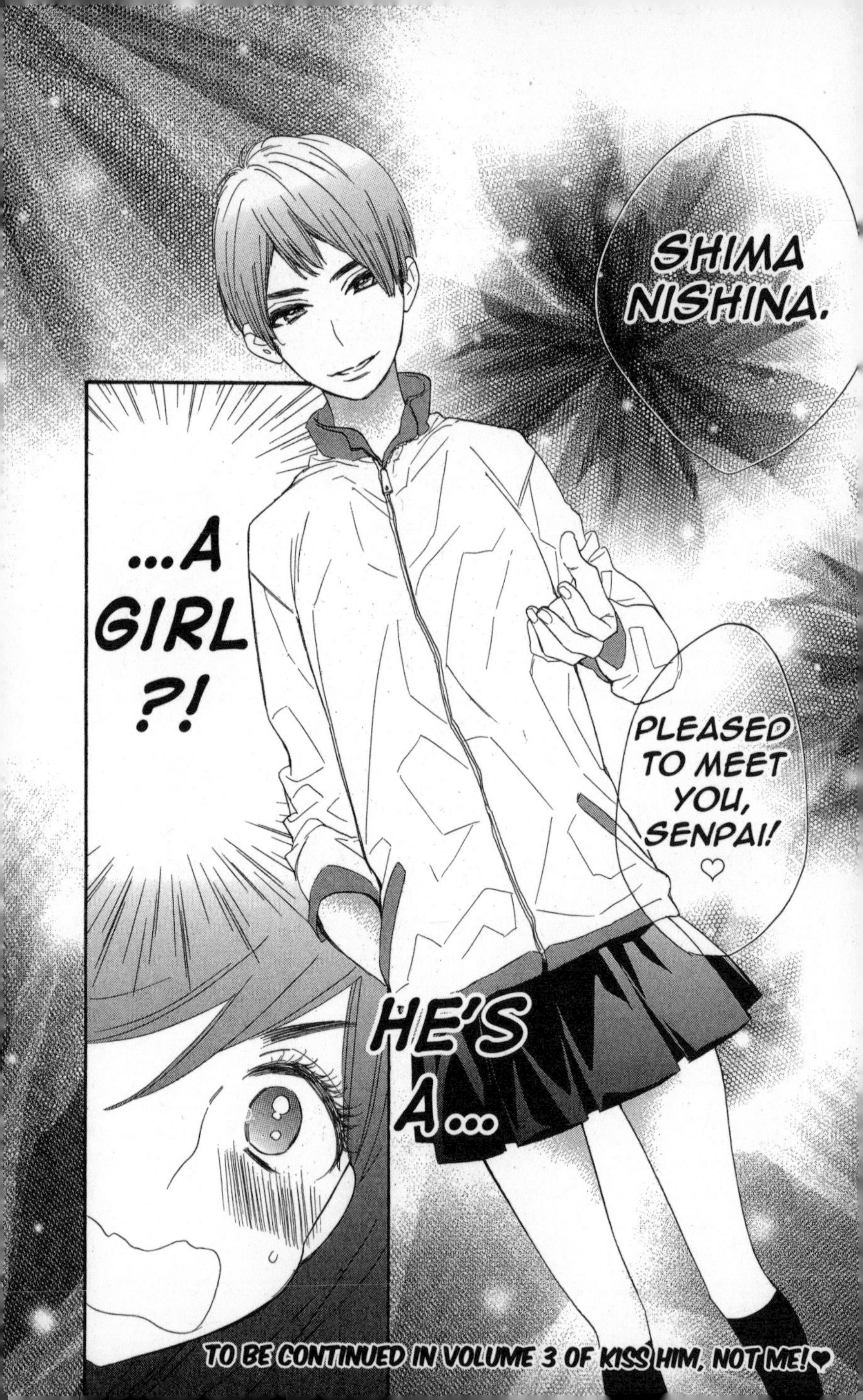
SHIMA NISHINA.
PLEASED TO MEET YOU, SENPAI! ♡
HE'S A...
...A GIRL ?!
TO BE CONTINUED IN VOLUME 3 OF KISS HIM, NOT ME! ♥

Thank you very much.
THANKS FOR READING THE SECOND VOLUME OF "KISS HIM, NOT ME."
Boing!
Boing!
Boing!
Boing!
THIS IS MY FIRST CONTINUOUS PUBLICATION, SO I'M VERY HAPPY.
Happy Dance
I have eight BL books released. I also have e-books! (Shameless plug)
WHEN IT CAME TIME TO DRAW THE COSPLAY AT THE SCHOOL FESTIVAL, I THOUGHT, "OKAY, IT'S FOR KODANSHA, SO I WANT TO DO 'ATTACK ON TITAN'!" WHEN I REQUESTED IT, THEY GLADLY GAVE ME PERMISSION.
I THANK THEM GREATLY FOR THAT.
You got approval!
Huh? Are you sure ...?
Seriously?
I can draw that erotic butt belt? Yesss!!
Voice in my head
INCIDENTALLY, I LIKE ARMIN AND JEAN.
You didn't ask, did you? Sorry.
ALSO, I ADDED THE HANDSOME GIRL, SHIMA, TO THE GROUP.
The most traditionally handsome face.
SHE'S GONNA DO VARIOUS THINGS TO STIR THE POT, SO LOOK FORWARD TO THE NEXT VOLUME. (ADVERTISEMENT)
Also, I'd like to have Mutsumi in cosplay if I get the chance...
Since I didn't get to this time.
What would be good?
THANK YOU TO ALL WHO WERE INVOLVED WITH THIS WORK, AND THOSE WHO SUPPORTED ME.
I HOPE TO HAVE YOUR SUPPORT FOR THE NEXT VOLUME AS WELL!
Junko
2014.01

Thank you! Nobue, Shinohara-san, Otsuka-san, Yuki-san, Nozomi-chan, Konbu-san, Aki, Eiki-san, Zao-san, Yuge, Supervisor Y-sama, Designer-sama, and everyone else involved with this book!

AUTHOR'S NOTE

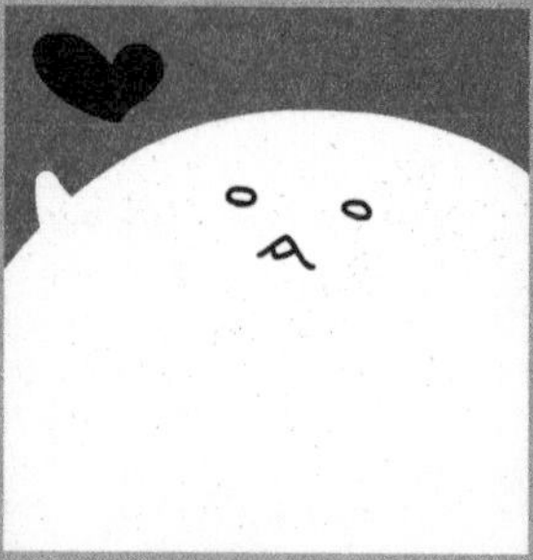

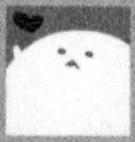

IF I HAVE MOE, I CAN GET MORE POWER THAN MY BODY NORMALLY HAS—I'M OVERCOME WITH MOTIVATION AND BECOME REALLY CHEERFUL! HOWEVER, IF MY SUPPLY IS CUT SHORT, I SUDDENLY GET DEPRESSED AND TURN INTO SOMETHING LIKE A FLESH-CRAVING ZOMBIE! SEEMS LIKE A BAD DRUG TO ME.

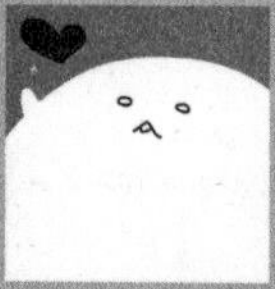

-JUNKO

I ♥ BL

Translation Notes

O-MO-TE-NA-SHI, page 50

Simply put, *omotenashi* is Japanese hospitality. Though the term has long been present in the Japanese language, it recently became a trendy phrase due to its use in a presentation to the Olympic Committee as a bid for the 2020 Olympics in Tokyo. In the presentation given by bid ambassador and TV personality Christel Takigawa, the term was spoken slowly and enunciated as "O-MO-TE-NA-SHI." It was this special (and somewhat cute) delivery that made the term popular in the Japanese media.

Kabedon, page 57

Kabedon is a combination of the Japanese word for wall (*kabe*) and the sound of a blunt impact or hit (*don*). This describes the action of a guy cornering a girl against a wall by facing her and hitting his hand against said wall behind her. This is a common trope in shojo manga popularized by *LDK* (which also happens to be published by Kodansha). For Japanese shojo readers, this is seen as a dramatic moment, which creates tension between two love interests.

Why meeee?!, page 86

The reason why Ah-chan says, "Is this 'Jojo'?!" in response to Kae is because what Kae originally said was "MURYYY" ("I can't" or "no way"). This is a reference to a sound made by Dio Brand in the popular manga series, *Jojo's Bizarre Adventure*. After turning into a vampire, Dio would sometimes scream WRYYYY as he attacked.

LINE, page 107

LINE is a popular chat application. It was originally developed to aid communication in the aftermath of the Tohoku Earthquake of 2011, but has since grown to become one of the most popular chat applications in Japan. One of the features of LINE is that it lets you know when a sent message has been viewed, which can sometimes lead to tension when a person doesn't respond promptly after viewing a message.

Hand warmers, page 131

These are no ordinary hand warmers. The Japanese name of this product is "A-ta-ta-ta-ta-ta-ta-ta-ta-kaairo." *Kairo* means warmer in Japanese and *atatakai* means warm. However, the extended string of syllables that create *atatakai* in the product name are a reference to Kenshiro from *Fist of the North Star*. In the series, Kenshiro's trademark special move is the *Hokuto Hyakurestu Ken* (North Star Hundred Shred/Crack Fist) in which he unleashes a barrage of punches while repeating "A-ta-ta-ta…" à la Bruce Lee.

The Gray Butler, page 147

This is a not-so-hidden reference to the *Black Butler* series.

Kiss Him, Not Me volume 2 is a work of fiction. Names, characters, places, and incidents are the products of the author's imagination or are used fictitiously. Any resemblance to actual events, locales, or persons, living or dead, is entirely coincidental.

A Kodansha Comics Trade Paperback Original.

Published in the United States by Kodansha Comics, an imprint of Kodansha USA Publishing, LLC, New York.

Publication rights for this English edition arranged through Kodansha Ltd., Tokyo.

First published in Japan in 2014 by Kodansha Ltd., Tokyo, as *Watashi Ga Motete Dousunda* volume 2.

ISBN 978-1-63236-203-2

Printed in the United States of America.

www.kodanshacomics.com

9 8 7 6 5 4 3 2

Translation: David Rhie
Lettering: Hiroko Mizuno
Editing: Ajani Oloye
Kodansha Comics Edition Cover Design: Phil Balsman